Light in the Heart of Darkness

EMDR AND THE TREATMENT OF

WAR AND TERRORISM SURVIVORS

Light in the Heart of Darkness

EMDR AND THE TREATMENT OF
WAR AND TERRORISM SURVIVORS

Steven M. Silver, Ph.D.
Susan Rogers, Ph.D.

W. W. Norton & Company
New York • London

A Norton Professional Book

Though both authors are employees of the Department of Veterans Affairs, this book represents their own views, are not those of the VA, and was not prepared using VA time or resources. The views expressed herein are not necessarily those of Francine Shapiro, the EMDR Institute, nor the EMDR Humanitarian Assistance Programs.

Library of Congress Cataloging-in-Publication Data

Silver, Steven M.
  Light in the heart of darkness : EMDR and the treatment of war and terrorism survivors / Steven M. Silver, Susan Rogers.
    p. cm.
  Includes bibliographical references and index.
  ISBN 0-393-70366-5
  1. Eye movement desensitization and reprocessing. 2. Post-traumatic stress disorder—Treatment. I. Rogers, Susan, 1953– II. Title.
RC489.ES98 S554 2001
616.85′21—dc21   2001045249

W. W. Norton & Company, Inc., 500 Fifth Avenue, New York, N.Y. 10110
www.wwnorton.com

W. W. Norton & Company Ltd., Castle House, 75/76 Wells Street,
London W1T 3QR

1 2 3 4 5 6 7 8 9 0

To
Al Brooks, M.S.W.
W. Peter Sax, M.D.
and
George Phillips Rogers, USN, WW II
David Stephen Silver, USN, WW II

CONTENTS

FOREWORD

Approximately ten years ago, it was reported (Janoff-Bulman, 1985; McCann & Pearlman, 1990) that both trauma victims and their therapists were often debilitated by having their assumptions "shattered." In the act of confronting their patients' realities, therapists were apt to discover that their belief in a universe in which they were safe and in control was not borne out. The lack of effective therapeutic tools compounded the problem by reinforcing a sense of protracted helplessness in the face of their patients' prolonged suffering. Such therapists were prone to developing what became known as vicarious traumatization and burnout, and many left the profession. We can only feel compassion for those men and women, as we do for the patients who were never healed. The breadth of experience and knowledge demonstrated in this book can help assure that these tragedies are not repeated.

While I was sipping coffee in college cafes, the Vietnam conflict merely an ongoing conversation topic, Steven Silver, one of the authors of this book, was fighting in that war. At the time, I did not know anyone personally who had gone to Vietnam. Indeed, neither I nor any of my acquaintances had any inkling of the motivations and commitments of those who did. But, as I later learned, there were many who believed it was their duty to serve; they believed that it would not be honorable to do otherwise. Barely out of their teens, their beliefs in personal invulnerability and of a benign universe where they were safe and in control were shattered long before our generation of therapists recognized it as a problem. Many did not survive. Many who did survive are still in psychological pain. While no one was left unscathed, many, understandably, prefer not to look back. However, as a Marine Corps officer and decorated combat veteran, Steven Silver has inspired me since I met him. Many years ago, speaking of his work as a therapist in the VA, he said to me "I'm still determined to get them all home alive." I feel gratified beyond words that EMDR has aided him in that service.

There is much to learn in the pages of this book. Dr. Silver, a multiply honored VA PTSD program director, and his colleague Dr. Susan Rogers have combined the latest developments in trauma treatment with the specialty wisdom of a field that has spanned many decades. Their use of standard EMDR protocols, innovative adaptations, and an integration of divergent methodologies will serve well therapists who work with victims of combat, terrorism, and torture. Both authors have served as program directors in the EMDR Humanitarian Assistance Programs and have trained diverse groups of clinicians in numerous countries. Their consolidation of the contributions of these clinicians, along with their sensitivity and understanding of multicultural issues, will make this book useful to therapists worldwide.

The goal of the EMDR Humanitarian Assistance Programs is to disrupt the cycle of violence that characterizes much of the world today (see Appendix B). We believe that by addressing the pain of the victims we can help stop the ongoing threat of retribution. When people are able to process the pain of the past, they become more open and responsive to present solutions. Trainings in Northern Ireland, the Balkans, and the Middle East have taught the same lessons: There is suffering on both sides of any war, and there are commonalities that can allow understanding if the pain can be addressed. Ultimately, there is the possibility of peace if the pain can be healed.

The EMDR Humanitarian Assistance Programs has organized a worldwide cadre of clinicians who are able and willing to go to the aid of any population in pain. Regardless of background or ideology, it is evident to most clinicians that those who are in pain will almost certainly inflict pain on others, that many perpetrators are those who have been previously victimized. As we treat the extant pain we not only liberate the victim, but we also spare others the consequences of unhealed rage and the need for vindication and vengeance. By so doing, we hope to spare future generations from unremitting suffering. We open the possibility of peace in our lifetime.

We are always at the effect of our ideologies and experiences. However, regardless of geographical location, clinicians can all believe in the possibility of what we can become with enough persistence, wisdom, and good will. Whether or not we believe that we live in a benign universe, with the help of this book we should be able to forge a future where we can exert some control for the common good.

—Francine Shapiro, Ph.D.

FOREWORD

About two years ago Steve Silver briefly mentioned plans for doing this book. I was pleased that his, and Sue Rogers', well-earned expertise in working with psychological trauma, and especially trauma related to war and terrorism, would be chronicled for the benefit of counselors and their clients. Their experience and ability in teaching, conducting research, and providing clinical services in this area are unsurpassed in general and with EMDR in particular.

I first heard of Steve in the early 1980s, when I began learning to work with combat-related PTSD. One of my first and most valuable educational experiences was watching a videotape that included Steve's discussion of Native American methods for healing from war trauma. As time passed and I became more involved in the field, I had the opportunity to meet Steve, and later Sue, whose knowledge and dedication to our work were inspiring. It is the chance to meet and work with people like them that makes a career profoundly rewarding. I am honored to be a small part of their sharing their work even more widely.

The writer of a foreword may find himself in one of several possible situations. Of those the most felicitous is to have a volume good enough to simply provide direction to its merits. Since that is the happy situation in which I find myself, I will take advantage of it and recommend that readers avail themselves of this book for its:

- authoritative discussion of the psychological effects and treatment of war and terrorism;
- comprehensive review of the research on the use of EMDR;
- expert suggestions on the general and specific use of EMDR;
- writing style and organization, which are clear, professional, and yet personal enough so that one feels that one is hearing colleagues who have much to say;
- template for cross-cultural clinical and teaching interventions to traumatized people;
- relating of the chance reunion of the two veterans, and the lessons of that meeting;
- telling of the psychiatrist who was forced to work with the oppressors of her people;
- showing how one veteran learned that what had separated him from others could become the link that connected them;
- comprehensive and emotionally powerful discussion of issues of countertransference in war trauma work;
- direction to a path toward integration of spirituality and science-based psychotherapy;
- documentation of how, in EMDR, very specific interventions for recurring specific situations can be proposed and the results can immediately be measured;
- introduction to Michael Paterson, a psychotherapist who is also a physically and psychologically traumatized former Northern Ireland police officer, and narration of his story of trauma treatment from his perspective as both a client and a therapist.

Among the many treasures of this book are the nuggets that open each chapter—brief, lucid comments from clients that relate the various aspects of traumatization and treatment. They have the immediacy and universality of haiku.

Read on, you will see how right I am.

—Howard Lipke, Ph.D.
North Chicago DVA Medical Center

PREFACE

This is a joint effort. When we started this book, I (Steven M. Silver; SMS) was director of the inpatient PTSD program of the Veterans Administration (VA; now the Department of Veterans Affairs) Medical Center in Coatesville, Pennsylvania.

In that same program, I (Susan Rogers; SR) worked as a psychologist and was also the research coordinator and assistant director. We had provided treatment to war veterans for many years—SMS since 1972, SR since 1982. We were trained in and used a variety of treatment methods before encountering EMDR, including Rogerian therapy, rational-emotive therapy, reality therapy, gestalt, hypnosis, implosive therapy, and neurolinguistic programming, among others.

In all candor, EMDR sounds, to be charitable, quite odd to most therapists the first time they hear of it. We were not exceptional in that regard. In 1989 I (SMS) was a member of the editorial board of the *Journal of Traumatic Stress*. The publication of Shapiro's research on what was then called eye movement desensitization (EMD; Shapiro, 1989a) in that journal came as a surprise.

Upon reading her paper, I contacted the editor, Charles Figley, Ph.D., and expressed my disbelief in the results. I thought either the journal was the victim of a hoax or some fundamental flaw existed in the research methodology. Though the editor reassured me the data were sound, I remained highly skeptical. When approached by other VA clinicians about EMD, my usual response was to voice suspicions.

It was not until a peer, Howard Lipke, Ph.D., of the North Chicago VA Medical Center, contacted me that I became at least slightly open to the possibility that EMD was a valid treatment. Lipke had taught himself EMD by puzzling out the procedure from that first article. Using this procedure, though admittedly not making use of Shapiro's full protocol, Lipke was getting very positive results with Vietnam War veterans. Indeed, the results he was getting surpassed those I obtained with exposure and cognitive therapies.

Now slightly interested, I attended the first EMD training weekend in Philadelphia. The following Monday I tried it with a patient who reported complete resolution of a combat experience after three sets of eye movements. I was astounded at this result (maintained in the decade since) and began using the new procedure with any veteran who was willing to try it.

I (SR) worked in the same PTSD program. I had recently completed data collection for a dissertation on PTSD treatment outcome when I read Shapiro's article. Having spent several years reviewing the available literature on PTSD treatment, my initial reaction to the description of what was then called EMD was, "This is stupid. In fact, this is so stupid I'll bet there's something to it."

I completed Level I and II training in 1990 and 1991 and eventually became a pro bono trainer for the EMDR Humanitarian Assistance Programs. My clinical work generated research inquiries and I became the principal investigator for a VA-funded research project investigating EMDR.

When Francine Shapiro began the development of EMDR, the primary focus was on posttraumatic stress disorder (PTSD). She developed a sensitivity to the plight of war veterans suffering from the condition, particular survivors of the Vietnam War. While developing the method, she visited with veterans at a VA Vet Center in San Jose, California. Afterwards, she said, "I got slammed in the face with the war I'd ignored. No one I knew had gone. I saw they were still dealing with it. And I saw the nobility they showed in their suffering." She went on to say, "My feelings were crystallized by a Vietnam veteran who was a therapist when he said that he was trying to do here what he tried to do over there—bring them home alive." (F. Shapiro, personal communication, 1994).

Shapiro hoped to see EMDR rapidly adopted by those working with veterans. In the early 1990s she offered to train VA clinicians and counselors for free, but her offer was rejected. Nonetheless, she continued her commitment to provide VA mental health professionals with EMDR and selected two VA psychologists to become EMDR trainers, Howard Lipke and me (SMS). A program for training VA clinicians followed. Dr. Lipke pioneered a method for training small groups, while I became an EMDR Institute senior trainer and utilized the large-group format of the EMDR Institute.

The forerunners of EMDR Humanitarian Assistance Programs (EMDR–HAP) were the pro bono trainings organized by the EMDR Institute in such war-ravaged places as Bosnia-Herzegovina and Croatia. We were active in these and later EMDR–HAP programs and provided EMDR training to numerous VA and other clinicians working with survivors of war and terrorism.

This book grew out of those activities. While it is not a substitute for becoming formally trained in EMDR, it is designed to provide a mental health worker new to EMDR with a basic understanding of that complex methodology, while also addressing the need for a more precise focus on treating trauma due to war and terrorism. In that regard, it addresses the needs of trained EMDR clinicians.

A deliberate decision was made to make this book primarily a useful tool for clinicians "in the trenches." Theoreticians, academics, and researchers will find much food for thought and possible areas for formal research. However, for those who are providing treatment for the most difficult trauma responses—those whose etiology is in war and terrorism—this book has as its main purpose to provide information and ideas from the real world of therapy.

Because EMDR is still new enough to be evolving, few of its procedures are carved in granite. There is much room for research, innovation, and variation. To tap into this ongoing growth and change, we invited the comments of many of our peers and friends from around the world who have brought light into the heart of darkness. We invite you to consider their comments, experiences, and modifications of the EMDR methodology as a rich vein representing hard work, sometimes painfully developed competence, commitment, and, not least, compassion. To avoid the repetition of "private communication" citations when making use of their input, we adopted the simple expedient of mentioning them by name. Where, for the sake of clarity, we quote them, the reader should understand we are making use of messages they sent to us for use in this book. They are listed in the Appendix with e-mail addresses.

Having said that, we wish to stress that the protocol for EMDR with trauma survivors developed by Francine Shapiro is the bedrock of this book. Readers who have not encountered EMDR before are best advised to become formally trained in the EMDR protocol before making use of the material here. This book should be regarded as a supplement to formal training and may best be seen as a specialist volume in a library built around Shapiro's 1995 text.

When discussing our individual experiences, we chose to write in the first person and identify ourselves through the use of our initials, SMS or SR, in the manner already encountered.

The reader will find the first chapter aimed at providing a basic understanding of the nature of trauma reactions to war and terrorism experiences. We discuss the nature of war and terrorism and why we include such apparently nonpolitical horrors as school shootings as acts of terrorism.

The foundation of EMDR work is the client. Chapters 2 and 3 present a case history and an interview with an EMDR client to emphasize this point. These chapters also introduce the methodology that we cover in more detail later on.

The role of therapists in EMDR is not that of automatons. Using EMDR requires solid clinical skills and can be quite demanding. Chapter 4 presents an interview with an EMDR therapist. Chapter 5 follows with a discussion of therapist attributes.

The next eight chapters cover basic EMDR methodology. In addition to reviewing the procedure, we point out those areas of particular concern to our topic. We then examine variations of the basic methodology developed in the field useful for survivors of recent events and for children. War and terrorism survivors may encounter high levels of emotional reaction during treatment and so we devote a chapter to abreaction procedures. The levels of intense emotion resulting in abreaction often come from powerful issues. We provide chapters on grief and loss, guilt, and anger and suggest ways of addressing and processing those issues.

Working with war and terrorism survivors can mean participation in relief work and a chapter on this activity is provided. Whether therapists go into the field or not, there are often cross-cultural issues to consider and a chapter is presented on that topic.

The last chapter is designed to provide a brief summary of the formal research corroborating what we learned empirically in the field. Therapists working with war and terrorism survivors may find it useful to review the literature. Familiarity with it is helpful when discussing assistance methods with authorities unfamiliar with EMDR.

Throughout the book we consider questions raised during EMDR training concerning our experiences with survivors of war and terrorism. Where we discuss perspectives and theoretical understandings, our goal is to provide information useful for the therapist or client in formulating how EMDR might be applied.

Oklahoma City, Belfast, Zagreb, Rwanda, Dunblane, Sarajevo, Columbine, Londonderry, World War II, Korean War, Beirut, Vietnam War, and many other places and events—we have been honored to work with survivors of these and with those who have helped the survivors. There is much to be learned from them. We hope this book will be one small part of that learning.

ACKNOWLEDGMENTS

It is a commonplace in books to state that many have contributed but the authors are responsible for any errors. The commonplace happens to be true.

First, we acknowledge the survivors who granted us the honor of their trust and the privilege of witnessing their courage in taking on this new treatment.

Second, we acknowledge the fine work of those who opened their hearts to us and let us pick their brains. If there is such a thing as evil—and working in this field tends to reinforce that idea—then there is also a thing called good, and these people embody it. We are proud to call them our peers and friends.

Third, I (SMS) would like to acknowledge my coauthor. I have seen her courage descending into the dark valley of Sarajevo and into the dark valleys of her clients' hearts. If a Marine may say so of someone not of the Corps, she has been *semper fidelis*.

Fourth, we would like to acknowledge the input, suggestions, and assistance of many others, some of whom would prefer to remain anonymous. Jim Goss, Lady Lobo, Col. Jacob Flannagan, Sidley Hawker, and Max all made their contribution in word and deed, if only in helping us maintain a proper focus on the book and life. We would particularly like to thank K. Soze, Ph.D., for his valuable insights on the role of belief systems in the modern world, and J. L. Lewis, Ph.D., for his organizational suggestions.

Fifth, we acknowledge the unending dedication and contributions of the EMDR Humanitarian Assistance Programs and all those EMDR clinicians who go into harm's way to provide help and training.

Sixth, our gratitude goes out to Francine Shapiro. She developed what history will undoubtedly come to judge as a significant contribution to psychotherapy.

Light in the Heart of Darkness

EMDR AND THE TREATMENT OF

WAR AND TERRORISM SURVIVORS

THE NATURE OF WAR AND

TERRORISM TRAUMA

"You don't know and I hope you never do."

This book describes the application of Eye Movement Desensitization and Reprocessing, or EMDR (Shapiro, 1989a, 1989b, 1995), to the treatment of war and terrorism trauma and is based on the authors' ten years of experience using the method. Though the focus of the book is on a specific form of psychotherapy, it contains information about war trauma that may be relevant to therapists working from a wide variety of theoretical orientations.

We have combined the psychological reactions to the traumatic experiences of war and terrorism. As will be seen later in this chapter, these kinds of traumas share some unique qualities. For purposes of brevity, we will generally use the phrase "war trauma" to encompass both.

Terrorism is, after all, war waged by those without the resources to conduct the application of violence for political ends generally recognized as "war." Rather than a battalion, a suicide bomber is sent. As in general war, man-made violence may be visited upon civilians or military. From a politico-military standpoint, the only features distinguishing war and terrorism are that in war there is an attempt to seize and hold ground, or deny its use, while in terrorism that goal is reserved, if present at all, for some distant future. However frequently

1

violated, recognized rules of warfare exist, while there are none for terrorism; terrorism has as its primary goal the destruction of the opponent's will. War certainly has that as a goal, but it may be subsumed to other goals, such as the taking of territory or the destruction of the enemy's capacity for waging war. For the victim of violence, there is no difference between war and terrorism. The explosion in the marketplace could just as well have been a car bomb as an artillery shell.

Terrorism is not just a function of conventional politics. It may be engaged in by anyone with resentment toward groups of others for a variety of reasons, real or imagined. With the identification of "others" being the key, mail bombings or mass shootings at work or school may be seen as acts of terrorism. Whether or not the perpetrator had in mind the psychological result of terror as opposed to the extermination of the others is not the critical point from the perspective of the survivors.

WHAT IS TRAUMA?

Trauma reactions have been the subject of energetic investigation since the inclusion of the diagnostic criteria for posttraumatic stress disorder (PTSD) in the 1980 *Diagnostic and Statistical Manual of Mental Disorders* (*DSM-III*; American Psychiatric Association). Much of the ongoing professional discussion about trauma reactions such as PTSD centers around the questions of whether they are more properly viewed as a function of the nature of certain events or as a function of the characteristics of the person experiencing the event, and to what extent the post-event environment plays a role. While there are biological models of PTSD, what follows is our attempt to integrate various psychological conceptualizations of trauma as a background for understanding the development of posttraumatic symptoms and for identifying effective means of treating disorders such as PTSD.

One of the more enduring elements of the psychoanalytic conceptualization of trauma is the suppression of disturbing experiences and the therapeutic value of bringing such experiences to the surface and exploring them. This model was the foundation for much of the treatment of veterans of the First and Second World Wars (Grinker & Spiegel, 1979; Sargant, 1997; Southard, 1973). Current support for this model can be found in the work of Pennebaker (1985), who demonstrated that writing about disturbing life experiences decreases anxiety.

In the 1980s a behavioral conceptualization of PTSD was presented (Keane, Zimering, & Caddell, 1985). In this model, the symptoms of PTSD were seen as conditioned responses to the unconditioned stimuli present during the traumatic event. The goal of behavioral trauma treatment is the extinction of anxiety and avoidance of unconditioned stimuli. This model, while providing a reasonable explanation for such posttraumatic symptoms as anxiety and avoidance of trauma-related stimuli, as well as hypervigilance, physiological reactivity, and poor concentration, was less successful at explaining guilt, grief, depression, emotional numbing, and the spontaneous reexperiencing of symptoms such as flashbacks, nightmares, and intrusive memories.

Another perspective is the cognitive model, which views trauma memories as a sort of "unfinished business." They command the individual's attention and demand completion or integration into existing schema. This model suggests a failure to integrate a unique experience is at the heart of posttraumatic symptomatology. In this case the goal of treatment is not a simple desensitization of anxiety, but something more akin to accommodation and assimilation.

There is a certain amount of overlap among these models, with the focus on completion and integration being common to psychodynamic and cognitive conceptualizations, and an increasing recognition on the part of behaviorists that subjective appraisals play a role in determining whether or not an experience leads to long-term dysfunction. Later revisions of the behavioral model place greater attention on the violation of an individual's assumptions about the predictability and controllability of events (Foa, Zinbarg, & Rothbaum, 1992). Other more cognitively oriented models, such as that proposed by Janoff-Bulman (1985), address a broader range of challenges to the individual's belief system. Still others focus on an individual's explanatory style as a factor that may perpetuate maladaptive responses to events (Benight, Swift, Sanger, Smith, & Zeppeling, 1999).

We view trauma reactions as complex responses, with individuals' immediate perceptions determining the degree of distress with which they respond. Some of the learning occurring during the event may be rapid and unconscious, as would be suggested by the behavioral model. However, the response does not stop there. Humans reflect on their experiences and draw conclusions about them that direct their future behavior. This is where personality type or previous experiences (there may be little distinction from a learning perspective), as well as the posttrauma environment, come into play in determining whether an individual resolves the trauma or becomes impaired by it. The posttrauma environment may be important in providing opportunities for processing an event and modifying the conclusions drawn from it.

Shapiro's modern restatement of these ideas is that trauma responses are a form of "information dysfunctionally stored in the nervous system" and that treatment involves the processing of this information. Her original 1989 explanation for the effect of her procedure, then called Eye Movement Desensitization, reflected her belief that she had developed an alternative method of "counter-conditioning" trauma memories. However, she also observed that her procedure led to a resolution of distress that was more rapid than would be predicted by the conditioning model. In 1992 she began speaking in terms of information-processing. Since she started with a single observation that spontaneous eye movements seemed to accompany decreases in emotional distress, she assumed that this was the effect of an innate information-processing mechanism. Her model, though possibly insufficient to fully explain the effects of EMDR, is the basis for much of the material presented in this book.

From this perspective, a trauma may be defined as an experience that is not, for whatever reason, processed. The brain may continually return to it, trying, in effect, to make it fit with the previously held beliefs and value systems. At the same time, the individual may try to avoid thinking about the experience for a variety of reasons: it is too horrible, too damaging of self, too disconcerting of the previous world view, and so on. This conflict is experienced by the individual as the intrusive and avoidant symptoms of PTSD.

Time does not solve the conflicts generated by a trauma. The needed resolution comes about as the experience—most particularly, its meaning—is examined and reconciled so that it might fit with the already existing belief systems of the individual (assimilation) or those beliefs themselves are finally altered so that the information presented by the new experience might be finally accepted (accommodation).

This leaves us with a definition of healthy functioning as the ability to process experiences—that is, to extract and store information that can serve as a useful guide to future behavior. This process involves a certain amount of "distortion"—some details are emphasized, others become vague or forgotten. Other life experiences can shape our perceptions at the time of the event or during later recollections.

This process can be illustrated by a case example. In describing one of his most traumatic war experiences, one veteran described his reaction to the explosion of a nearby grenade. It was the first time he had ever seen a "chicom" (Chinese communist grenade) and he mistook it for a small soft drink bottle. Much of his reaction was based on this misperception. He picked it up and casually tossed it into the branches of a nearby banana tree, only to have it explode and knock him over. Certainly this event meets the current *DSM-IV* (American Psychiatric Association, 1994) stressor criterion as involving an immediate threat of death or physical harm.

It is clear from this description that he was encountering a novel object. His brain scanned for the closest match in his repertoire—a small soda bottle. He threw it and experienced something unexpected and aversive. The optimal outcome of this experience would be that he would learn to distinguish between harmless and dangerous objects, that he would have a new category—objects that resemble soda bottles in some ways but not in others and that can explode if not handled properly. This may certainly be seen as matter of discrimination, but it can also be seen as a process of accommodation and assimilation. If he were to ignore the implications of the experience and continue to treat such objects as if they were soda bottles, he might get killed. If he were to begin treating all soda bottles as if they could explode, there would be some possible negative consequences, but they would be lesser consequences.

Note that, to some extent, it was his previous belief system that set him up for the shock. Had the grenade resembled a firecracker he might have been less inclined to pick it up and less surprised when it exploded. Furthermore, his response to the event goes beyond a simple reevaluation of what is safe and what is not. Upon reflection, he may also conclude that his failure to see the grenade for what it was in the first place is evidence that he is stupid. Again, previous experience will have an influence on his interpretation of the event. If he came from a supportive family, he might feel frightened and embarrassed for a little while but eventually recover, given the strength of his positive self belief systems. If he came from a family where he was constantly belittled, the event with the grenade would likely have a broader effect.

He may see himself as an incompetent soldier who is a danger to himself and others. The incident, while perhaps leading directly to an aversion to bottle-like objects, also leads indirectly to a tendency to avoid other people or situations that place him in a position of responsibility. While he is still in the combat zone, he is likely to have difficulty avoiding such situations, so the events following the grenade incident may have a moderating effect (failures reinforcing the idea that he's incompetent, successes reducing it). It is not possible to appreciate the meaning of the grenade event in isolation; instead, it is necessary to examine its meaning in light of experiences that followed or preceded it.

What result would we want for this individual? First, we would like him to be able to distinguish between grenades and soda bottles. Emotion plays a potentially positive role in this. The fear he felt during the explosion serves to assist him in making correct choices in the future. This need not be entirely on a conscious, verbal level. The knot in his stomach when he sees something resembling the grenade will be sufficient. We would also like him to be able to make use of this experience without involving his entire sense of self-worth, to be able to conclude that his mistake was based on a lack of familiarity, not a lack of intelligence.

He might resolve this conflict without intervention, simply by reviewing the experience or talking to someone about it. On the other hand, the process of resolution could become inhibited by avoidance. He may avoid thinking about the experience, because not just the event itself but also the implications of the event are disturbing. The conflict between what he would like to believe about himself (competent and intelligent) and the implications of the experience (incompetent and stupid) are threatening.

In another example, a child survives the shooting rampage of a peer that leaves others dead or wounded. The impact of the event on the world view may be enormous. Though the child survives, the child's belief system may be shattered in several significant ways. The perception of safety within the school is challenged by the reality of the gun shots, and the reminder of vulnerability is triggered each day by seeing the newly plastered and painted bullet holes in the hallway walls. Indeed, the impact of the event may be generalized, so that no place is now regarded as safe.

Arguments about how safe the current environment is have little meaning to the child or, for that matter, the adult survivor. Their experiences may provide them with new learning, in which degrees of safety are not the issue. From survivors' point of view, the real issue is degrees of *danger*. Their perceptions of the immediate world have been shaken, so that they cannot share common, reasonably realistic evaluations of the environment. Now, everywhere is threatening.

For a child other perceptions are likely to have been affected. The view of parents, siblings, and teachers as protectors may have been overwhelmed so that the child is left with a sense of isolation. No one can help, everyone is powerless, and the child is alone. This may even grow into a sense of abandonment. While the child huddled in a coat closet hearing the sounds of gunfire, a seed was planted and may have quickly taken root and grown: "The people who say they love me have left me here."

Logic is not the issue. Simply explaining the reasons why the parents did not come running into the building to rescue the child may be insufficient, though necessary. From a child's perspective, the existing beliefs, perspectives, and paradigms are built not on logic but on experience. Mommy and Daddy have always been there for them; therefore, they always will be there. This belief is challenged by their experience, which is what makes the experience traumatic. The problem for the child is that the alternate belief, "I am all alone," is terrifying. It is particularly terrifying in view of the surrounding experiences.

It is important to remember that, even in situations where the traumatic reaction has lasted for decades, the individual usually already has the information needed to resolve the internal conflicts. Trauma survivors can often see the irrational or unreasonable nature of the judgments they have made about themselves. They typically know, even before meeting a therapist, alternative, rational, and functional ways they could be thinking: "I know I couldn't do anything about the situation and I know I should just accept it, but I can't."

After all, most trauma survivors, long before they see a therapist, have received a great deal of advice and opinion from others, which often simply parallel their own thinking. Family and friends, self-help literature, and their observations of how other survivors of similar experiences are dealing with those experiences provide information: "It wasn't your fault. You did the best you could. Everyone makes mistakes so you shouldn't be so hard on yourself. There's no need to be afraid now because it's over."

If the information necessary for resolution of the trauma experience is already largely present, what keeps an individual from accessing it? This is a critical point, one with which both therapists and their clients have struggled. After all, the very intensity of the conflict discussed thus far might be expected be serve as a powerful motivator to make use of the information and thus alleviate the distress.

The most likely explanation is the sheer power of the experience. Remember, when we are talking about a challenge to someone's existing belief system, we are referring to their most fundamental beliefs. Once altered by a powerful experience, the new beliefs are not easily modified or discarded, no matter how logical the alternative presentation might be. The client's ability to *process* the experience, then, is impaired by the *meaning* of the experience—the more radical, in terms of preexisting beliefs, that experience, the more likely processing is to become stymied.

When considering the impact of the meaning of an experience it is important to take into account the totality of a person's belief system. For example, a child may have learned the world is essentially chaotic and unpredictable. The child may also have learned that she or he can handle effectively whatever is encountered in life. To learn that the world is unpredictable is not necessarily the same as learning that one cannot deal with it. On the other hand, a very protected child who learned that she or he will always be protected and kept safe by others but who developed little sense of personal mastery over life may find it overwhelming to encounter a moderately stressful experience without external supportive resources. These extreme examples—children learning the world is chaotic usually do not develop a strong sense of self and mastery—point out the difficulty in predicting who, in a given experience, may have trauma reactions. To put it another way, whether or not an experience is traumatic is not a function of what the experience was; instead, the degree of trauma relates to the degree of difficulty in assimilating the meaning of the experience. This is one of the reasons why it is possible for two people to go through the same experience but only one to be traumatized by it.

A case example illustrates this point. I (SMS) had in my group therapy a veteran whom I was also working with individually. The primary combat experience the veteran was unable to resolve was an incident that occurred as his unit was sweeping through an area of relatively open dry rice paddies while heading toward a river. As the radio operator for his company commander, it was his job to stay with the officer and keep the radio always available and functioning. Things had been relatively uneventful. Ahead, their lead platoon had just entered into a tree line bordering the river, while to the right and left the other two platoons were checking out other tree lines. Helicopters, including gunships, circled overhead and the company commander was busy with the radio, talking to the platoons, their supporting units, and his commander. The veteran remembered that, standing out in the open with the officer in the middle of the dry and dusty rice paddy, he was a little bored and envied the members of the platoons who were at least in the shade of the trees.

Suddenly the tree line to their front, several hundred yards away, erupted in a series of explosions and gunfire. Red and green tracers seemed to be emerging from every portion of it. Then what appeared to be "a hundred" (but later proved to be no more than twenty) North Vietnamese soldiers came running out of the tree line, heading directly at the radio operator and his officer. He thought he was going to die. He could not run for cover, since he had to stay with his officer and keep the radio available. His impression was that the enemy soldiers were all coming straight toward him and there was nothing he could do about it. However, the officer was using the radio to get assistance and the gunships and supporting mortars began almost immediately to attack the oncoming soldiers, and the platoons on either side of him opened fire as well. In a matter of seconds it was over, with all the enemy soldiers dead or wounded.

He remembered, when discussing this experience in individual therapy, having been so afraid "I peed myself." When he realized what he had done, he dumped a canteen of water down his front, ostensibly to cool off, in an effort to hide the stains. His overwhelming feeling from the experience was helplessness. He stated that whenever he got into situations that he saw as at all threatening, he would feel like he was back in that rice paddy and there was nothing he could do.

He had not described this incident in group because of his shame about how he had reacted. While working on it in individual therapy, he finally decided that "If I'm ever going to get over this thing, I have to be able to talk about it." He decided to talk about the firefight in group therapy. During the next group session, when I asked if anyone had anything to start off with, he talked about the experience, beginning with what it meant to him and his anxiety about talking about it in front of others, especially other veterans. Reassured by the group, he began to describe the battle in detail. There were two new men in the group and I could see one of them was becoming more fixated on the veteran.

As the veteran finished his story, the new man leaned toward him and said, "Red?" The veteran looked startled for a moment and then stared at the new man. Finally he said, "L-T?" When the other man nodded, both men stood and hugged each other.

The new man, L-T, had been the officer, the company commander. What was interesting was his perception of the event. He barely remembered it. What he remembered was that the lead platoon and the NVA blundered into each other, with the Vietnamese soldiers having just crossed the river as the Americans were walking toward it. As both sides opened fire, the Vietnamese ran past their startled American enemies and emerged from the tree line intent on breaking contact by getting across the rice paddies to a denser area of woods. It was a critical mistake, for the company commander could see them clearly and was able to call in the supporting fire needed to stop them.

L-T never felt in danger. What he saw was a small group of enemy soldiers out in the open and relatively helpless and too far away from him to be much of a personal threat. Having at his command enormous firepower and using it effectively gave him a sense of mastery over the situation. Though he was later given a medal for his actions, as far as he was concerned he was "just taking care of business." It was a chance, he said later, to show his competence to himself.

His memory of his radio operator, nicknamed "Red" in Vietnam, was that "As always, he was cool, calm, and collected. Red never got rattled and always had the radio up and running."

The two men were literally shoulder to shoulder in the same situation. For one it was traumatic; for the other it was an experience that tended to be ego-enhancing. Later on, after his promotion to captain and reassignment to another unit, a portion of that unit was ambushed and he tried unsuccessfully for the better part of a day to relieve his men. His inability to do so was interpreted by him as a failure and became the primary source of his PTSD.

The meaning and therefore the impact of the experience were different for the two veterans. Red knew that he was not really helpless, neither at the time nor since. However, that knowledge was based upon his life experiences in the environment of "the world"—that is, the noncombat, ordinary life arena. The idea of helplessness was introduced in the rush of twenty oncoming enemy soldiers, a far more powerful conveyor of an idea than day-to-day functioning. Required to literally stand still and do nothing and thus permit ongoing communication, he perceived himself as not doing anything, helpless.

The problem became not just that he perceived himself as having *been* helpless. Given that he had, from his perspective, become helpless at a most critical time, he had little faith in his ability to handle any other situations in his life. Over time, this idea of helplessness became more and more pervasive and, of course, self-reinforcing. Believing that he was helpless, or even just might be helpless, led him to conduct his life business with decreasing expectations of success, which led to a greater number of failures, which made the idea of helplessness even more powerful.

This case points out two important aspects of PTSD that clients and some therapists overlook. First, PTSD is not the result of seeing horrible scenes. While scenes may be indeed horrible, the problems arise from the unresolved conflicts. Second, the conflict is active now; the unresolved issues and conflicts do not recede with time. Time only provides an opportunity for resolution or for the situation to be exacerbated by subsequent life events. In and of itself time does nothing.

What this means is that the event is not the source of the traumatic stress reaction but its meaning. An example of this occurred with a client I (SR) worked with. She had been a nurse in a field hospital in Vietnam. One night she felt something brush her hair. Assuming it was a bug, she swatted at it and went on about her work. The next morning soldiers came on the ward investigating sniper activity that had taken place during the night and showed her where a bullet was embedded in the wall. At that point she realized that it was a bullet that brushed her hair and not a bug. Shaking and sick, she went to her bunk. Later she developed intrusive memories about the moment when the bullet passed her as well as an aversion to having something touch her hair unexpectedly. The trauma occurred when she learned she had been in danger. Her previous therapy had stayed within the traditional confines of the trauma event, the bullet grazing her hair, and had failed to obtain resolution. Had we used EMDR, she would have focused on whatever parts of the event emerged. In her case, the most disturbing part of the experience was learning how close to death she had come and most of her processing would be done at that point.

While war trauma does not appear to be affected by such variables as race and culture (Adelaja, 1976), the degree of group cohesion and support does tend to reduce psychiatric casualties during the war (e.g., *Cyprus*: Volkan, 1979; *Israel*: Sohlberg, 1976). However, regardless of the degree of group cohesion, combat trauma reactions tend to persist over time unless successful treatment is provided. Again, this is true across cultures (e.g., *Canada*: Klonoff, McDougal, Clark, Kramer, & Horgan, 1976; *Israel*: Merbaum, 1977; *Japan*: Meguro, 1972; *USA*: Archibald, Long, Miller, & Tuddenham, 1962).

War trauma, like nonwar trauma, may have a delayed response (DeFazio, 1978). Perhaps the initial relief of surviving mutes the manifestations of the psychological trauma, or the survivor may be attempting to "gut it out," believing that with a little time things will return to normal. Or survivors may believe their nightmares and startle response are normal and to be expected and they just have to learn to live with them. Some survivors have focused on "catching up" or getting on with their lives, setting a furious pace for themselves that serves to block at least some of their symptoms.

While war survivors may describe themselves as essentially symptom free immediately following their leaving the war, close examination of their histories often shows early manifestations of problems. Nightmares, avoidance of war reminders, frequent changes in employment, difficulty finding pleasure in life, a general muting of emotional responsiveness, a "workaholic" approach to the job or school, and difficulty in forming and maintaining relationships, are often very common and typically overlooked as indicators of worse to come.

Whether or not the reaction is delayed, the result of war and terrorist trauma is typically more complex, severe, and chronic than that found in noncombat reactions. Trauma resulting from the experiences of war and terrorism differs in degree from that typically encountered in civilian trauma in a number of ways. It should be noted that we are speaking in broad terms and that there are always exceptions. Keeping that in mind, let us point out several potentially unique elements of war trauma.

The first quality of war trauma is the duration of exposure. Time is an important variable in terms of its contribution to erosion of an individual's capacities and modification of her or his perceptions while enduring combat. The physical and psychological exhaustion typically experienced on the battlefield can lead to a state in which an individual views the present situation as disconnected from the rest of life (soldiers in Vietnam referred to "the 'Nam" and "the World," as if the two existed in separate universes). This may lead individuals to disregard previously developed value and belief systems, with powerful consequences once they leave the war zone and attempt to pick up those belief systems. Indeed, prolonged time in combat may result in an increased perception of danger, so that the perception itself, if allowed to escalate to a great enough degree, may become a stressor (Noyes & Klettie, 1977).

A society dealing with terrorism is, in effect, in a war zone with no "rear area." A glance at the situation in Northern Ireland or Rwanda illustrates this point. Terrorism served as a vehicle to promote change in both places and, as is typical for terrorism, its application was ongoing. This is very much like the situation in a formal combat zone.

The second quality of war trauma is the likelihood of multiple traumas. While a survivor of a civilian trauma, say, an assault or a plane crash, may experience a terrible event, war survivors typically have undergone several terrible events, any one of which would be traumatic by itself. While in Sarajevo, we encountered mental health professionals who had, during the two years of war, undergone the traumas of having to send their children away, living in fear of being overrun by the Serb forces, undergoing daily shelling and sniper attacks, seeing friends and family die, and experiencing several brushes with death themselves. They had also experienced cold, starvation, and ineffective help from the international community, and they were all the time aware that the people trying to kill them had been their friends and neighbors. In addition to this, many of them had continued to work during the war and had tried to help their clients cope with their own war experiences. Again, terrorism is often not a single event but a series, and simply living in a particular place, such as Sarajevo or Belfast, may greatly increase the chance of an individual's being traumatized more than once.

The third quality of war trauma is that it is man-made. Survivors of natural disasters and accidents deal with terrible events whose origins are clearly external to humankind; they typically are referred to as "acts of God." War and terrorism are conducted by people and as such carry an additional existential load. God may be questioned for permitting people to commit the acts of war, but it is people placing their fingers on the triggers, detonating the bombs, planting the land mines, and firing the artillery. The fact of fellow humans' committing such a deliberate act has an added impact on an individual's world view, understanding of relationships, and sense of what it is to be human.

The fourth quality of war trauma is the tendency of a survivor to be both perpetrator and victim. The role of victim in war is obvious. The position of perpetrator is unfortunately one that is often not clearly understood and often not willingly approached by therapists, as it is likely to generate a major problem in countertransference. War survivors may be perpetrators in two ways, which we have termed "objective perpetration" and "subjective perpetration."

Objective perpetrators are those who have committed acts that by any reasonable moral scale, including that of the individual, are considered wrongful. For example, the soldier who mutilates enemy dead would be regarded by others and himself as a perpetrator of an atrocity. These actions, when committed by essentially normal individuals, are usually the result of the stress and impact of war accompanied by a breakdown in military discipline and leadership. In a blind moment the individual responds to the fear, anger, anxiety, confusion, exhaustion, and peer pressure, common to the battlefield. The normal behavioral safeguards are dropped and an act of perhaps previous unimaginable savagery takes place. The survivor is left with blame, guilt, and questions about his or her own trustworthiness.

Subjective perpetrators are those whose actions are within the broad guidelines of their society and culture but violate their own deeply held moral principles. Killing the enemy, for example, is, on a societal level, often laudatory. However, for a given individual, seeing the remains of an enemy soldier whose life he had just taken may result in a judgment that finds him in violation of rules in place long before the war. A common example of this is a soldier who has killed and feels that he has committed a wrongful act, for his religious upbringing has taught them, "Thou shalt not kill." Efforts by others with apparent moral authority, such as military chaplains, to provide intervention often fail, with the authority being discredited as hypocritical. Also, the survivor may see him- or herself as unworthy of intervention or salvation. This makes the individual's resolution even more difficult, as resources such as the church are seen as closed off to him.

In terrorism, this objective/subjective duality is less common. However, it may still exist, in that the victim may also be the supporter of one side or the other engaging in acts of terror. Certainly, the possibility of terrorism triggering revenge terrorism exists.

The fifth quality of war trauma is the conflicted duality of the survivor's roles, both powerful and powerless. Typically this results in an expectation of resolution and a corresponding degree of frustration when that resolution is not achieved. A nurse serving off the coast of Vietnam on a hospital ship had enormous power, literally that of life and death, as she conducted triage among the incoming wounded. Not only did she make decisions about who would get what kind of medical care and how rapidly, but she also performed medical procedures ordinarily reserved for doctors. On the other hand, as she put it, "I could not turn off the war." Powerful on one level, powerless on a metalevel, she was left uncertain as to her own abilities and competencies.

In situations of terrorism, the victim is, on the one hand, helpless to prevent such acts from occurring. She or he may be leading an essentially normal life—working, raising a family, and otherwise dealing with all the usual challenges of life. Success in life, in other words, gives a sense of mastery that is directly opposed by the person's perception of helplessness when and where the next act of terror takes place.

The sixth quality of war trauma is the experience of witnessing what happens to others. As noted above, this kind of trauma is typically repetitive in nature. A war refugee does not see something bad happen to others once, but many times. Particularly in limited geographical areas, such as a town or city under the siege of terrorism, a person is likely to encounter multiple scenes of carnage. There can develop a sense that the trauma experience is unending and that the world is a chaotic place in which a person is essentially helpless to keep bad things from happening. Along with this may come guilt. When others are injured or perish, the survivor naturally will wonder why. The need to believe in a "just universe" may be so great that, rather than abandon that belief, the individual will judge himself or herself as having in some way "cheated" and thereby survived.

Survivor guilt also may be generated by the individual's perception of what he has done with that survival. The justification of living is a challenge war survivors are continuously confronting, for each stage of their life is accompanied by the remembrance of others who did not live to that age. For some survivors this can lead to a life in which little is done, so as to avoid the guilt. This effort always fails, for life itself is an accomplishment, a possession, granted to the survivor but denied to the others. The unconscious response to this realization can be a form of "slow-motion suicide," in which the survivor sabotages anything of value life brings her or him while at the same time engaging in behaviors, such as substance abuse or violence, whose consequences are self-destructive. These behaviors may steadily escalate over time, as the pressure for some sort of final solution increases.

The seventh quality of war trauma is the societal impact of the war or terrorism. It is almost cliché to cite the negative response of American society to its returning Vietnam War veterans. We tend to think of WW II veterans as having been welcomed with open arms; however, some have spoken of the unhelpful attitude they encountered on returning: "People only wanted to hear 'war stories.' Their attitude was, 'What have you got to gripe about? We won, didn't we?'"

The harrowing experience of having loved ones in danger is not something people often wish to think or talk about. This can lead to an avoidance of reminders of the war, such as veterans, and a preference for silence about the experience. Survivors can become discouraged from discussing their experiences and gaining assistance from others.

The nature of war is such that all who live through it, whether directly exposed to battle or not, are, in effect, veterans. Its physical, political, social, and psychological repercussions may affect people for generations after the guns go silent. Indeed, these repercussions may serve to cause the guns to speak again unless they are dealt with.

Acts of terror provoke the same kinds of responses, with the increased likelihood that the individual members of what would otherwise be an individual's natural support system have, themselves, been victims. In this situation, all the members of a society may enter into an unspoken agreement to maintain a "conspiracy of silence." This effectively increases the probability that long-term trauma reactions will develop. Again, the similarities between these two sources of trauma, war and terrorism, far outweigh any differences. Indeed, those differences are primarily of interest to the political scientist; for the mental health clinician, the results are indistinguishable.

The qualities of war trauma may be found in particular noncombat trauma experiences, but is the severity, frequency, and sheer number of these qualities typically experienced by a war survivor are generally far in excess of that seen in civilian trauma.

Treating war trauma responses calls for highly effective approaches available coupled with the ability to respond to some of the highest demands that can be made on a therapist. On the other hand, treatment approaches effective with war trauma are readily adaptable and useful for noncombat trauma. This simple reality makes the study of war trauma and its treatment important for all clinicians.

Chapter 2

CASE PRESENTATION

"Doc, you cleaned my head out real good."

J was initially admitted to the VA hospital with a provisional diagnosis of depression. Presenting complaints included nightmares, flashbacks, headaches, chest pains, insomnia, panic attacks, depression, poor concentration, intrusive memories of combat, and decreased interest in activities. He identified certain types of weather, clothing and scenery as triggers for his war memories. The precipitating event for hospitalization was a surprise phone call from a Korean War buddy whom he thought he had seen die after being bayoneted in the chest.

Though the phone call had been positive and pleasant, soon afterwards J began experiencing intrusive memories of the war. He began to isolate himself from his family and coworkers and spent long hours working alone in his office at home. A period of deterioration culminated in a flashback while he was giving a presentation at work. He was diagnosed with combat-related posttraumatic stress disorder and referred to the PTSD program for treatment.

History-taking revealed that J was the youngest of seven children and had begun to work after school while he was still a student. When he graduated from high school he enlisted and served as a machine gunner with the Marines in the Korean War. His combat exposure was high and included the seven-day battle of Hill 221, in which his unit survived multiple enemy assaults. He contracted malaria and was

18

wounded in action. After treatment he was returned to active service. He was honorably discharged. He married and began to raise a family. His military history was confirmed by military records.

Though his history showed a better than average level of overall functioning, there were some exceptions. He had twice attempted suicide and was hospitalized for a "nervous breakdown" in 1960. Later he was to explain that this hospitalization followed an incident in which he had been snowbound in a store along with some Korean customers. At that time he was treated with Thorazine and electroconvulsive therapy. He returned to his family and had a successful career.

I (SR) was his therapist when he was first admitted to the PTSD program. He was treated with individual therapy focused on war experiences, group therapy, and anxiety and anger management classes. At various times he was on several medications, including tricyclic antidepressants, SSRIs, and Tegretol. He had undergone a full cardiac evaluation with negative results. Headaches had also been evaluated and a CT scan had revealed no abnormalities. He responded well to cognitive treatment and was discharged to outpatient group treatment.

He was readmitted to the PTSD program a year later complaining of an increase in intrusive recollections of the war. I had just completed EMDR training. Though he would be my first EMDR client, I elected to approach J about using this new therapy because, despite the severity of his trauma and his symptoms, he had long periods of stability in his history, was very intelligent and insightful, and had a high level of motivation for treatment. Moreover, we had a good working relationship. From my perspective, he was a good first EMDR client.

We decided to start with the incident in which he saw his friend bayoneted in the chest. After a brief discussion, he identified the most disturbing aspect of the experience as the thought that he had not reacted to the loss of his friend and had not bothered to check later to find out whether he had survived. The negative cognition was "I am a bad friend," the positive cognition was "I'm a caring person," the most powerful emotion was guilt, and the SUD (subjective units of disturbance; Wolpe, 1991) level was eight.

His reaction to EMDR during the first treatment session was surprising to me. His facial expressions showed that he was reexperiencing the event, but at the same time he also seemed to be observing himself. He remarked that he was fascinated by the connections that were coming up during the processing.

At one point in the session, when a loud thunderstorm broke out directly over the building, he became confused about whether the sounds he was hearing were real or part of the memory. I assured him that there was a storm outside.

A bit later, he somewhat sheepishly said, "I know there's nothing there, but I have to do this," and turned to look behind him. This was clearly related to part of the battle when his position had been overrun. As a machine gunner he had to maintain a field of fire in front of him, but he knew the enemy was coming up from behind. Nonetheless, he had remained at his post and continued to fire to his front and did not, then, look behind him for the enemy. He said that he could feel the hair standing up on the back of his neck, then smiled and said he was reminded of his cat, whose fur would stand on end when she was frightened.

Later he reported that he was beginning to get a headache on one side next to his eye. I was beginning to worry that I was doing something that had triggered a migraine. Because I was uncertain about whether this was an artifact of the eye movement or part of the memory we were working on, I asked him whether the headache had come on gradually or suddenly. He said it had just started, so I asked him to focus on the sensation. After two sets of eye movements his face lit up and he said, "I know what this is. My helmet got shot off!" After another set of eye movements he reported that the headache was gone.

The turning point came when he remembered how he had felt at the moment when he saw his friend injured. Prior to this session he had been unable to recall how he had felt when this happened. Now he said, "I was devastated." He was able to understand that this incident had occurred in the middle of a very complex battle and that he had no time to linger over his feelings. Later on he had been so sure that he had seen his friend killed and was so upset by this that he had not wanted to ask any questions. Integrating this information eliminated the distress related to this and the veteran reported that the positive cognition "I am a caring person" seemed completely believable.

J and I worked on several other war memories during his hospitalization with good success. His depression, isolation, and intrusive symptoms were significantly decreased. Somewhat unexpectedly, he also reported an improvement in concentration that was particularly noticeable in the group education sessions. He described the effect as being like having "a whole new head."

We gained corroboration of his treatment gains unexpectedly. One Monday morning, shortly after this treatment session, I (SMS) arrived to find a message from J's wife requesting that I call her. I did and she began the conversation with the question, "What have you people done with my husband?" Concerned that something negative had happened over the weekend during J's visit home, I began to reassure her that all reasonable care was being provided to him. She interrupted, saying that during his visit he had suggested they go shopping at a nearby mall. I did not understand why this was so significant until she pointed out that in their 40 years of marriage he had never suggested they go to a crowded area such as a shopping mall and would seldom accompany her when she asked him, and then only with the greatest reluctance. She was, she said, very happy with the change and wondered how it come about.

At this point J asked me (SR) about an early discharge because he was feeling so much better that he wanted to see what would happen when he went home.

He seemed to be doing quite well until he was readmitted four years later. This time the precipitating factor was a diagnosis of prostate cancer and his primary complaints were feelings of anger. J had been told that, though a variety of treatment options were available, the prognosis was not good. He was angry about the fact that the cancer had not been identified earlier. This time the focus of treatment was not on combat memories but on his feelings about his own death. Again, EMDR seemed to resolve his distress. His serenity about his illness made quite an impression on the other veterans in his therapy group. He was discharged and left the program feeling confident about his ability to enjoy the rest of the time he had available with his family. He was again referred for outpatient follow-up.

As time passed and I stopped hearing from J, I began to assume that he had died. It was eight years after the first EMDR session that I went to the annual PTSD program picnic and saw him walking up with a big smile on his face. His first words to me were, "Doc, you cleaned my head out real good," and he proceeded to describe a long list of activities that he had been enjoying with his family. He also talked about the medical ordeal he had been through with surgery and radiation. He had safely passed the five-year mark without a sign of a recurrence of the cancer. Despite the stress he had been under with this life-threatening illness, there had been no further recurrence of PTSD symptoms related to the material he had worked on. It has been six years since his last admission and he continues to do well.

This case is not remarkable in terms of the effects of EMDR with long-standing PTSD. It had been about 40 years since J's trauma experience when he encountered EMDR. His rapidity of response is not unusual, either. What is different from most cases is our knowing of the occurrence of a posttreatment life-threatening situation. His presentation on his third admission was specific to that situation and the difficulty he was having dealing with it. Admission to the PTSD program was made as a preventative, since experience over the years with others treated with non-EMDR therapies had led us to the expect that there would likely be a recurrence of PTSD symptoms. This did not happen. EMDR remained focused on his illness and no links developed going back to his war experiences. Even with major subsequent major life stressors, then, the original trauma experience remained resolved.

INTERVIEW WITH AN EMDR CLIENT

"Isn't that what Memorial Day is all about?"

What is EMDR like for the client? Obviously, there is no single answer to this question, since each client processes experiences and material in a unique way. Nevertheless, following a case from the client's point of view offers clinicians working with war and terrorism survivors an opportunity to hear things from "the other side of the desk," and this is always desirable.

We are fortunate that a client of another therapist, upon hearing that we were writing a book, came forward and offered to recount his experiences with EMDR. I (SMS) quickly agreed, for as you will see from the interview, "John" is in a unique position to comment, given his past experiences as well as his current occupation as a nurse working with psychiatric clients. All the names in this interview have been changed, as have some historical specifics, in order to maintain the anonymity of the people involved.

Let's start with a little preservice history. What were things like before you went into the Navy?

My premilitary years were largely unremarkable. I was raised in a nurturing and loving family and taught the need to support and respect others. High school was never a priority and my grades reflected this ambivalence toward the need for education. Most of my teenage activities revolved around the Boy Scouts, the Presbyterian Church, automobiles, and teenage girls. I was a motorhead for much of my adolescent years spending most of my time drinking beer, talking about auto racing, going to auto races, and racing automobiles.

Sounds pretty normal. Was there a tradition of military service in your family?

All the men in my family served in the military, all in the Navy, and the expectation was that I would follow tradition with a tour of duty in the Navy. My dad was a World War II veteran and my only brother served in the sea-going Navy in the early '60s.

You elected to become a Navy corpsman, what the Army would call a "medic." Given that corpsmen often were assigned to Marine units, was there some special reason for this choice?

I remain unclear to this day as to why I desired to fill the shoes of the corpsman. I had no understanding of the responsibilities of these individuals prior to speaking with my recruiter and the information he gave me was not a bit helpful. During my senior year in high school I developed an interest in emergency care and volunteered with the local community ambulance service. Perhaps this was the basis for my interest in the medical field. I would like to think that this decision was based on my pacifist leanings and a genuine desire to serve my country when she needed me most but to do it in a way that would not place me in the position of having to take a life. Fact be known, I think my decision was purely as an impulsive act. I did not take the advice of the people I solicited guidance from.

You went into the Navy in . . .

1967.

What was training like to be a Corpsman?

Following boot camp I was transferred to Hospitalman "A" School located on the main base across the road from Recruit Training. Corpsman school was a 17-week clinical and didactic course of instruction that turned a group of 60 adolescent sailors into "life-saving gods." The majority of our classes were taught by senior corpsmen. Most of them had served time in Vietnam and looked upon us with a great deal of sorrow. I didn't understand it then. The courses stressed the how-to more than the why. It was crucial that we be able to inject morphine but it was not necessary for us to understand the chemical properties of this powerful drug. We were instructed in the technique of emergency tracheotomy with no mention of the inherent hazards of this procedure. Any qualified otolaryngologist will attest that this procedure should not be performed outside of an operating room or by anyone with less than extensive experience and understanding of the anatomy of the neck. This kind of information must not have been important enough for us to know at that time.

How did you get assigned to the Marines?

My first duty assignment following Corps School was at the boot camp dispensary at Great Lakes. I worked the sick call area, the outpatient pharmacy, and the pneumonia ward. Nothing important happened during this period of my life other than meeting my wife-to-be.

In October of 1968 my orders were dropped for WESPAC. This meant my ass was going to Vietnam. Following a 30-day leave at home I was assigned to the Field Medical Service School at Camp LeJeune, North Carolina. This five-week school is the Navy's method of preparing the corpsman for assignment with the United States Marine Corps. Classes were provided in weapons familiarity, emergency procedures, field tactics, Marine Corps history and indoctrination, and guerrilla warfare training. The intention of FMSS was to prepare us for combat. FMSS did *not* prepare us for combat.

In early March of 1969 I joined a hundred or so others for the long and winding road to Vietnam. The flight was a Boeing 707 contracted by TWA to fly kids to the war zone. The plane landed at Danang Air Base at 10:30 A.M. on the morning of March 12, 1969. The day was hot and humid and it continued to be hot and humid until at least March 12, 1970.

What were your overall impressions of the war?

From my perspective, Vietnam was a mix of utter boredom and absolute terror. The country was hot and dirty and the people did not think much of Americans. I always considered Vietnam to be like a Boy Scout camp from hell. Contrary to what the media would have you believe, the Vietnam experience was not absolute and total warfare. Enemy contact was a rare occurrence. But as rare as this was, the fear was constant. The anticipation of waiting for the firefight to start was excruciating to say the least. I know experienced combat veterans who survived a full year of combat duty without ever actually seeing the other team. I participated in major operations in the heart of the badlands that resulted in no contact at all. There were times that all hell broke loose, the fighting was violent and intense, and stopped as quickly as it started. This was typical—the rule, not the exception.

But in the face of all of this, based on my experience, the real enemy that we dealt with was the unseen horror of the booby trap. These devices, typically made of American dud ammunition, would lay dormant like inanimate objects waiting to maim or kill. You rarely saw them, you couldn't capture or shoot them, they did not respond to *Chu Hoi* (*surrender*) flyers, would not take bribes, and never seemed to fail to detonate. I was in constant amazement that the damn things would frequently fail to explode for us but always blew up for them. This type of warfare takes a great toll, both physically and psychologically, upon the injured, the witness to the crime, and the one that has to put the pieces back together.

Whether intentional or not, the booby trap employed by the Viet Cong was one that rarely killed but typically caused horrible and disabling injury. One device in particular was most consistent in its horror. By placing an unexploded 105 MM howitzer shell in the ground at ground level and running a trip wire from the base of the shell across an open pit a foot square, detonation would usually remove the intruding limb at the knee and the arm on the same side as the explosion, and result in a magnitude of lesser burns and wounds. I have seen many of these work and they always worked the same. They were highly reliable, extremely economical, and definitively effective. By the very nature of the physics of an explosion, dirt, gravel, and shrapnel would be driven far into the limb, necessitating the removal of much more of the leg than initially thought. A blast causing a below-the-knee amputation leaves the survivor with a prosthetic device that is relatively easy to master. Amputation above the knee, by the very dynamics of prosthetic design, leaves prosthesis fit and ambulation difficult. I often wondered if they realized this when they designed these horrible devices.

The response of the patient to this kind of injury is devastating. Those that remain conscious, which is the majority, immediately recognize permanent disability. There is no time to adjust to it. Boom, it's all over, it's done, and it's gone. I have been told that the instantaneous vaporization of a limb causes the peripheral nervous system to collapse, preventing pain. I can attest to the fact that this premise is utter bullshit. Rest assured, the pain is intense. The mixture of pain, fear, the anticipation of the consequences, and the doubts of the future are devastating. They always yell and scream, ask questions that have no answers, and without exception, they cry out for their mothers. Each and every time.

Where were you assigned and what kind of unit were you in?

I was assigned to a Marine rifle company. Our tactical area of responsibility was in an area largely made up of rice fields, some cultivated and some not, and areas of scrub brush. A large mountain range, part of the Annamite range, was to our west and southern borders. Several large rivers traversed the area. Free fire zones, places where you didn't have to ask permission to blow stuff up, were the really bad places. The official name for this area was the An Hoa Basin; we had more colorful names for it. Most of our time was spent conducting security patrols in our tactical area of responsibility, walking around, day in and day out, trying to make contact. Contact is a military term for getting into a fight. Our patrols were either short night and day security patrols or two- to three-day mini operations called the platoon patrol base (PPB). We would operate in groups as small as four- or five-man squads or company-sized operations of 125 or so. Each platoon was made up of 40 or 45 people when at full strength, which was not a common occurrence.

The corpsman's position of safety was very precarious to say the least. Of all the jobs in the platoon, the corpsman was in one of the more risky ones, followed closely by the radioman and platoon commander. It goes like this; when the shooting starts everyone gets down. The corpsman gets up. The enemy shoots the first soul that gets to his feet. Get the picture? When someone is wounded you can't wait for a lull in the fighting to tend to their wounds; care is needed, and expected, immediately. The Vietnamese learned very quickly the game of snipe and wait. The sniper would wound one of the grunts. He would then shoot to kill the first person that was seen standing erect. This person would either be the platoon commander, the radioman, or the corpsman. Nine hundred and five corpsman were killed in action during the Vietnam War.

As awful as that experience was, and even with all the pain it has caused over the years, I can honestly say that those days and nights were the most rewarding of my life. I functioned quite well in my position and can honestly say that there are people alive today because of my actions. I was wounded two or three times and personally decorated for valor. The down side is that regardless of how well we worked, no matter what we did, sometimes it was not enough. Sometimes the Marine died and sometimes he died on your watch. There is absolutely nothing as devastating as losing one of your Marines.

The burden of responsibility was enormous. The problem was that we received absolutely no training or preparation of any kind that helped us deal with the emotions that arise during an event like this. The Marines placed us on a pedestal that reached to the heavens.

They felt that we could do no wrong. They knew that they could count on us each and every minute of the day. It was an awesome feeling with a commensurate amount of responsibility. We didn't know what to do when things went wrong. Many of us brought these feelings home with nowhere to go and no one to help us to deal with them. Thirty years later the feelings are still there.

After thirty years you took yourself in for treatment using EMDR. Were there particular experiences that you focused on?

On the 28th of May 1969, I was one of two corpsman assigned to the third platoon. I was selected to fill the senior corpsman position [of the company]. This promotion necessitated a transfer from the platoon to the command group. The third platoon left the perimeter and went to Hill 25 and immediately set about preparing their positions for the evening. During the night the NVA proceeded to surround the hill and assault it from all directions, breaching the perimeter from numerous directions simultaneously. The command group and the first platoon of Alpha Company responded as a reactionary force. The reactionary force had to breach the NVA lines in order to reach the third platoon currently being overrun at the top of hill 25. Once they reached the American lines, Alpha Company was able to reinforce the third platoon and with the help of Cobra gunships and light from a flare ship, the NVA were driven back in the direction from which they had come.

The fighting continued for several hours. When the NVA were finally pushed back and the perimeter was secured, the NVA continued with random fire from the southwest. One of the Marines from the first platoon was shot in the chest and nearly died from his wounds. I inserted a chest tube and relieved his tension hemothorax. We had a hell of a time finding the entrance wound in his chest. I finally covered him with a poncho and with the help of a flashlight found the entrance wound in his armpit. He was medevaced on the second chopper that night and apparently survived his wounds.

Dave Black, a tall 20-year-old from Virginia, sustained multiple gunshot and fragmentation wounds to the lower extremities. Although he had been previously bandaged, I reinforced his dressings, checked him for further injury, and moved on the next.

The next morning the casualties were counted. Four Marines lost their lives and 18 to 20 were wounded sufficiently to require evacuation.

At some point in the early morning hours, as the sun was coming up, I remember looking to the west and seeing the dead lying on the west side of the hill. Michael, Peter, and Billy were lined up in a row. I can remember that Billy's legs were bent at the knee and were pointing up at the sky. Apparently he died lying on his side and when he was carried up the hill, he was laid on his stomach. Rigor had set in and his legs were bent at a 45-degree angle. I had forgotten this until only recently when the memory came back while doing EMDR.

I remember Billy the best of them all. He was in my squad and was the best damn pointman I ever saw. After the sun was up I was approached by Fred and informed that the incoming chopper was refusing to take Billy because of the unexploded ordinance in his chest. I guess I can understand this now, but at the time I was furious over the refusal to fly him out. Even more infuriating was the Captain's comment that we should blow the RPG in place. I remember how angry Fred became, ranting and raving about the Captain's comments. Wasn't the Corps supposed to bring all their men back? The solution to this problem was easy: cut the thing out and send Billy home.

Fred and I really didn't discuss this; there was no formal plan. We tied a rope to Billy's leg and dragged him to the far east end of the hill. I can remember now how nobody got involved in what we were doing. No one even asked us what we were doing. In retrospect, I think they knew what we were going to do, but they just couldn't condone this and none of them had any interest in getting involved.

We cut Billy's shirt off, which exposed the problem. It was almost surrealistic the way the fins and rear shaft of the rocket were sticking out of his chest. It had entered the right side of his chest at about the level of the sixth or seventh rib and the entire head of it, about twice the size but the same shape as a coke bottle, was buried inside his chest. I remember noticing the absence of hemorrhage at either his chest or at the site of the blast injury on the left side of his neck and wondered which injury came first. He may have had other injuries buried in his clothing or covered by dirt, I didn't look. My focus was on his chest.

We didn't take a lot of time. While Fred stabilized the rocket, I probed around the wound trying to figure out what to do next. I set out a scalpel and small blade and my surgical scissors.

Billy's skin was absolutely waxen and colorless. There was no bleeding at either wound site. I remember making the first incision along the head to foot axis extending the wound from the chest defect about three inches toward the axilla. I remember—distinctly remember—the blade separating the tissue exposing fatty tissue. This was a post-mortem incision so there was no bleeding. I repeated the incision inferior to the opening, continuing to extend the wound in order to expedite the removal of the rocket. I then cut several ribs with the scissors above and below the rocket along the line of incision I had made and physically separated the ends of the ribs with my hands, making the hole large enough to enable the rocket to slide from thorax. This was extremely hard to do. The noise the ribs made as they separated and broke is a sound that has remained with me to this day.

We then laid some gear on his legs to weigh him down, tied a rope to the shaft of the rocket, walked to the bottom of the hill, called out "fire in the hole," and yanked on the rope. When the rocket came out of Billy's chest it made a popping sound like a cork does coming out of a fine bottle of champaign. The rocket seemed to sizzle when it hit the ground but did not go off. We dragged the rocket to the bottom of the hill and turned it over to the Marines to deal with. I think it was blown in place. We bagged Billy and carried him to the area where the choppers were landing. The whole thing lasted about ten minutes.

It was then that I found out that Dave Black had died of his injuries. This affected me in a big way. When I sent Dave off on the chopper he was talking to me. Now he was dead. I have spent the intervening 30 years trying to determine why he died and what I did wrong.

What kinds of problems were you experiencing in the years after that?

I entered into therapy in the mid 1980s when I found that my behavior was causing problems in my life and with my work. The way in which I did things had been a topic of discussion on a number of occasions but I think most of my family, friends, and associates chalked it up to "that Vietnam thing." I remember well the time that I overheard one of the nurses at the emergency room where I worked say, "I wish Memorial Day would get here so we could get this over with." I found that most of my problems tended to get worse around Memorial Day. At the time I assumed that what I was feeling was due to the upcoming Memorial Day festivities. I was unable to link Memorial Day with the date that it occurred, on or about 28 May.

The man who helped me sort this out was a very talented therapist affiliated with the local Vet Center. He was able to educate me into the why and wherefore of combat trauma and taught me how to deal with these things on a daily basis. I will never be able to thank him enough for the many things he did for me. I remained in therapy with him for about eight months, perhaps the longest eight months of my life. I found out, among other things, that trauma can sometimes be more painful when experienced the second time than it was the first.

There are a number of things that puzzled me greatly. Startle reflex is the one thing that I fully understood from the beginning. Over the years my startle response has been disturbing, frightening, thought-provoking, and even humorous.

The thing about the steaks is really fascinating. I initially thought I was a vegetarian in hiding. I never ordered a steak when we ate out, unless steak was the only option. My wife rarely cooked steak, and more rarely a roast—she tired of throwing the leftovers out. I thought I just didn't like it. Through therapy I came to realize that the problem was not in the steak, but what I had to do with it. Apparently the act of cutting was the problem; cutting into Billy's thorax was what I was really seeing.

Although sleep disorder is commonly seen in the combat survivor, I was usually able to sleep, eventually. The problem for me was going to sleep. Once sleep began, I slept like a rock. For years I would remain awake perhaps as late as 3 A.M. before going to sleep. This made waking early very difficult. I do not ever recall dreaming at night.

I thought about the war all the time. The mere act of looking out my office window and gazing upon the trees would take me back. Watching aircraft fly overhead was another way to change time zones. I thought about it all the time.

I was also experiencing a great deal of guilt. More and more of my time was spent volunteering my services to each and every group, organization, or cause that asked for help. I would travel the 100 miles to Washington once a month to work a 12-hour shift as a volunteer guide at the "Wall." I was active in my local volunteer fire company, I gave my time to the American Gold Star Mothers, the County VVA chapter, the Military Order of the Purple Heart, the American Heart Association, County and State EMS activities, the County CISM team, and I donated blood. I traveled 1,900 miles each Memorial Day to volunteer at a Vietnam Memorial in northern New Mexico. I spent Veterans Day in Washington. This seemed to be a natural thing to do at the time and never did I even consider that I was trying to give something back and atone for what I perceived as sins.

I could no longer function in the emergency room setting. It was too close to a painful period in my past, at least that is the way I saw it at that time. The typical day-to-day activities weren't the problem. The motor vehicle trauma clients and the victims of violence were. Working around the severely injured became a significant problem. When combined, the odors of blood, gasoline, and urine would make my skin crawl. For days after dealing with a major trauma like that my intrusive recollections would go through the roof. My sleep would be sporadic at best, and I would isolate and withdraw.

I found that over the years I learned to deal with much of what I was doing. With the help of my therapist I understood what I was doing and why I was doing it that way. Life was now much more manageable and living was more enjoyable. But the time came to try again and see if I could do more than just cope with my problems. I found out about EMDR. I was referred to an EMDR therapist named "Ann." I made an appointment with her for the initial session.

There was no small amount of anxiety related to this first appointment. I found myself confronted with the thought of having to bare my soul to someone that I didn't know and being afraid of dragging all of this stuff back out into the open again.

I did not have to go through all the preliminary work typically associated with the therapy process. Dr. Ann took into account my experience level and knowledge of exactly what I wanted to get done and developed my treatment plan based on those elements. We were able to place a focus right on the problem and didn't have to spend a lot of time sorting things out. After some thought I decided to focus on the guilt associated with the removal of the RPG from Billy's thorax, the loss of and unexplained death of Dave. I decided to focus on the RPG thing first.

What was the image that you had for that experience?

The image I was most able to bring up was when I made the first incision in Billy's chest, when I tried to open the wound so in could remove the rocket from his chest. The image was clear and sharp, in color, and easily recalled.

What were the negative and positive cognitions?

We never got to those. If I remember correctly my SUD was seven or eight on a zero to ten scale. The guilt that resulted from these feelings was overwhelming. She asked me to bring up the image in my mind and to follow her fingers as she moved them back and forth in front of my face.

Perhaps she picked up on the emotions triggered by the picture and decided to go ahead and start the processing without worrying about the whole assessment phase.

That might be. I concentrated on the image and it came up as easily as it had in the past. Ann's fingers began to move and I followed them with my eyes. After about the third or fourth pass I began to feel something, a feeling and a sensation that I find hard to put into words. I can tell you this—it was as intense a feeling as I have ever experienced. The feeling seemed to come from deep inside me and move over me like a wave of heat. I bawled like a baby. This was serious emotion. The strangest aspect of it was that I had absolutely no control over it. I cried and shook like I don't think I have ever done before. The image began to fade as I cried. All of this took place in less that a minute and a half. Ann stopped moving her hand as soon as I began to react (not that I could have followed her hand anyway), and I slowly calmed down. Although I had just spent a few moments crying like I had never cried before, I wasn't sad. I don't know what I felt.

It seems like you went into the abreaction pretty quickly. Was that the only major reaction you had working on that memory?

This process continued in cycles. Ann would ask for the image, do eye movement, I would react sometimes and sometimes not, and then we would discuss the image and the feelings that they generated. It was so odd, the image started to change, and in fact, it led me to different feelings and different images, some really intense, and some not.

What did you notice changing, if anything, during the course of treatment?

The first image I worked on, the image of the parting of the flesh with the scalpel, changed from a sharp, easily retrievable color image to one that was devoid of color, low contrast, a black-and-white image. Where the former image was intense and vivid, the new image was more clinical, like looking at a controlled surgical situation. It was not a moving image; it was more like a photo. The SUD level when concentrating on this image was now at somewhere around two or three. I even found it hard to pull the image up into memory. Now a year later, I sometimes cannot find that image at all.

I also had an image of Billy laying with the KIAs, his legs stiff with rigor in the air. The image was dull, not colorful, sort of surrealistic in a way, and was devoid of anything but the three bodies, the grass, and the sky.

The new image of Billy lying on the ground is now more reminiscent of the image one views on the TV screen, not surrealistic or "dreamy" like it was before. The colors are brighter; the surrounding scenery is more vivid and more detailed. The legs are not visible in the new image and the three bodies are not clearly recognizable as such, looking more like bumps on the hill. And most surprising is the sun; the new image as I see it is a sunset scene. Keep in mind that I was looking west in the morning and the sun was rising in the east, behind me. The image I was now seeing was one with the sun setting in the west. My SUD level was in the two or three range following this eye movement session.

The change in my perception of that night, at least in relation to how I felt about Billy, was equally dramatic. For years I had carried with me the guilt of having abused Billy's corpse. The last memory of a friend should be a good one. The last memory I have of Billy was when I mutilated his corpse.

I covered quite a bit of ground with this memory, going from the guilt of having mutilated him and ending up with issues related to Billy's parents. My guilt was related to the pain that his parents felt and how my parents would have felt had I been killed in the horrible manner that Billy was. It also had much to do with my fear of being mutilated in the way in which I felt I had mutilated Billy.

This new insight gave me a new perspective, a perspective that what I actually did for Billy was make it possible for him to return to his family intact, to make his return home a reality. The end result of this process was that I now see what I did for Billy and not what I did to him. I am now able to feel a sense of satisfaction for what I did. I was able to see that his family was able to have him return home. I will never enjoy a sense of pride in what I did early that morning in the spring of 1969, I never will. What I can do is accept the fact that I did a great justice for Billy and his family and made it possible for him to return home.

This resolution, accomplished in a single session, reveals the negative cognitions associated with the experience and how the positive cognition evolved. I know you tend to be skeptical of things. How did you react to your own accomplishments?

I walked out of the hospital that evening feeling like I just had my ass kicked. I was exhausted, but at the same time felt like I had just shed the anchor that had been weighing me down for years, holding me back from moving forward. What I did while driving home that evening proved the point.

On the way home I stopped at a local restaurant and ordered a steak; the waitress asked what kind, I said it didn't matter, just a steak. My only prerequisite was that it be well done. I turned down the offer of salad, vegetables, and a beverage. I told the confused girl that I wanted a well-done steak on a plate, a steak knife, and a glass of water. I didn't even want any bread. She looked at me like I was crazy.

As confused as she was, the poor thing complied with my request and served me the steak. A steak dinner is a meal that I normally would avoid like the plague. It was not that I disliked the taste, it was cutting the steak that was the problem. The steak arrived and was placed in front of me. I stared at it for a while, digesting it with my eyes. I picked up the steak knife; I remember the wooden handle and shiny stainless steel blade. I placed the knife on the steak and with no little bit of thought applied the pressure necessary to cut the beef. The knife effortlessly separated the meat, cutting the steak into two equal parts. I then proceeded to cut the steak into increasingly smaller pieces. This done I put the knife down and stared at my handiwork for a while. Carefully and deliberately I picked up a piece of steak with my fork and placed it in my mouth. I tasted the steak and found that it tasted just fine. This was steak, a rather good steak, steak that I had cut with my own steak knife. It was not flesh. It was beef and nothing but beef. It was not Billy. I finished the steak, paid my bill, and went home.

It sounds like you were pretty much finished with this experience.

I spent the next several days thinking about what I had done that evening. Over the next week I kept trying to bring the old images up with little success. I had no intrusive thoughts to speak of; in fact, I spent very little time thinking about that period in my life. When I consciously tried to bring up the old images in my mind, I had great difficulty doing so. The times I could bring the images up they were vague and unimpressive. I was, and remain to this day, totally amazed.

We worked on this event for several more sessions and continued to finetune the thing. Each successive EMDR session yielded less and less of a response. Eventually there was nothing to focus on. I couldn't bring the old images up anymore and the new images caused me no distress. It was time to move on to part two.

This was your experience with Dave Black. Can you give us a little more about your relationship with him prior to the night he died?

Dave Black was a 20-year-old black man from Roanoke, Virginia, and was, to most of us, the guy on the Marine Corps recruiting poster. It was so unusual for someone so gung-ho to be so quiet. Most of the gung-ho types were loud and boisterous. Not Dave. A quieter Marine I can't remember. The one memory that comes to me most often is of Dave sitting cross-legged on the ground on his poncho liner cleaning his M-16. I think Dave cleaned that damn rifle every day. I also remember his heroics.

We were attempting to cross a berm when the NVA sprung an ambush and opened up on us from spider holes on the east side of the berm. To this day I don't understand why no one got hit. Luck must have been on our side that day. I can still see Dave standing on the top of the railroad berm firing from a standing position. He would stand up, draw fire, and return fire when he saw where the NVA fire was coming from. He did this several times. I was with the radioman in my favorite position, flat on my stomach, watching this like it was a John Wayne movie in real time. I can see Dave firing that M-16 like it occurred yesterday. Dave was known among his peers for this kind of behavior.

The night he was wounded, after I arrived I started an IV of Ringers lactate solution. I can also recall someone had placed battle dressings on his legs and I think I reinforced them. I do remember he was alert and oriented and he talked to me every time I checked on him. He did not appear to be that badly injured.

Dave kept asking that I spend time with the others because he was OK. I agreed with him and directed most of my attention to the others. He was evacuated on the first medevac chopper some time in the middle of the night. He was OK when he left my care, at least I thought he was. Captain Jones advised us the next morning that Dave had died of his wounds. I have spent the past thirty years of my life trying to figure out what I did wrong that night. In retrospect I can attribute most of my problems over the years to losing Dave Black.

So you had started with a memory that was relatively less powerful than this one. How did processing go on this one?

When the time came to focus our attention on Dave's death, Ann asked me to pull up an image of him. Try as I could, I found it difficult to find an image of Dave that night. So much of the night's activities were a blur. I was really having a problem with this one. Part of the difficulty may have been anxiety. I was now visiting the most painful experience of my life and quite frankly, I was scared shitless. I was hopeful for relief from my pain and, at the same time, afraid that it wouldn't work.

I was finally able come up with an image of Dave lying on the ground. He was wearing a green T-shirt and camouflage trousers that were now dark and wet with blood. Ann asked me to focus on this image. We did EMDR on the image for quite a while that day and over the next two or three sessions. I was unable to move anywhere with this event and became more and more frustrated each time we tried. It seemed like I was on the edge and ready to jump but something was holding me back. I was getting nowhere. After several frustrating sessions without results and with my vacation coming up, we decided to give it a break for awhile. Following my vacation we planned to get back into it.

It was a few days before I was to leave for New Mexico that I came up with an idea. I vacation in northern New Mexico every summer, visiting friends and attending the Memorial Day activities at the Westphall Memorial east of Taos at Angel Fire. Spending a week in such a peaceful and serene environment seemed to me to be the best place in the world to do what I needed to do. If I was ever going to have success with this, Angel Fire would be the place to do it. In addition, I was going to be there through Memorial Day weekend, which included the thirty-first anniversary of that night. I was curious if the combination of the two, the place and the time, would enable me to get over the hump and finish the work that had been started.

I was knowledgeable enough about EMDR to know that it's not advisable to perform it on yourself. I also know the possibility of digging up other things, things you are not consciously aware of, while doing EMDR. This combination without access to my therapist could also be risky. Considering the possible benefit, I thought the risk was acceptable.

Ann and I discussed this at length. She was initially opposed to the idea, but I told her I did have access to counseling support services where I was going and she reluctantly agreed. Both Ann and you provided guidance and suggestions. Considering what I had put up with over the past thirty years, I didn't think it could make things any worse.

Well, I thought it was not a great idea at all. My big concern was not that you would have a big abreaction and wouldn't be able to handle it. Instead, I thought you might run into a block where a therapist might be useful in getting you passed it.

That's what happened at first. I tried EMDR a number of times in a variety of places. I tried it at the Memorial, in my hotel room, in the woods, even on top of the mountain at 14,000 feet. I just couldn't get it to budge, it just wouldn't move. It started to happen several times but it just wouldn't break, it was like something was blocking the process and preventing it from happening. I even tried it at 9:30 P.M. on the 28th, as close as I could get to the exact time of the event. I just couldn't make it happen. I put the idea aside and went about visiting my friends.

I spent a lot of time traveling with an Indian friend named Will. I happened to be in the middle of writing a paper for school that focused on alternative health care choices. I asked Will if it was possible to visit with his Kaseke, the Pueblo holy man. Will said that would not be possible, due to the old man's age, but recommended we see an old friend of his named Sam.

Sam is a Northern Comanche, on hiatus from his home in self-imposed exile working on his own spirituality issues. He is the pipe carrier and man of great spirituality for his people. He is also "contrary," a philosophy and way of being important in his community's daily life. Sam is a veteran, having served a tour of duty in Vietnam with the Army.

We found his home at the end of a long and dusty road. After formal greetings Sam invited us inside. Will had asked him to talk with me about spiritual healing and Sam proceeded to do just that. The conversation was quite lively and certainly a learning experience. It was at this time that I gave Sam the gift I had brought for him. Tradition dictates that a gift is given when visiting new friends in the Native American community. I had picked up a hand of tobacco at a smoke shop in Taos and Sam was most impressed with his gift. As a result of this, Sam invited Will and me to join him for a sweat lodge later that evening.

On the ride back to Taos, Will educated me about the Native American practice known as the sweat lodge. This age-old ritual, steeped in spirituality, culture, and Native American heritage, is a very important part of Native American society. The focus of a sweat is healing, commune, prayer, and cleansing. The practice goes back the origins of the Native American culture and is practiced in one form or another in most if not all Nations across the country. It is truly an honor for a white man to be invited to participate in a sweat.*

The lodge in Sam's backyard was a tent-like structure large enough for four people. The framework for the structure was made from willow branches and the covering was a combination of quilts, canvas, and dirt. A fire pit, centrally located in the center of the dirt floor, was to receive the stones being heated in the fire adjacent to the lodge. Sam had placed carefully selected stones into the fire and was in the process of heating them to a warm red color. Will told me that Sam had gathered the rocks from "special places" visited over the years and would only select rocks that spoke to him. Most of them were brought with him from his home reservation in South Dakota.

When the lodge was prepared and Sam was satisfied with the work the fire was doing for the stones, we stripped to a towel and in precise order, entered the lodge. I went first, entering the lodge and crawling around the periphery from the left to the right. Will came second followed by Sam. When we were all seated Sam closed the doorway, making the inside totally dark, and began to pray, first in his native tongue, then in English. Sam next went outside and brought in seven stones, one at a time, glowing red in the dark. Lastly he brought in a

*Readers can find more about the sweat lodge tradition in Silver (1994) and Silver and Wilson (1988).

bucket. Pouring water on the rocks would produce a searing hot steam that seemed to permeate the soul. The use of the name "sweat" is literal.

This process was repeated for three or four hours into the night until a total of 28 stones were placed in the pit. Prayers were offered along with songs and stories. At one point in the sweat Sam asked Will to share a pain. Will talked of difficulties in his life and losses he experienced. He sang in the native tongue and prayed to Grandfather, asking to be given peace in his life. Combat experience and family loss played heavily in his prayers. Sam then asked me to offer a pain.

Without thinking about it I talked about of Dave Black. I told them what a friend he was and how brave he was in battle. While I was talking Sam offered prayers by singing in Comanche. It was then that the idea came to me. While he was singing I attempted to place myself into a eye movement pattern by flicking my eyes back and forth from two imaginary points at the extremes of my visual periphery. Although the lodge was dark, the stones produced enough light that I was able to find two spots to use as reference points. Almost immediately, after no more that five or six repetitions of eye movement, I began to feel the sensation well up deep inside me. My emotions opened up and I cried and shook violently, for how long I do not know. I can vaguely remember hearing Sam's singing in the background.

I wish, I truly wish, that I could remember what I was thinking about while this was going on. For the life of me I cannot. It was exactly like it was when I was working on the Billy thing; the emotions flowed from my body with an intensity that is unimaginable. How long this went on I don't know, but it eventually subsided. I was left exhausted. I can't remember what happened following this; I was so wrapped up in my emotions. The sweat continued without my active participation. I felt totally exhausted.

When one of Sam's dogs entered the lodge the sweat was declared over. We crawled from the lodge in the reverse order that was used during entry. Although it was a warm evening, coming into the night air from the heat and humidity of the lodge was like walking into a refrigerator. We talked and laughed about anything and nothing. The thing I most remember upon leaving the lodge was the sky. The stars shone with a glory and majesty that leaves one with an assurance that life is really worth living.

The therapeutic power of a sweat lodge should not be underestimated, but power is power. If someone is not adequately prepared for the experience and what they might end up confronting, the effects could be devastating. Nonetheless, this is a very good example of integrating a culture's therapeutic tools with EMDR. What were the results of this?

In dealing with the removal of the RPG from Billy, I had tangible elements to evaluate. I was able to cut into that steak and either feel it or not feel it. I could test the results. I still shake my head in amazement when I think about it. I can still bring these images up in my mind. Although it is difficult sometimes to find them, they are still there. When I am able to bring them up my stress level is nearly zero. It really doesn't bother me anymore. I can still feel bad for Billy, that will never change. I am still able to mourn his loss, but now I am able to mourn for him when and where I choose. I control it now, it does not control me or what I do with it.

I don't have the freedom to do this with Dave's loss. Guilt being the strange bird that it is, I'm sure it will show up at some point in time if it is still there.

How long ago did you start working on the death of Dave? Has anything happened since that night in the sweat lodge that has given you any indicator of whether or not the experience really was processed?

It's been more than a year since I started working on the loss of Dave Black. I have lived through another anniversary of his loss and the loss of all the others that night. The only thing I can say is that it doesn't hurt me like it did before.

There was one more thing that I had to do in order to bring this all full circle. I felt I needed to visit Dave.

I was able to locate where he was. One dreary day in September of last year I made the journey to Arlington National Cemetery and found the grave of Dave Black. He now lies under a tree in the Southeast corner of the cemetery within sight of the Marine Corps Memorial. He is there with a number of others that died before their time, taken from us at such a young age. I drank a toast to Dave, left a flower, one my Purple Hearts, and moved on with my life.

I don't know whether this was truly effective in helping me to alleviate the guilt associated with the loss of Dave Black. I will in time. I do know that I see him differently today. I have the feeling that I am in control of my feelings now. He is now in place along with the others that I remember, both the living and the dead, from my time in Vietnam. I still remember him and I honor him as I do all the others. I make it a point to do something on Memorial Day to honor them all, as I did again this year. It just seems the thing to do on Memorial Day. Isn't that what Memorial Day is all about?

Thank you.

INTERVIEW WITH

AN EMDR THERAPIST

"I was fascinated that a therapeutic approach could be so weird yet be so effective."

Whaт does it mean to be a therapist using EMDR with survivors of war and terrorism? We discussed earlier some of the issues faced by therapists; here we focus on the work itself, what it is like, and how therapists function. Our vehicle for this is an interview I (SMS) conducted with Michael Paterson. His story may help other therapists to understand EMDR and what a clinician doing this work experiences.

Tell us about your background, Michael.

I became a police officer in Northern Ireland in 1979, at the age of 22 years. Civil unrest had been on going since 1969 and had claimed the lives of civilians, police, and army alike, and had severely injured countless others. I served in two rural areas prior to being transferred to Belfast prior to my marriage in September 1981. Three weeks later I was in an armored vehicle that was attacked by the terrorist group, the Irish Republican Army. Their attack with an anti-tank rocket and gunfire resulted in the death of my colleague and me losing both my arms and receiving severe injuries to my left leg.

How did you go from there to being a therapist?

My career in the police service was effectively over. After a period of coming to terms with my loss, I commenced study at university towards a bachelor's degree in psychology, completing that in 1987. I then went on to attain a Ph.D. by research, in 1991. During this time, I became involved as a volunteer counselor with a mental health charity and with a local bereavement care organization. At the same time, I was working as a civil servant, but had kept in touch with developments in clinical psychology.

That path from being survivor to therapist is not uncommon in our field. How did you become involved in EMDR?

I became aware of EMDR as a strange new type of therapy for PTSD. I recall asking someone to "tell me more about this eye movement thing." At this stage, my knowledge of EMDR was little more than a passing interest, but when I commenced a doctorate in clinical psychology in 1996, I had an opportunity to read more about EMDR. I was fascinated that a therapeutic approach could be so weird yet be so effective. Driven by curiosity and faith in a colleague's testimony, I decided to enroll in an EMDR Level 1 training.

During the practicum I reprocessed the incident in which I was injured and was surprised to see the previously vivid images fading. A tightness in my stomach appeared to have sadness attached to it, but by focusing on this feeling I found the emotion increasing and tears appearing to travel from my stomach to my eyes: these tears were the same as I had shed only once before—in hospital 17 years previously! At the end of the Level 1 training I felt euphoric, as if a weight had been lifted off me. Two days later my processing arrived at a new understanding, an issue that I later addressed at my Level 2 training.

Your personal experience with the therapy during the training seems to have been a major influence on your acceptance of it. What were your experiences with it like when you began to work with your clients?

When I first started using EMDR with clients, I found that it fit my style quite well. I particularly liked the EMDR protocol's structured approach that indicated when to return to target and when reprocessing was complete. For me, the protocol gave a sense of security and distance that allowed me to dive into the mire of pain and distress being felt by my client, with whom I was tied into empathically. I also relished the client-led focus of EMDR, as it permitted

clients to generate their own images and emotions without me imposing upon them my perception of their problem.

*Clearly you became very proficient at EMDR—you are a trained EMDR
Institute Facilitator and an Approved Consultant in EMDR Europe. The
obvious question, given your personal experiences, is how did you return to
working with police officers?*

With having served in the Royal Ulster Constabulary, the police
service in Northern Ireland, I shared the *esprit de corps* and have always felt part of the organization. During my clinical psychology
training I had the opportunity to work in the RUC's Occupational
Health Unit, treating serving officers and civilian support staff. I was
delighted to return to this environment with an understanding of the
subculture and the pressures of policing in a divided society.

What were your experiences like with these clients?

Many of my serving officer clients presented with PTSD and I
treated them successfully with EMDR. Interestingly, I found that sin-
gle-incident traumas were rare in this population. Police officers
throughout the world are exposed to unpleasant experiences on a regular basis and usually deal with these by some form of emotional
avoidance. In Northern Ireland, where "normal" police work has
been interspersed with terrorist atrocities, the frequency of gruesome
incidents has been all too regular. In many cases, clients have presented following cumulative traumatic stress. Here, a relatively minor
incident, such as an unprovoked assault at a domestic dispute, can
have such salience for the officer that core assumptions about the
world are altered and PTSD is triggered. The resulting nightmares
and intrusions often relate to a series of unpleasant incidents attended
over the officer's years of service. Following my clinical training I
accepted an appointment as a clinical psychologist treating retired
and retiring RUC officers.

*Your point about multiple traumas contributing to the PTSD and the
relatively minor event serving as a trigger parallels what we see with combat veterans. You have a case illustrating this point, but I wanted to get
back to an interesting point. You now primarily work with retiring or retired police officers. Have you been able to identify anything about this population that is unique?*

When the officer retires from police service, symptoms do not
necessarily disappear; sometimes they are exacerbated. In some cases,
PTSD is triggered where the officer had not previously experienced

the disorder. Research I and my colleagues have conducted with retired RUC officers indicates that PTSD is present in nearly one in
five retired officers, with subthreshold PTSD present in many more.

*Has your experience led you to a particular approach when doing
EMDR?*

As with serving officers with cumulative psychological trauma, I
have found that by identifying the traumatic experiences throughout
the client's life, and the meaning each has had for the individual, I
am able to find a starting point for EMDR therapy. Where, for example, the client has had a series of experiences with the associated
negative cognition "I'm vulnerable," I address, initially, the first
traumatic memory, even if it has a low SUD score or predates the
traumatic experiences during police service. I feel that this deals with
the roots of the distress the client is currently experiencing, and thus
prevents feeder memories maintaining the SUD levels of the recent
traumas.

With my EMDR clients, as with other client groups, I would often
see reprocessing of a body sensation without any apparent related
emotion or image. I have adopted a variation on the EMDR protocol
where this sensation appears stuck after three sets of bilateral tones.
This variation, which I think of as a cognitive interweave for the
body, is derived from the ego state work of David Grand (e.g., Grand,
1998). I ask clients to notice the color of the area of discomfort and
then to identify an area of their body where they feel comfortable,
even a small patch. I then ask them to identify the color of the comfortable area, then request they notice the two colors and be aware
of what happens. Invariably the discomfort subsides, usually after
three to four sets of tones, with the comfortable color having overcome the uncomfortable one. At this point I take the client back to
target to open the next channel for reprocessing.

*Let's turn now to the case you wished to present and then return to you.
Tell us about the case background.*

During the early 1970s, murders by terrorists and serious injuries
were an all too regular occurrence in Northern Ireland. Police and
army were often the victims, particularly if their duties were on a
part-time basis and they lived a predictable life in the community.
Whilst murders and injuries were ongoing, efforts were made to
maintain a normal policing environment. Police officers would, on
occasion, be sent to do a foot patrol alone in an area where the risks

of attack by a gunman or violent mob were high. In later years, policing with military support became the norm where risk was high, but normal policing continued in relatively safe areas.

Throughout "The Troubles" in Northern Ireland, police have been duty bound to provide a police service. Many have been exposed to horrific scenes, not only as investigators but also as victims. For the majority of officers, there have been multiple exposures to unpleasant scenes of crimes. Officers often coped by using alcohol to suppress their arousal: discussing emotions was not a macho thing to do!

F, a police officer with 27 years' experience, presented with characteristic PTSD symptoms relating to incidents he had attended more than 25 years previously. Until a number of months before I met him, F was functioning well in a training role in the police service.

PTSD symptoms appeared after F was assaulted by a colleague at work. The attack was encouraged by a band of onlookers. F did not suffer any physical injury, but did complain to his line management and was told emphatically that "it was just horseplay." F went on sick leave, never to return to work. He was medically retired over one year later.

It is interesting that a relatively minor incident could trigger PTSD. For F, the event involved a threat to him, and his response involved fear, helplessness, and horror. On the face of it, who could believe that a minor assault would trigger PTSD? When I took a detailed history, it was clear that the assault on F held similar meaning for him to several earlier experiences.

By similar meaning I assume you were identifying the negative cognition. How did the past and present experiences tie together?

I identified several key incidents in F's police experience that were distressing him in the present: all had the negative cognition "I'm vulnerable." They included the murder of part-time soldier—F had to pick up the pieces of his shattered skull; having to do a foot patrol alone in the center of a town with a high population of terrorist sympathizers; being left behind by colleagues in a dangerous area; driving a vehicle when a colleague was shot and injured beside F; and a soldier shot dead beside F in a public order situation with a jeering crowd "baying for blood."

The assault at work took place in front of a group of onlookers who encouraged the attack. This apparently linked to the incident where the soldier was shot dead and the crowd delighted in it. The assault engendered a sense of vulnerability, also present in the earlier experiences. In addition, the sense of being alone, deprived of support from colleagues, also manifested following the assault at work.

It seemed to me that F's PTSD was as a result of cumulative exposure to a series of psychologically traumatizing incidents. All it took was for one additional experience, with the same meaning for F, to create a paradigm shift. For me, I saw the effect of F's cumulative trauma history as being similar to building a tower of children's blocks: things were more unstable as the number of blocks grew. Although I was only trained to EMDR Level 1 at this time, I was conscious that early feeder memories could prevent reprocessing of later traumas. I started using EMDR with the first policing trauma, the murder of the part-time soldier.

How did he respond to EMDR?

The first EMDR session was particularly frightening for F—and me! He experienced a dramatic abreaction where he saw the body of the dead man coming toward him. This continued for a long set with nothing shifting, and panic was setting in. In a moment of inspiration I instructed F to ask the body what it wanted from him. Although F had difficulty in forming the words initially, this got things moving and the trauma reprocessed.

Did you try anything else first? Had you tried this kind of intervention or cognitive interweave before with anyone?

I didn't try anything else first. To me, after the Level 1 training, you "just keep out of the way when the train is rolling." I had never before used a cognitive interweave, but had used imaginal confrontation with various clients in a CBT framework. It seemed like the sensible thing to try at that time.

Prior to experiencing EMDR myself, I was unsure what to expect. At Level 1, my experience was interesting, and enlightening, as it showed me that affect that can be locked in from the time of the trauma, and led me to believe that an abreaction would not be too unpleasant for a therapist to witness or a client to suffer. With my client, I had expected to perhaps see a few tears, some increase in arousal, and reports of unpleasant images, but nothing on the scale I witnessed.

Although my Level 1 training encouraged keeping clients in touch with the experience for effective EMDR, the client was too distressed to continue. In hindsight, with the knowledge I have now, I would have asked my client to try an emotional distancing technique, such as placing a transparent wall between himself and the approaching body.

On the other hand, there is no arguing with success. Reframing a threatening situation is a good intervention and your encouraging F to ask what the body wanted moved the perception from being just one of a fearful reaction to one of learning, of information-gathering. Even if it had not altered processing, F's response at that point might have provided good clinical information. How did treatment go from there?

The subsequent traumas were all dealt with sequentially, and each session had a spectacular abreaction. By then I was well used to it and comfortable with extreme emotion. My EMDR practice benefited greatly from this early "baptism of fire," and I have gone on to use EMDR in hundreds of sessions with traumatized police officers.

Getting back to F for a moment, have you been able to follow up with him? How is he doing today?

Now he is functioning well. He is following technical training toward a professional qualification and leading a full life. He did report that his partner found it strange for him to be decisive and no longer dependent on her. This resolved over time.

I understand what you meant about the first session being "particularly frightening for F—and me!" This case is a good illustration of how powerful abreaction, while certainly distressing for the client and therapist, may also be a key part of the processing and should not be suppressed but responded to in a manner that encourages processing and resolution. Since your clients have multiple traumatic experiences, where do you usually start?

I have found that EMDR works well with multi-incident traumas. The best way to approach this, for me, has been to start with the earliest trauma that has the same meaning for the client, and work forward to the most recent incident.

The treatment of cumulative psychological trauma undoubtedly benefits from the use of EMDR. I find it difficult to comprehend how I could work effectively, avoiding burnout, with this population using only prolonged exposure and cognitive restructuring.

What has it been like for you to work with other police officers? Any positives or negatives you have encountered?

Because of my perceived membership in the police in-group, and my "badge" of injury, I am accepted readily. Sometimes clients with

PTSD report feeling "like a fraud" because I have visible injuries and they do not.

Being a survivor can result in some additional "wear and tear" on thera-pists who can, even when their own experiences are resolved, more clearly picture particular scenes and events. You mentioned "burnout." How has that been for you?

I have found that my knowledge of the police subculture has been both beneficial and detrimental to what I experience in session. I usually form mental images of the client's experience as it unfolds. This helps me understand what else may have been going on at the same time, but also creates a more vivid, and often uncomfortable, picture. The vividness of my images is enhanced where some clients have reprocessed traumatic memories relating to incidents in which I was involved personally. Also, image intensity is greater following my cu-mulative exposure to the same incident through several clients' per-spectives of the experience.

Clearly I am at risk for vicarious traumatization. To protect myself, I note if anything has been triggered in me and address this with EMDR at a later time. I am conscious of the harm it could do to my family in terms of my mood and irritability. Where an unpleasant image remains with me after a session, I select two points at opposite sides of the visual field and do sets of eye movements until the image fades and cannot be recalled easily.

By the way, a long time ago, before there was EMDR, I was asked to consult on a British soldier who had experienced a flashback while visiting relatives in Philadelphia—the row homes were similar to a neighborhood in a town in Northern Ireland. In any case, one of his traumas was of a police vehicle being blown up in front of his armored car, I believe by a command detonated mine, and his involvement in recovering body parts. I noted your police officer having to do similar work. I wish I'd known then what I know now. I wrote the case up and sent it to a British psychiatric journal as a "heads up" and to suggest maybe PTSD was happening to the folks working in Northern Ireland. The manuscript was rejected, with the editor noting that stress reactions were not really an issue among members of the British Army or the RUC, since no one had reported any.

The British "stiff upper lip" has now gone soft, it would seem. A large number of ex-military in the UK are taking a class action suit against our Ministry of Defence for not providing psychological sup-port to help them when they experienced PTSD. More recently, the

Police Federation for Northern Ireland (the police trade union) has also initiated an information-gathering exercise for a class action against the Police Authority for a similar failing. The RUC did not have an Occupational Health Unit prior to 1988—the Troubles commenced in 1969! They should have listened to you, Steve—you may have saved the British taxpayer millions of pounds.

Well, maybe, though what I was hoping for was to open the lines of communication between those of us working here in the States and our peers in the UK. I'm very happy you agreed to share your experiences with us. I think your work should reassure therapists who are concerned with issues like abreaction and vicarious traumatization as well as giving them some useful clinical ideas. Any last thoughts?

For me, as an ex-police officer who has served in an ongoing fight against terrorism and been maimed in the process, being able to use my knowledge and skills to improve the quality of life of many of my former colleagues leaves me with a sense of personal pride, achievement, and satisfaction. Through my work, I still contribute to the *esprit de corps* I hold within me.

Chapter 5

THE THERAPIST

"I don't plan to, but sometimes I feel like running."

9/27/00
E-mail
To: Steve Silver, Ph.D.
From: D. West, Ph.D.

Steve, when I was an intern and you were helping me work on the issue of getting the vets to accept me, the question came up of the challenges of, "You weren't there so how do you know?" and the fear they might have of overwhelming me.

Yesterday, the first scheduled vet of the day was talking about how his daughter had three crabs and he came down in the morning to find one of them dismembered with claws scattered all over the cage. He couldn't understand why this upset him so much. Then the memory came to him of being in Vietnam and after a helicopter crash opening a box that he thought contained helicopter parts and finding body parts. He cried uncontrollably. Then he mentioned his 12-year-old daughter's comments to his wife that it wasn't fair that her father was sick. She didn't go to war so why should she put up with it?

My last veteran of the day talked about his second tour in Vietnam and how he really didn't care about much at that point. They were sweeping a village looking for VC and he entered a hut. There were people in a bunker below the hut and he told them a number of times to come out. They didn't. He threw in a grenade. He never checked to see who was down there, but he is sure it was a woman and a couple of kids. He tries not to think about it.

When I was an intern you told me to tell the vets that "Maybe your pain is too much to handle alone, but we could handle it together."

Both of these veterans have severe PTSD. Both are working and holding responsible jobs. The amount of tension and anger within them is enough to ignite a major explosion. I understand how it is too much for them to handle alone.

Sometimes the pain overwhelms me and I am not sure how long I can continue to do my part in a way that makes this all safe for them without destroying myself. Tuesday one of the vets was talking about how hard it is to trust and invest in a therapist and then they leave. He had been working with one of your therapists who had died and the loss took a toll on him. He wanted reassurance that I wasn't going anywhere. I don't plan to, but sometimes I feel like running.

Not sure why I am sending this to you. You were very helpful to me with this when I was an intern and when I was driving to work this morning and dreading it every mile as I got closer, you came to mind. I just needed to share it. Hope you don't mind.

9/28/00
E-mail
To: D. West, Ph.D.
From: Steve

Nietzsche once said something about taking care when gazing into the abyss because the abyss is gazing into you. We go into the dark places and the dark can seep into our hearts as it has for those we seek to guide out of those places.

Charles Figley asked me once several years ago how it was I was still doing this work. I was surprised by the question but he rattled off the names of everyone we both knew at the time we started in the early '70s and many who came onboard since and they are all gone— administrators, working with different kinds of clients, teaching, but no longer working directly with war survivors.

> I didn't have an explanation. I don't believe I am or was stronger than all those other folks. I floundered around for an explanation. Charles sat and listened and smiled and then he said, "The reason is, you win." He's been studying how therapists deal with working with trauma survivors and he figures the way to be able to remain in this field is to be successful. Otherwise you have to leave or just do hand holding.
>
> He may be right about that. Just trying to endure these journeys could eventually break anyone's heart. But if you are bringing someone back with you . . . it makes a difference. So maybe the answer is not pulling back but actually pushing deeper in so that the pain has a payoff.
>
> Do what you need to do to gather your strength and to protect yourself—write to me if that helps!—and pay some attention to yourself. Like I said a long time ago, in a very profound sort of way, everyone is a veteran of the war. Everybody was torn up by it. And still is. Welcome home.

This correspondence took place while we were writing this book. Shortly following it, Dr. West (not the psychologist's real name) and I (SMS) met at a conference and our conversation continued. She described feeling so beaten up by the horror of what she was hearing that she was not addressing the trauma experiences of her veterans and was sliding into what was referred to as "hand holding." Her insight was that she was using the excuse of working in an outpatient setting as a justification for not going deeper with her clients. She has been facing a growing sense of helplessness and despair in her own work—to the point where she has begun to consider leaving that work. Her experience takes us to a critical question: what are the issues that erode a therapist's ability to do this work and how can those issues be dealt with?

She is not alone in raising this question. At our trainings, we are asked by therapists, supervisors, and teachers of therapists to cover not only the skills needed for trauma work but the issues generated for therapists by the work. These requests have increased over the years. Dr. West's openness on the subject served as the catalyst for this chapter.

TRAUMA WORK

Figley is not the only one to note the negative effects of trauma work on therapists. There has been a growing body of literature devoted to the topic of secondary traumatization (e.g., Figley, 1995; Haley, 1978, 1979; Kishur, 1984; Silver, 2000; Stamm, 1995). Therapists' reactions to their work can range from transient countertransference to the development of symptoms that mimic those of their clients', with intrusive recollections, avoidance, and hyperarousal. In our experience the development of full-blown PTSD symptoms among therapists is rare. What is more common is the tendency for therapists to distance themselves emotionally from their work, with a resultant loss of effectiveness.

In all therapy work, there is risk in empathizing with clients, though empathy is a tool of critical importance. When working with trauma survivors, therapists' empathy serves as a way of breaking out of the isolation and withdrawal common among such clients. To feel what clients feel is to feel their pain, anger, sorrow, and guilt. Therapists may receive an emotional battering and be left with sense of helplessness when clients are slow to respond to treatment. As with clients, so it is important for therapists to ensure social support and self-care.

CHARACTERISTICS OF WAR AND TERRORISM TRAUMA

There may be some aspects of war and terrorism that therapists need to consider before working with this population. We discuss these points not to suggest that therapists, such as ourselves, who work with war and terrorism survivors are superior to other therapists. Our intent simply is to point out the unique elements of work with these particular clients that experience has taught us are worth carefully considering. We recognize that there are unique elements with any specialized population.

Haley (1979) remarked that, "For the therapist war is hell for three reasons: (1) confrontation with one's own personal vulnerability to catastrophe; (2) the challenge to one's own moral attitudes about aggression and killing; and (3) the almost unbearable intensity of the transference and countertransference" (p. 1). This combination of sources of stress means therapists face a number of simultaneous internal challenges. These challenges can be complicated by additional factors.

By their very nature, war and terrorism are designed to impact not just on individuals, but whole societies and cultures. Therapists trying to work with the survivors of these events often have to deal with institutions, political forces, and a variety of other elements external to the client and often contributing to the severity of the situation.

Of these various sources of stress for therapists, coming into contact with individuals who have committed acts of violence against others is among the most difficult. Many therapists find they are no longer able to simply categorize their clients as victims or perpetrators, but are forced to recognize both aspects simultaneously. It is impossible to maintain empathy with clients without examining one's own capacity for passivity and cruelty. This is not necessarily bad for the clinician, but it can be a confusing and stressful process to go through. It is unrealistic to expect therapists to be unaffected by what they hear, but the fact that trauma clients are very sensitive to the reactions of others can deprive the therapist of a sense of privacy while they sort out their own reactions.

THERAPIST SKILLS

Bob O'Brien, a VA psychologist and EMDR Institute Facilitator, makes the point that survivors of war, especially soldiers, often carry levels of PTSD with degrees of complexity greater than that encountered with other populations:

> You must be already skilled and trained in dealing with complex, severe PTSD. You don't want to get into the situation of opening up the wounds and being in over your head. These clients, while not unique in the business of complex PTSD, are more complicated than most. This is because it is likely that clients were repetitively traumatized by very violent life-threatening events. In addition, clients were likely to have been responsible for sending men to their deaths and for inflicting death, injury, and pain on other people in a very deliberate and calculated way. This is, unfortunately, what combat is about.

The key attributes needed for this work are: empathy, self-awareness, flexibility, a moral sense, and a willingness to learn. We will consider these separately, but it is clear that they operate synergistically.

Empathy

The basic principle of empathy is one repeatedly addressed during the basic training of mental health professionals. With a therapy as client-centered as EMDR, empathy is critical in the process of making decisions about how quickly to proceed, what to target, and so forth.

It can be extremely difficult for others to develop empathy for survivors of war, simply because of the extreme nature of the events. Moreover, clients may be both victim and, at least in their own perception, perpetrator. Survivors of terrorism present some therapists with a similar problem, particularly where the terrorism is a function of internal, societal conflicts. The divisions existing within that society that permit and encourage acts of terrorism affect the therapists who live within the society as well as the victims. Keeping political, ethnic, religious, racial, tribal, and other divisions out of the therapy office and out of the way of empathizing with the client is challenging.

Self-awareness

We regard self-awareness, a desirable attribute for any helping professional, as particularly important in this field. Therapists treating war and terrorism survivors are likely to encounter disturbing stories and experiences and their own reaction to these things must be continually monitored and dealt with. Some therapists note that they seem to pick up some of their client's sense of alienation from ordinary society and report that it is easy to hear normal social conversation as trivial after spending a day listening to their clients talk about their experiences.

A simplistic view of EMDR—it is a mechanical procedure and therapists don't need to hear clients details—overlooks the reality that the level of involvement is as deep as with any other psychotherapy and there is the potential for even greater stress loads for the therapist.

Our ideas about secondary traumatization run parallel to our ideas about trauma in general. When therapists listen to their clients they may be hearing a lot of gory details, they may be picturing the scenes in their minds, they may even be reminded of some painful experiences of their own, but these are probably not sufficient to cause secondary traumatization. Secondary traumatization is more likely caused by a sense of helplessness. Just as many war survivors were helpless to protect other people from harm, many therapists feel helpless to protect their clients from pain. What is more, as they listen to their clients' experiences, many of the therapists' beliefs are being challenged. They must have a response to this challenge or they too can become vulnerable to impairment. While few therapists actually develop all the symptoms of posttraumatic stress disorder, many begin to look for ways to protect themselves from what they hear, either by disengaging emotionally or by entering with their clients into an unspoken conspiracy to avoid confronting the trauma.

Therapists cannot avoid the trauma and maintain their effectiveness. Therapists who work with traumatized clients and who do not engage the trauma end up contributing to their clients' despair. Trauma survivors have such a strong tendency toward self-blame that they are likely to explain a lack of progress as evidence that they are doing something wrong or that they can't be helped. They may also perceive the therapist's avoidance as evidence that their trauma is too awful to be discussed. These reactions are compounded if the therapist practices the most extreme form of emotional disengagement—judging the client.

Clearly, it is part of trauma therapists' job to monitor their own reactions and to be alert to signs of wear and tear. One of our psychology interns, after a little initial nervousness, found that she could work quite comfortably with war survivors. Later, when she was hired as an assistant on a research project with the same population, she noticed that she was feeling a great deal of distress about what she was hearing. After some discussion about it with another psychologist, she realized that one requirement of her new job—obtaining pre- and posttreatment trauma narratives from clients and later transcribing them for coding—contributed to her reaction. The fact that she was hearing about trauma experiences without being able to offer any direct intervention was making her feel helpless. She negotiated some modifications in her job, including having someone help her with the transcription, arranging opportunities to discuss her reactions to what she was hearing in supervision, and giving her access to the therapist's notes after the assessments were complete so she could see the progress subjects were making.

Empathy is as critical a requirement for the conduct of EMDR as for any other psychotherapy. The decisions to proceed or pause, to follow which lead, to move with what degree of speed, whether to provide a cognitive interweave or other intervention, the integration of other psychotherapeutic techniques, and the fundamental decision as to when to initiate the processing all demand a close, empathic understanding of the client. Therapists using EMDR often comment on the fact that they find themselves more tuned in to their clients than they are with other methods. This may be partially due to the need to attend closely to clients' verbal and nonverbal communication.

Even though it is possible for an EMDR session to be initiated without therapists being told all the details of the event, they often end up hearing them anyway. Once clients have experienced resolution of the trauma, they sometimes find that their resistance to divulging the details of the event has disappeared, and so they take the therapist through the story.

The speed of EMDR treatment, coupled with a high degree of empathy, means that both client and therapist may find themselves suddenly confronting painful or shocking material. The opportunity to "brace" oneself, to prepare for what might surface, is greatly reduced while doing EMDR. For instance, I (SMS) was working with a Navy veteran who in Vietnam had been assigned to small boats used for patrolling rivers. We were working on the veteran's reaction to a commander he had perceived as incompetent. The particular incident targeted was a disagreement he had with the commander over the best way to recover a body they found floating in a river. They had argued about the possibility of the body being booby-trapped and how they might go about ascertaining if it was safe to recover it. The client was asked to "go with that" and eye movements were resumed.

Therapist (TH): OK, let's pause. Take a breath. What are you aware of now?

Client (CL): I was really pissed at him. He wouldn't listen. The other chief (*another member of the boat crew*) agreed with me, but he wouldn't listen. So I went into the water with a line to tie it off.

> TH: So think of that, and let's go. (*Therapist resumes EMs. The client's eyes suddenly widen and his eye movements stop. I get his attention back by wiggling my fingers. Eye movements are continued until the client appears to be tracking smoothly.*) All right. Take a breath. What do you get now?
>
> CL: Oh, shit, I just remembered. I looped the line over the body and then pulled on the arm and all the flesh came off in my hand, down to the bone. I can still feel it in my hand.
>
> TH: I want you to focus on that sensation in your hand. Got it? (*Client nods.*) Good, go with that. (*Resumes EMs*)

It reads smoother than it was. I recall that my jaw literally dropped as the client described the image and physical sensation. There was not anything particularly new about that story, and I had heard, and would hear, much worse. However, mentally I was not expecting that particular imagery. My attention was on the identified issue, the conflict with the commanding officer.

This is an example of what can happen to a therapist; often the degree of shock or traumatization can be much greater. The empathetic bond and speed of EMDR processing suggest therapists need to understand their own vulnerabilities and be willing to admit to the impact of trauma work. When one's own ability to deal with vicarious traumatization is insufficient, outside resources must be mobilized.

Flexibility

Flexibility refers to therapists ability to adapt to the needs of their clients. Empathy refers to understanding where the client is and what is needed; flexibility means having the ability to provide it. Essentially, clinical flexibility requires thorough clinical knowledge. Without that knowledge therapists will find that their ability to be flexible is curtailed.

When in a high-pressured situation, such as delivering therapy with survivors in the environments such as war zones, many therapists are tempted to fall back on what they know best and are most comfortable with. Their therapy can become rigid as a result of the stress they encounter, a phenomenon not unique to the field of psychotherapy. One of the best ways of ensuring flexibility is through consultation with other therapists. For some therapists this process produces stress and they tend to avoid it. After all, as one therapist said, "I have enough to handle with dealing with my patient. I don't need to deal with a bunch of other therapists as well." This statement itself is a measure of flexibility lost.

Viewing consultation as a source of stress often comes from previous experiences. Consultation in these settings should be conducted on a peer, mutual basis, with the emphasis on assistance, not on hierarchy and judgment. It helps to educate therapists making use of consultation as to its procedure.

A Moral Sense

Where morality is used to provide strength, it is a powerful attribute for a psychotherapist. Some therapists use a purported sense of morality to avoid working with survivors of war and terrorism, but for most a sense of right and wrong is vital and gives meaning to their work.

As supervisors and consultants, we are asked as to how do therapists confront not simply a series of horrible pictures, but this violence, this ultimate outrage of human behavior? In a practical sense, therapists fight the violence by trying to eliminate its effects. If the chain of pain is not broken, inevitably it will wrap itself around more people. This requires the therapist's moral sense. If the therapist is not engaged morally, then the struggle is nothing more than an exercise and it will be simply a matter of time before the therapist gives up.

A Willingness to Learn

Learning is, of course, about the clinical skills needed to function effectively. It is also about what has happened to the client. The client is the teacher. Therapists who approach the therapeutic relationship convinced they already know everything there is to know run several risks. They may not listen to their clients. This can become especially dangerous when clients belong to another culture.

An additional risk for these therapists is they will not listen to other mental health professionals. Additional tools and skills will not be accessed, understood, or utilized, with possible damage to clients.

The final risk is that their assumptions may be wrenched apart by the reality of what they may encounter in the course of treatment of their clients and the experiences they hear about. Both may lead to disillusionment and cynicism, if not despair.

EMDR AND THE EFFECTS
OF TRAUMA WORK

When EMDR was first introduced, some therapists expressed the hope that it would provide protection from hearing all the details of traumatic experiences. After all, assessments were relatively tightly focused and clients were encouraged to be brief in their reports after each set of eye movements.

Experience has demonstrated that EMDR provides no insulation from clients' experiences. While a client might have been fairly brief in their initial presentation of an experience, during the course of processing details may be revealed as part of clients uncovering process or abruptly during abreactions. Many clients who were initially reticent to discuss the details of their experiences, once they achieve resolution, often describe in extreme detail the experiences. We think this occurs because the client, on some level, is demonstrating to themselves their resolution of the experience—if they can teach that which they formerly avoided, then they have mastered it.

A case example illustrates this point. A Navy veteran received EMDR treatment for his PTSD resulting from an explosion and fire onboard his ship. The disaster took place in an area of the ship he had been transferred from two weeks previously. All his friends were working in the area at the time and all were killed. He was one of the first on the scene. In years of therapy, all he described were the events leading up to his arrival at the hatchway to the area— hearing the warning klaxons, the call to General Quarters, his run to the area, and the sight of the body on the other side of the hatch when he opened it. He had never discussed anything after that point.

I (SMS) was asked by his therapist to do EMDR with him. During his first session he reported only a small amount of change. During the second session he spontaneously began to describe the recovery of the bodies from the blasted and burned area. He did this in a matter-of-fact tone. I was astounded by this and it must have showed for he looked at me quizzically and asked, "What's going on, doc? You're acting like you've never heard any of this before."

I told him that he had not told me any part of what he was now talking about (nor, according to over ten years of medical records, had he ever told any other therapist). His expression changed to mild surprise and he said, "I don't know why not, it's not that big a deal." He continued to describe what it had been like and, in detail, how they performed their necessary and grisly task. I recognized he had a need to finally talk about the experience and let him proceed.

EMDR enhances the opportunities for therapists to learn from their clients. The nature of the protocol, in which clients are encouraged to report on the flow of their ideas, creates an immediate feedback loop, which allows therapists to observe each client's unique manner of problem-solving. This can have a positive effect on other therapeutic work, even when EMDR is not being used. In this way every client becomes a teacher, each session a lesson.

TRAINING

Assuming that prospective therapists have all the attributes described above, the next step is specialized training in war trauma. Certainly we recommend training in EMDR, but there is more to be considered. Let us consider things from the broad to the narrow and provide a sense of direction for therapists by providing a series of questions.

1. *What do therapists know about war and terrorism?* Being a survivor of war and terrorism is not the issue, for reasons we have already discussed, but understanding the events of war, the impact of terrorism, and the results of these experiences is important.

2. *What do therapists know about this particular war or terrorism?* While therapists do not have to be a military expert or historian, basic information about the chronology of events, what has been happening "on the ground," and how people have been trying to deal with the situation provides a context for the understanding of clients' experiences.

3. *What have therapists learned about violence and killing?* What are their views on it? Getting past the pat answers is the key, for understanding both clients and the circumstances. Have therapists taken the time to clarify their own thoughts, feelings, and morality about killing? This is a consideration best done before starting to work with clients who may have had to make life-and-death decisions, who may have had to kill, in circumstances of intensity difficult to imagine.

4. *How familiar are therapists with trauma reactions?* There is no one reaction. What do therapists know of the range of responses? Have they pushed the boundaries of their knowledge beyond the literature by participating in responses to disasters, critical incidents, and other traumatic situations? Every such experience helps prepare therapists.

There is no single format for answering these questions, but one indispensable element is competent and experienced supervision. Supervisors can help ensure that therapists confront the questions and can provide guidance in the hunt for the answers. Supervisors may help therapists explore such issues as countertransferance and develop their attributes.

A Model for Training

In addition to various mental health students, doctoral candidates in psychology fulfilling their clinical internship requirements at our medical center often elect to do a rotation with the PTSD program. We have been fortunate in that many of the most talented therapists in each intern class have selected this rotation. We have also worked with those whose initial talents were not as great but who became very excellent therapists. A small number have had major difficulties during the rotation. Some of them have been urged not to work with these kinds of survivors. This is as it should be. Any training program established to prepare therapists to work with a particular population should also be evaluative in nature, with the goal of redirecting therapists who, for whatever reason, should not be working with that population.

Feedback from these interns, other mental health students, and from mental health professionals we have trained in other settings has provided us with some general guidelines for training.

Ongoing evaluation begins with gathering baseline information on the therapist. While much of this is of the paper variety—previous training and experience, credentials and certifications—the most critical baseline is drawn from two sources: (1) the impression the therapist gives upon being interviewed by an experienced supervisor and (2) observations of therapy sessions. Live supervision is best, of course, supplemented by video- or audiotapes, which are excellent teaching aids through the course of training. We particularly pay attention to therapists' reactions when under stress. Whatever the stress load they encounter in a training setting, it will be worse when in the clinical setting without the sorts of supports and pacing that are normally a part of training.

The training program should provide opportunities for formal education in the field of traumatology, with an emphasis on the issues of particular concern to war and terrorism survivors. This may include a recommended reading list, extracts and papers from journals, attendance at inservice trainings and presentations, and the like. Whatever format is used, the supervisor should ensure that time is spent discussing the material and its connection to "real life."

As for the topics, the chapters of this book evolved from the trainings we have conducted for mental health professionals and might serve as a starting point. Beyond becoming comfortable with the EMDR methodology, some of the most difficult areas for new therapists are responding to clients with high levels of emotion, guilt, anger, and to those who were involved in perpetrator activities. Additionally, cross-cultural issues, a problem endemic in psychotherapy, should be addressed.

Caseloads should be carefully arranged in terms of both number and level of difficulties. We have found a gradual approach to be quite useful. If methodological difficulties are encountered, they can be addressed early on without the difficulty affecting too many clients. Ideally, the cases should be introduced one at a time with a period of several days between each. This gives the therapist an opportunity to develop a thorough treatment plan and review of procedures with the first few cases without major distractions. The total number of clients should be kept low, since the therapist will need extra time for case formulation and will be actively involved in ongoing education.

Case selection should be performed by the supervisor. Since the therapist will be working in an unfamiliar area, starting with the simplest presentations is advisable. Realistically, war and terrorism survivors are seldom truly simple cases. Thus, selection will be on a comparative basis, with emphasis placed on the fewer number of traumatic experiences, complicating factors (e.g., additional or ongoing life events), and additional diagnoses in the client's presentation. This will necessitate the supervisor's conducting an evaluation of the client beforehand.

Undergoing several evaluations can be trying for trauma survivors, so the supervisor should openly discuss the reason for the evaluations and the role of the therapist in training. The fact that the therapist is in supervised training should be clearly stated, and only with the client's agreement should the therapist and client be brought together. Ordinarily there is little difficulty in securing the client's consent. The open presentation of the training aspect is reassuring. It also helps to note that the purpose of the training is to benefit other survivors by enabling the therapist to acquire the skills needed. Also, given the close nature of the supervision, the client will have, in effect, the benefit of two clinicians, rather than just one. When clients refuse to work with a therapist in training, that position should be respected. In our experience, clients usually base decisions about their therapists much more on the interactions of the first few therapy sessions than on the therapist's degrees or training status.

Adequate time for supervision needs to be scheduled and considered inviolate. The therapist should also be permitted to consult with the supervisor whenever desired. Several hours a week of one-to-one contact between supervisor and therapist are typically needed. Supervision sessions generally will focus on two areas:

1. *The therapist's current caseload.* The therapist should be prepared to present on each individual client and describe not only what is currently happening with the client but also what is predicted. Supervisors, using their own observations and those gathered from other clinical staff, can critique these reports and make recommendations.

2. *The broader field of trauma treatment.* The educational topics noted above will tend to occur naturally in the course of discussion. If they do not, the supervisor should bring them up. It is useful to have readings to suggest for each topic in case the therapist needs or would like to pursue the subject in greater depth.

Group supervision can be useful but is not a substitute for individual supervision. It is often hard for new therapists to express their doubts, problems, and concerns in front of peers. This difficulty may be influenced by the culture of the therapists in training and needs to be taken into account.

Some therapists in training may find they are having extreme difficulties working with war and terrorism survivors. There are three broad areas which might be causing these difficulties. One of the keys in responding to these areas is to ensure that therapists have them presented and discussed at the start of training. Therapists should be encouraged to discuss any concerns they might have with these issues.

If the problems are due to an unusual lack of basic therapy skills or knowledge, it is often possible to provide additional assistance in alleviating those lacks. This is a relatively rare problem since therapists seeking specialized training generally have therapeutic experience and have acquired the skills and knowledge needed.

Sometimes therapists have unresolved experiences of their own that impinge on their work. This issue is best confronted openly. "Getting one's own house in order" is a logical first step for any therapist and discovering the need for it in training, rather than later when therapists are working with less support and with more clients, should not be presented to therapists as a failure. With resolution of their experiences, and the knowledge gained by that resolution, these therapists may become excellent practitioners.

A very few therapists discover that working with war and terrorism survivors is simply not appropriate for them. Perhaps the intensity of the experiences have is too disturbing, the concentration and empathy is too demanding, or their interests shift to other areas. Again, this issue should be confronted openly and presenting the possibility at the start of training assists the discussion. As with any specialized area in psychotherapy, working with war and terrorism clients is not appropriate for all therapists.

We believe there is no end to learning as a therapist to survivors of war and terrorism. Our clients always have something more to teach us. Formal training, however, must come to an end. We work toward supervision evolving to consultation. No therapist, no matter how skilled or experienced, should work in this field without having a consultant whose judgment they respect. Our procedure is to encourage therapists we have trained, whether in prolonged internships or in brief weekend workshops, to seek out consultative relationships wherever they go or to make use of us until they can develop those relationships. Serving as a bridge until novice therapists can develop consultation relationships provides us with feedback about our training that improves the level of our future training. It also gives us the satisfaction of knowing that our therapists are, in fact, putting to use what we have taught.

Therapist as Educator

The clinician may have an additional role to play on a community level. Ernest Baringer, a paramedic and 20-year counselor for war survivors, has noted that in many communities emergency service workers are already at or past the breaking point because of work demands and ongoing psychological stress. The ability of these front-line people to function in the face of, for example, a terrorist bombing be impaired. Responding to such stress in Israel, Alan Cohen and his colleagues have educated those in positions of authority, such as school administrators and teachers, about the nature of trauma reactions and assisted them in developing emergency response programs.

Clinicians familiar with the effects of high intensity stress may be of great service to their communities before traumatic events take place by educating local authorities, their mental health network, and people generally about the problems faced in these kinds of situations, as well as the tools useful for dealing with them. These clinicians can assist in ensuring that the community's emergency response plan includes a mental health component. This process of lending expertise has the added benefit of familiarizing local authorities with clinicians trained in EMDR and traumatology.

Chapter 6

OVERVIEW OF

EMDR METHODOLOGY

"This is the damndest thing I've ever heard of—but what have I got to lose?"

There are eight broad phases to EMDR. Only three make use of eye movements or other bilateral stimulation. Clinicians wishing to gain the most from EMDR will find that they are best served by viewing it not as a technique, but as a way of looking at clients and their problems, an approach into which the tools of other therapies may be incorporated.

Over time, the theoretical model of EMDR has evolved from a relatively simple desensitization one to a fairly complex information-processing one. Shapiro (1995) regards her current model as a heuristic method that permits prediction of results while at the same time providing a structure from which to work when those results do not occur. In simple terms, the essential EMDR model holds that life experiences are processed as incoming information by the brain. Shapiro's (1995) working hypothesis depicts trauma as an experience that causes an imbalance preventing adaptive integration of the experience. EMDR is assumed to work by stimulating the client's neuro-physiologically-based information-processing system.

EMDR therapists commonly use the word "processing" when referring to the eye movement portion of the approach, especially since additional, alternative bilateral stimulation techniques have been clinically identified.

The eight phases of the EMDR approach are client history, preparation, assessment, desensitization, installation, body scan, closure, and reevaluation. Eye movements or other forms of stimulation are used during the desensitization, installation, and body scan phases. Since a full description of these phases can be found in Shapiro (1995), here we merely emphasize several key aspects of each phase, which are expanded upon in subsequent chapters.

Client history, as the name suggests, is the information-gathering phase, in which the therapist seeks to identify the initial experience leading to the current problems. Past occurrences of the current problem are sought, along with the negative, self-limiting belief systems resulting from those occurrences. The duration of the presenting problem or symptoms is important in determining when the onset occurred and what event might have been the catalyst. Present triggers tapping into unresolved previous life experiences are identified.

Preparation of clients includes educating them on the nature of EMDR work, providing them with self-management tools for stress, and testing the eye movement and other bilateral stimulation procedures. While explaining EMDR, therapists use metaphors that can later be used during processing to help clients stay focused and to provide a reassuring reminder of how processing works. Typically, a "safe place" exercise will be taught, along with other stress management techniques, for closing down incomplete sessions or for use between treatment sessions. The addition of eye movements, originally thought to enhance the effects of the exercise, also serves to familiarize clients with this aspect of the procedure before trauma memories are addressed.

Assessment occurs as the therapist identifies the experience to be targeted for processing. When the client has identified several similar experiences, he or she is asked to select one representative incident. By processing this memory, it may be possible for the therapist to take advantage of a generalization effect. The client is asked to identify the picture that represents the experience or the worst part of it. Then the client is asked to identify the negative cognition that comes to mind as he or she focuses on the picture. The most useful negative cognitions are statements that reflect an irrational self-limiting belief ("I am no good") rather than a description of the situation ("The war was awful") or an emotional reaction ("I'm scared"). Once the negative cognition is identified, the therapist immediately asks for the desired positive cognition. As with negative cognitions, useful positive cognitions are about the individual ("I am OK"), rather than about external events or other people. The "felt" believability of the positive cognition is assessed using the Validity of Cognition (VOC) Scale (Shapiro, 1989a, 1995), a simple seven-point Likert-like scale where one indicates that the positive cognition is felt to be completely false and seven that it is felt to be completely true. The VOC is measured while the client focuses on the experience and its representative picture. The client is then asked to identify the emotions felt when focusing on the picture and the negative cognition. A SUD scale rating by the client of the intensity of the emotion provides an initial measure of the disturbance generated by recalling the experience. The client is asked to locate where this disturbance is felt physically.

Desensitization begins with having the client focus on the representative picture, the negative cognition, and the physical sensation identified during assessment while following with her or his eyes the therapist's hand as it moves back and forth in front of the client's face. After a number of repetitions, the therapist will stop and ask for whatever has come into the client's awareness. The client may report changes in any aspects of the targeting experience or the emergence of a different memory. When new material comes up, the therapist will direct the client to focus on it and resume the eye movements. This pattern continues until the client reports no further disturbance. The client is then instructed to return to the original memory in order to determine if any disturbance is present. If it is, the client resumes eye movements while focusing on the disturbance.

Installation is performed after desensitization is completed. During this phase, eye movements are used to enhance the believability of the positive cognition. The initial positive cognition may be replaced by an emerging, more empowering self-belief. The client focuses on the positive cognition while at the same time recalling the original experience. The eye movement sets are repeated, with the client providing feedback using the VOC scale and his/her own sensations. This continues until the positive cognition is described as feeling fully believable or as long as the client is reporting positive gain.

Body scan is the phase during which the work of desensitization and installation is checked for completeness. While recalling the original experience, the client is asked to scan his or her body and report any sensations. Eye movements are used to enhance any positive sensations or dissipate any negative ones.

Closure marks the process of ending a session. Whether or not the targeted experience is fully resolved, there will come a point where a treatment session has to be stopped. If needed, the tension and anxiety reduction techniques taught during preparation are utilized. The client is given a homework assignment that involves monitoring dreams, thoughts, and behaviors and noting in a logbook any changes in old memories, the emergence of new ones, and so forth. This material will be examined during the next session. A good debriefing is provided, including a reminder that the information-processing system being "jump-started" by EMDR is internal to the client and may now do some processing on its own. Therefore, whatever comes up, even if it is distressing material, is good news in the sense that the client is continuing his or her own processing and healing.

Reevaluation is the phase opening each subsequent treatment session. The therapist takes the client back to the experience targeted in the previous session to ascertain if it was fully resolved or if more processing has occurred. Any residual distress can be processed in this session.

As in any therapy, progress can become blocked. In general, these blocks are belief systems that have to be dealt with before further processing is possible. This situation occurs in non-EMDR therapies as well, and the same principles for dealing with it apply. The block is identified wherever possible and made the new target for therapy. In EMDR, identifying the block is accomplished by the somewhat innovative technique of asking the client. Additional tools, including changing the focus of awareness, are available for the EMDR therapist encountering blocks and will be discussed later.

Cognitive interweaves (Shapiro, 1995) are often used to break through a block or to reach a plateau of resolution sufficient to permit ending a session. This technique involves the therapist introducing a new idea or perspective to the client and then having him/her do eye movements while focused on that idea. Cognitive interweave interjections are very brief and are particularly useful with clients whose reactions and self-belief systems are chronically negative.

Variations in the protocol described above have been developed for particular populations and problems and several of these will be discussed in later chapters. At this point, it is worth noting that these variations have been developed as a result of clinical experience. EMDR clinicians have shared their experiences and provided feedback as to what works and what does not. While the EMDR theoretical model has remained intact, Shapiro has been willing to consider and teach variations of her original protocol (indeed, to change it in response to the experiences of other clinicians). This is one of the aspects of EMDR that many therapists find particularly appealing. These variations now exist, or are evolving for recent trauma, children, dissociative disorders, pain management, and other conditions.

When considering termination, therapist and client examine a wide range of material to insure completeness of the work. This includes the original target memory as well as any other experiences that emerged during processing. If the targeted experience was selected as representative of a cluster of similar experiences, these are examined to be certain that they have been fully resolved. It is also important to examine the current triggers that have brought up feelings, thoughts, and sensations associated with the target experience. If those triggers have any remaining ability to cause discomfort, they can be targeted as well.

The resolution of past trauma is not magical; it will not provide a person with neglected social skills, for example. Thus, it is important to provide follow-up, so that such deficiencies can be identified and rectified. Additionally, the resolution of past experiences may permit the client to engage in new behaviors, access new relationships, and otherwise become involved in new activities. This encountering the "new" may elicit additional unresolved experiences that have not been anticipated.

This brief summary serves as a review for trained EMDR clinicians and an orientation for others. It should not, we reiterate, be considered sufficient for treating clients. Therapists interested in applying this methodology to their clinical work would be professionally and ethically correct in using formal training provided by the EMDR Institute, one of several doctoral graduate programs in psychology offering the training, or other venues recognized and accredited by the EMDR International Association. EMDRIA is the professional and scientific organization of EMDR clinicians and seeks to provide an ethical framework for the development of EMDR.

Chapter 7

CLIENT HISTORY

"I was just like everyone else before."

The goal of developing a client history in the basic EMDR protocol is to begin to find the origin and threads of the presenting problem. Additionally, this phase offers an opportunity for the development of the therapeutic relationship, of which we will speak more in the next chapter.

TARGET SELECTION

Ordinarily, the therapist is interested in identifying the first occurrence, or the earliest remembered occurrence, of the presenting problem. When treating trauma reactions, therapists tend to focus on the presented trauma as the first or primary occurrence and often limit their development of the history to that particular experience. However, war-related trauma usually consists of multiple stressor experiences, any one of which might have been sufficient to result in PTSD. It is not uncommon, then, for several incidents to be feeding into the current problem or problems.

In many cases it is possible to develop a trauma list simply by asking clients to tell the story of their war experiences chronologically. The goal is to obtain not a detailed description of every event, which could be overwhelming for clients at this stage, but rather, a thumbnail sketch of the events that clients identify as most significant.

The development of a trauma list has several advantages. It helps the therapist spot any gaps in the client's timeline, which may indicate significant periods of dissociation. It allows the therapist to observe the client's tolerance for the emotions that accompany discussion of the memories. It can be helpful for the therapist to get a sense of the sequence of events, since the meaning the client attributes to a specific experience may depend to some extent on the experiences that preceded it. Since many clients will never have reviewed their experiences chronologically, the development of the trauma list may provide a structure for understanding their own reactions. In some cases, clients will begin to develop some insights during history-taking, which can enhance the efficiency of processing later. The trauma list also provides a handy reference to guide decisions about the order of memories to be processed, and it can help the therapist identify clusters of similar experiences. The trauma list obtained at this stage may not be complete, as clients often identify more incidents during the course of therapy.

The development of the trauma list also provides some opportunities for teaching about trauma reactions. When given the task of "telling the story," some clients may ask whether they are supposed to include the events that were most distressing at the time they occurred, the events they think may be contributing to their current behavior patterns, or the ones that show up most often in intrusive form. These distinctions in themselves may be a useful topic of discussion.

While some clients are able to provide the therapist with an orderly chronology, others find this task quite difficult. When asked about their experiences, they may start with one event and spontaneously associate to other related events. Though clients sometimes apologize for letting their attention stray in response to these apparently simple questions, this type of associating can be quite informative and should not be truncated in the first few sessions. Clients should be reassured that this is a natural process and that the therapist can help them structure their thinking when needed. The therapist can always go back to obtain information about the sequence of events later, while taking advantage of the client's tendency to associate now. In most cases, these experiences will be linked to each other thematically, and these themes are likely to be encountered later during processing.

The identification of clusters of similar experiences for processing is considered desirable in EMDR, as it may allow the therapist to process one memory in a cluster and take advantage of a generalization of resolution to other memories in the cluster. It is important to realize that by "similar incidents" we are asking not for identical situations but for experiences that have resulted in similar feelings and thoughts.

It is helpful for the therapist to be attentive to clients' negative appraisals of themselves, whether in the context of discussing war experiences or current problems, as these ideas may show up later as the negative cognitions to be used during processing. Even if negative appraisals do not recur, a good EMDR clinician will make note of them as material to be checked on after primary processing is completed as a way of ensuring that all aspects of a trauma experience have been resolved.

The client history should include identification of any significant pre- or postwar traumas, as these may also show up during processing. Nor should the history-taking be limited to negative experiences. Therapists should be assessing the client's positive resources at this stage. Identified positive experiences and resources may serve as the basis for cognitive interweaves.

Once the trauma list has been developed, the therapist must make a decision about which memory to target first in treatment. While it is possible for the therapist to simply work through the list in chronological order, therapists more often choose to work on clusters of similar experiences, starting with the earliest incident in the cluster. The reason for targeting the earliest recalled example of similar experiences is that, as with noncombat trauma, the tendency of the client will be to go back in time to earlier examples of the same situation during processing. It is simply more efficient to begin with the earliest incident.

Many trauma survivors doubt their ability to process their experiences. They will often be more willing to take on a trauma memory that is not the worst example. Resolution, even a partial resolution, of a less difficult experience may result in a generalization of treatment effects to the more powerfully traumatic experience, making it much more accessible. Indeed, having met with success using EMDR with one experience, even just a mildly threatening one, the client will often feel encouraged to take on another, more powerful one.

RESISTANCE TO
SHARING INFORMATION

War and terrorism survivors are sometimes reluctant to share information. This may be due to the need to develop a stronger relationship before divulging details of their past. However, there are other reasons as well.

Clients may be concerned about legal and other repercussions. Their behavior at the time of the incident might cause them to be concerned about criminal prosecution. Additionally, they may be concerned about possible revenge or retribution from others for their acts or for simply discussing the experience with anyone else, including a therapist. This issue is particularly acute when the trauma experience involves domestic terrorism.

There are two responses the therapist may use for these kinds of concerns. The first requires obtaining knowledge of the legal mechanisms, if any, that might come into play. For example, a Vietnam War veteran who believes he participated in an atrocity might be informed that the U.S. Government is not prosecuting any war crimes from that time, the Vietnamese government neither is in a position to do so vis-à-vis American citizens nor has expressed any interest in doing so, the statute of limitations for many offenses expired a long time ago, and information provided by a client is protected from disclosure by a variety of legal barriers and professional ethics.

The second response comes out of the nature of EMDR. Since processing is internal to the client, it is not necessary that any incriminating details be shared with the therapist. In explaining what will happen during the assessment phase, when the particular experience is identified for targeting, the therapist can point out that all that is needed is the client's affirmatives to questions, such as, "Do you have a picture of the experience or the worst part of it?" What the picture is does not have to be revealed. It is often helpful to walk the client through a hypothetical case and show how the information can be provided that enables processing even while the therapist remains ignorant of the specifics. Indeed, it is better to inform the client that, if he is concerned about the consequences of revelation, it is better not to provide the therapist with details than to provide a false history.

The benefit of not speaking of the specifics of an experience was perhaps best demonstrated by the work of EMDR clinicians with survivors of terrorism in Northern Ireland. The climate of concern, if not suspicion, was such that it was somewhat rare for therapists to discuss with one another their work with traumatized individuals. For example, we noted that therapists wishing to consult on cases involving police were careful not to discuss these cases in detail while their colleagues were present. Other therapists were careful not to discuss publicly their work with individuals who had been targeted by one of the various paramilitary factions. Given the sensitivity about working with individuals involved in "The Troubles" even as victims, it is not surprising that therapists found it helpful that clients could resolve traumas without divulging details.

"FALSE" HISTORY

It can be difficult to obtain objective verification of war memories. By their very nature, these kinds of experiences may be distant in both time and place. Witnesses may not be available and verified histories from objective observers may be totally lacking. Incidents of terrorism typically are more readily verified, though exact details may be confused or withheld by authorities.

Clients may misremember experiences for a variety of reasons. Traumatic experiences may be of sufficient power in themselves to interfere with memory, and the phenomenon of clients' "filling in the blanks" is common and natural. While the shock of the experience may result in psychogenic amnesia or simply confusion, and while the individual may invent details of an experience unconsciously, these distortions are not engaged in deliberately.

I (SMS) worked with a war veteran who remembered failing to radio for supporting fire during an enemy attack on another unit. In the middle of processing he suddenly stopped and stated, "Wait a minute. I wasn't on the hill. There's no way I could have seen what was going on with them. I don't know if I was at the stream or across it in the trees, but I wasn't on the hill when the attack came. Where the hell did I get the idea I was on the hill?" His exact location when the other unit was attacked was never definitively identified, which may have been due to his almost continuous movement during the battle. However, the primary issue, his survivor guilt about not being able to help his friends in the other unit, was ultimately resolved.

For the therapist, the primary question is a relatively simple one: Is the conscious recovery of accurate memory a necessary prerequisite for resolution? It might be argued that such a goal is, in many situations, unattainable. In any case, during EMDR trauma experiences can be resolved without a full recall of details.

There may be situations where the client is deliberately supplying false information. There are several reasons why a client might engage in this type of misrepresentation.

First, the client may be attempting to protect the therapist. The client may have concerns about the therapist's reactions to his experiences, about exposing the therapist to horror that seems beyond human endurance. "Vicarious traumatization" is a growing area of concern within the trauma treatment community (one of the earliest examinations of the impact of trauma on those other than the survivor may be found in Kishur, 1984; recent discussions of the perils of trauma work are Figley, 1995, and Stamm, 1995). A trauma survivor may be particularly sensitive about traumatizing others as a result of describing the experience.

Second, the client may be attempting to avoid possible negative reactions from the therapist. Countertransference issues in trauma treatment were first and probably best articulated by Haley (1974, 1978) and have been an ongoing topic of discussion among clinicians (e.g., Silver, 2000). There is no doubt that trauma survivors are acutely aware of the reactions of others toward them, and bitter experience may have made then hesitant to relate the actual nature of their experiences. To avoid those reactions from the therapist a client may withhold or distort the information provided.

Clients often present guilt issues in somewhat coded form at first. They may make passing references to things that they are not proud of or aren't ready to discuss. The therapist must be attentive to these messages and respond to them, even if only in general terms, such as; "I'm ready to hear whatever you have to say when you feel the time is right." If the therapist does not respond to these subtle signals, the client may lose the nerve to bring these issues up again.

Third, the client may be responding to a need to present the experience as different from how it actually was. This may be a reflection of the ongoing struggle the client is having with the experience and its meaning or of a need to protect others who were involved, even the deceased, who live on in their reputations.

Quite often the therapist is unaware of these kinds of distortions during history-taking. In terms of using EMDR, none is fatal to the process. In fact, the kinds of thinking resulting in distortion of the history may be part of the resolution. For example, after completing an EMDR session, one veteran began to describe a more complete version of a combat incident than had been previously reported. It included his freezing while under fire, which he had reported, and being unable to assist a wounded comrade, which he had not. When asked as to why the additional information had not been mentioned previously, the veteran stated that he had been afraid of the therapist's reaction. He knew the therapist was a Vietnam War veteran and assumed he would react as some other veterans had when hearing of similar occurrences. He said he now had a more realistic understanding of himself and was aware that after this incident, his first major combat action, he had learned to handle his feelings. He had gone on to be a very good soldier. He said, "That's just what can happen to a new guy; no training in the world can prepare you for what it's really like. Besides, it's not so important what *you* think of me as it is how *I* think of me."

Unconscious reasons for distorting history are, of course, the stuff of psychotherapy. Again, if such things have occurred, it is all grist for the EMDR mill. The therapist may suspect distortions of this type have taken place, but it is not necessary to take the time to dispute and clarify the history. It is the client's interpretation of the experience, not the experience itself, that is the focus of treatment.

RESOURCES IN THE CLIENT'S HISTORY

This is not to say that information provided by the client should simply be accepted without discussion. The client's recall of the experience will also provide the therapist with a sense of the resources available for healing. The therapist is interested in determining if other information, even if not currently being made use of, is available to the client. For example, the war veteran who describes himself as guilty for actions in combat may not have complete information about the nature of the situation he was in, the role of others' decisions, the effects of combat exposure on physical and psychological functioning, and so on.

Using EMDR as an approach, the therapist ascertains what information the client needs that is not presently available to him. One example is a veteran who had been assigned to an officer coordinating helicopter support. When the officer was killed, the veteran, at that time new to his job and unfamiliar with the procedures involved, tried to call in supporting gunships as his unit came under attack. No helicopters appeared for almost 20 minutes. The therapist asked how long it would have taken for the support to arrive had everything gone perfectly. The veteran shrugged and said it would have been "right away." The therapist gave him the assignment of asking the members of his therapy group who had served as helicopter crew as to what a realistic expectation of support would have been. The veteran somewhat reluctantly agreed and did so. The question provoked a fair amount of discussion among the former aircrew members and, as the information came out, the veteran revealed more and more of the situation. Eventually it was determined that, under the best of circumstances, it would have been unreasonable to expect the gunships to arrive in less than 20 minutes. Even if the experienced officer had been the one making the call for assistance, the results would have been the same because of the distance and time required to get helicopters into the air. The information discovered in group therapy was useful in itself in gaining a partial resolution of the trauma reaction; however, a thorough integration of the information was accelerated with EMDR.

This example highlights an important consideration for the therapist. As the client history develops, it may become clear that there are information resources the client needs for successful resolution. It is useful for the therapist to have a good general knowledge of the experience of war and terrorism prior to developing the client history. Understanding the primary protagonists, major events, and historical background provides a context for the client's individual experiences. Developing that understanding will also help the therapist identify additional resources that may be useful. The key is identifying resources useful in the development of new cognitive structures. The client history may reveal the client's familiarity, or lack thereof, with these resources.

For example, one veteran assigned to a particular task believed it was because he was considered incompetent at his primary job, that of being a field medic. Referring the veteran to others who were also medics or to books written by former medics helped him discover that his belief was erroneous.

What if the information uncovered tends to corroborate the client's negative self-belief? Though it may seem paradoxical, this is actually a positive step forward. It is important to remember that the EMDR approach emphasizes not the experience itself but, rather, its current meaning for the client. When the negative behavior is corroborated by other sources of information, the next step is to develop its current meaning for the client. "What does it say about you *now* that you committed that action? What kinds of judgments do you make about yourself *now* when you think about that experience?" Here we are beginning to lay the groundwork for the more specific focus developed during the assessment phase.

FACTITIOUS PRESENTATIONS

To return to the issue of false history, there is one other area that needs to be addressed—an overt, factitious presentation made in an attempt to obtain secondary gain, such as disability compensation. No psychotherapy is immune to the influence of secondary gain.

It is unfortunately true that a proportion of purported cases of PTSD are actually factitious or a function of malingering. While this is a phenomenon to be found in the aftermath of virtually all mass trauma situations, it is typically overlooked by mental health professionals. Verification of experiences is most often not done, and mental health professionals tend to take the client's word for what has happened. In many circumstances, that is the only option—records or witnesses may not be available, time constraints and the numbers of people requiring immediate assistance preclude prolonged background checks, and so forth. Nonetheless, even in these circumstances mental health professionals should take the time to learn about the experiences they are responding to and should take advantage of the expertise available. For example, while it may be impossible to obtain a war veteran's military records, it may be possible to consult with those who have knowledge of the war, the units involved and their organizations, and the nature of the conduct of operations. Literature and reference works provide the context that supports a veteran's story.

Therapists should use common sense. We have encountered veterans who reported stories like walking from Hanoi to Danang in Vietnam in five days. This story, apparently accepted by numerous VA staff, should have been disputed after a simple glance at a map— never mind the ongoing war, which would have made such foot travel more than slightly difficult. Mental health professionals tend to believe their judgment of the reality of a described experience is infallible; the contrary is true. Because of the nature of the calling and their training, mental health professionals believe their clients. Additionally, some therapists accept even the most outlandish stories because they fit their own preconceptions, or because they are afraid of confronting the fakers, or because they are unwilling to take the time to check the story.

Verification of experiences is useful for several reasons. One, it helps to dissuade those who are faking from taking up valuable time and resources. Two, it helps to legitimize the helpers in the eyes of those whose trauma reactions and experiences are real. Third, the information gathered is often helpful for the legitimate client in gaining clarity around their memory of the experience. Fourth, it cuts down on staff frustration and burnout, since the fakers take a disproportionate amount of time and effort but show little or no improvement. Fifth, failure to confront those who are faking can contribute to societal antipathy toward those who really have experienced trauma (Burkett & Whitley, 1998).

Beyond those who are simply faking their experiences or reactions are those who have, in fact, been traumatized, but who have become focused on secondary gain issues. An examination of the client's history may suggest that the client has anxiety about being successful in therapy because of the consequences, including loss of identity, loss of the therapist, loss of compensation, loss of the social support system of other survivors, and so on. However, EMDR does offer a possible approach for dealing with such issues. If the therapist believes that secondary gain is involved, it may be possible to extract a core belief that has the client essentially frozen in place. For example, a focus on disability payments may be at least partially due to a fear that the client will be unable to gain employment, learn new skills, or cope with his disability's physical consequences. These fears can be targeted for processing.

An open and frank discussion of these fears, initiated by the therapist, is often useful. Reality-based alternatives may be introduced to ensure that the client is aware of other, healthier possibilities. For example, the Vietnam War veterans who believe that getting rid of their symptoms will mean they won't really be veterans or that in some way they will forget their friends who died in the war may need to hear that "dropping the pain does not mean dropping the flag." Becoming a healthier veteran may mean being able to honor one's friends by leading a better life and by being in a stronger position to ensure that they are not forgotten. Healing PTSD means being able to help other veterans more effectively, which may mean saving lives.

The identification of role models is often useful to dispel the myth that giving up their trauma reactions means giving up their identities, social network, and so forth. If the client is unaware of such survivors, then the therapist has an opportunity to provide meaningful information and education. Enrollment in a group therapy with other survivors at varying stages in their recovery may provide a new perspective.

As we have seen, any discussion of client history forces a consideration of subsequent phases of the EMDR approach. After all, the development of the client history does not take place in a vacuum. It is designed to gain as complete a picture as possible of not only the identified traumatic experience but also all the other related experiences and current triggers that have been a part of the self-perpetuating psychological structure.

Chapter 8

CLIENT PREPARATION

"Why does this seem scarier than combat?"

There is a tendency for war and terrorism survivors to avoid initially their most emotionally powerful experiences. This may reflect a fear of the potential pain of abreaction, as well as concern about the dangers inherent in being out of control in terms of self-protection. The need to be on guard and ready to take defensive action may deter clients from approaching trauma memories. They fear being vulnerable while caught up in the potential flood of emotions. For these clients, preparation takes on added importance. In particular, the therapist will wish to stress the client-centered nature of EMDR and the fact that the client can stop the procedure at any point. Along with this, tension reduction techniques are very useful, including some opportunities for "field practice," so clients begin to have confidence in their ability to maintain control. Clients' fear of being overwhelmed and losing control in a manner dangerous to the therapist can be addressed in the same manner.

THE THERAPEUTIC RELATIONSHIP

War trauma can pose special challenges to the development of a positive therapeutic relationship. When people witness interpersonal violence their ability to trust others may be damaged. They develop a

86

keen interest in safety and control, which leads them to be attentive to signs of danger not just in the environment, but from other people. They may have experiences in which authority was used abusively or people were killed because of a lack of competence. Moreover, they tend to be isolated by the extraordinary nature of their experiences. Since EMDR requires individuals to confront their most painful memories and since the therapist is dependent on the client's ability to provide honest feedback during the procedure, the quality of the working relationship is important to the success of treatment.

Traumatized clients' internal world is typically chaotic. They are fearful of being overwhelmed by their feelings, of losing control, and of hurting themselves or others. Should they perceive a lack of competence in their therapist they may respond by becoming resistant or by dropping out of treatment. Some clients try to solve this dilemma by seeking out therapists who have had war experiences of their own. While this may have a sort of immediate appeal and may be consistent with the philosophy of the self-help movement, the issue is complex and deserves fuller examination.

The most obvious advantage for the veteran therapist* is that there is a certain degree of instant rapport with veteran clients. Traumatized individuals often feel isolated from those who have not shared the experience and gravitate toward those who they assume will have an automatic understanding. Veteran therapists have a technical familiarity with the event that can guide their decision-making and make the work of therapy more efficient. They can also serve as powerful models for recovery.

However, there are also some disadvantages in the use of veteran therapists. There are fewer of them, and clients may remain symptomatic while they take the time to search for one. Therapy with another veteran can increase a sense of specialness that contributes in the long run to isolation. More importantly, the assumptions underlying the expected "instant rapport" may be false. While the general aspects of the war experience may be relatively common, the traumatic aspects are unique to the individual. It has been said that,

---

* For the sake of convenience in the discussion that follows, the terms "veteran therapist" and "civilian therapist" will be used in the broadest sense to indicate therapists who have shared in the experience of war or terrorism and those who have not.

"Even two men in the same foxhole do not have the same experience." The belief that the therapist will automatically understand and affirm the client's views may be misplaced, a discovery that can be quite disappointing. There is also some risk for the veteran therapist, in that any unresolved traumas of their own can be triggered by their work with other survivors.

It is probable that civilian therapists initially will have to work harder at building rapport. On the other hand, they may be able to make an advantage of their own distance from the experience by using it as a springboard for discussion. By openly admitting the limits of their experience, they may temporarily place the client in the role of teacher, by asking, "I wasn't in the war, so tell me about it. What was your job? How were you trained? What equipment did you use?" Such questions demonstrate a willingness to get involved in the details of the client's experience.

Civilian therapists may sometimes find themselves the object of transference as a representative of a society the client has come to see as sheltered, ignorant, and even indifferent. They must be prepared to address this issue. On the other hand, by using a calculated amount of self-disclosure, they have an opportunity to serve as a bridge between the client and the civilian community.

Civilian therapists may be less vulnerable to having their own memories triggered by their work with survivors, though they may be vulnerable to secondary traumatization, in that their own belief systems can be challenged by exposure to their clients' experiences.

The EMDR approach, while usually requiring a strong therapeutic alliance, can also serve to build the relationship. Particular emphasis on the concept of a "team effort" empowers the client, and the time spent explaining EMDR and how processing might be experienced may legitimize the therapist: "Well, she told me this might happen, so maybe she knows what she's talking about."

THE FIVE C'S

The therapeutic relationship is built through the implementation of five Cs. These are competence, compassion, commitment, containment, and coaching.

Competence means not only having skills, but knowing the limit of those skills. Being honest with a client about one's abilities is reassuring. Survivors of war and terrorism, in part because of the nature of their trauma experiences, are often acutely sensitive to others. It is extraordinarily easy for them to spot someone who is trying to "fake it." Beginning therapists often take this to mean that they should not work with this population until their skill levels are fully developed. This restriction, however well meaning, is not necessary. If one has not had a lot of experience with a particular group of survivors, then having a consultative relationship with an experienced peer is invaluable.

It is important to let the client know what the therapist *does* know, as well as what his or her skill limits might be. The following dialogue illustrates how this can be approached.

TH: Well, Ann, I've given you a lot of information on EMDR. I need to tell you that almost all my work with it has been with people whose trauma was different from yours.

CL: Does that mean you don't want to do it with me?

TH: No. I just wanted you to know that this stuff is something that I haven't used EMDR with before. So I've been communicating with some other therapists, folks who are doing a lot of work with this kind of trauma and people I trust, and they've given me some ideas on how to approach this. Because it is new to me, you and I are going to have to make an extra effort to keep communicating with one another so we stay on track. Does that seem reasonable?

CL: Oh, sure. I thought you might be getting ready to bail out on me. I'd hate to have to start over with another therapist.

TH: (*Laughs*) Look, if there's something you need and I can't do it, I'll tell you. And if that happens to be another therapist, I'll tell you that straight up too. But I don't have any plan to do that. I just wanted to let you know that this is a little new to me, OK?

CL: Yeah, it's OK. Tell the truth, it's new to me, too.

Compassion, the simple act of caring, is particularly relevant. War and terrorism survivors have experienced the lack of compassion firsthand. They may also have encountered attempts to sweep their experiences under the rug afterward. Therapists convey compassion in a variety of ways consistent with their personalities. Trying to fake this will fail with this population and effectively discredit the therapist.

One caution should be remembered. Some therapists are emotionally generous and genuinely effusive in their demonstrations of compassion for their clients. Such therapists should seriously consider being cautious in how demonstrative they are with war or terrorism clients, especially with new ones. Someone whose emotional responses may be muted and who tends to regard others with at least caution and often suspicion may find being confronted—and that is often how it feels—with a therapist's tears and hugs may be disconcerting. Anything out of control is dangerous in the view of the survivor, and that includes the therapist. As the therapeutic relationship develops, the therapist may then ease the restraints and even serve as a model for the client, particularly in tolerating emotions.

Commitment means that the therapist is going to work with the client and not back off. Survivors of war and terrorism typically will forgive all kinds of mistakes by the therapist, even marginal competence, if they believe the therapist is committed to them.

Again, it is important to remember that war and terrorism trauma often involves what the client perceives as a lack of commitment on the part of others. The security guard who did not take his job seriously so the bomber got through, the officer who was more invested in taking care of himself than his troops, the country that did not seem to care what happened to its soldiers—all of these past lapses make present commitment imperative. Current authority figures often are tested by these survivors for just this reason.

The therapist conveys commitment by demonstrating reliability. This does not mean just that scheduled appointments are kept. It also means demonstrating a commitment to treatment. Does the therapist have sufficient commitment to stay with the client even when processing uncomfortable, even harrowing, material? The client must believe the therapist can be relied on to go with him or her no matter where the processing might go. Again, this is accomplished not just in words—they *are* important—but by acts.

Containment is a close relative to competence. It is the need for the client to have limits, boundaries, and safeguards established. War and terrorism typically involve multiple traumatic experiences. With the speed and power of EMDR processing, it is easy for a client to feel overwhelmed by an avalanche of rapidly connected and accessed experiences, thoughts, and feelings. Much of the preparation phase of EMDR is devoted to developing tools the client can use for containing unfinished material. Many EMDR therapists neglect to spend sufficient time with these tasks. Containment is also used within a session. The therapist, because of time or client limits, may decide to steer processing away from certain material or to close down processing during a particular session.

Communication with the client is very important. A clear statement of what is being done and why, with the door left open for discussion, will provide the client with understanding and a continued sense of control. Particularly with regard to the necessity of responding to the dictates of the clock, therapists will benefit from informing the client during preparation of the possibility of going into closure for a session with material unfinished and explaining what the procedures will be in advance.

Coaching means providing encouragement and education both within and outside of the treatment session. The kind of cool professional distancing adopted by some mental health professionals while working with their clients may be interpreted by the trauma survivor as indifference or worse. Especially when tapping into abreactive material, a greater level of activity by the therapist is appropriate and sometimes necessary.

Coaching also includes identifying possible experiences the client may encounter during treatment and educating the client as to how to respond to those situations. Occasionally therapists are reluctant to address potential problems for fear of creating a self-fulfilling prophecy. With trauma survivors this reluctance can have catastrophic consequences. The therapist has to realize it is unlikely that they will introduce any new negative ideas to clients who have come to expect the worst in all situations.

From the client history the therapist will be alerted to patterns of behavior the client has engaged when subjected to stress. Fighting, substance abuse, increased isolation, suicidal gestures and behavior, and so on, once identified, should be made part of the therapeutic contract, so the client can be coached into practicing alternative methods of coping.

This is especially important with suicidal ideation. Rather than side-stepping the subject, directly addressing it gives the therapist an opportunity to provide the client with additional tools for dealing with situations when such thoughts might occur.

MECHANICS AND TERMINOLOGY

During client preparation, the clinician acquaints the client with the mechanics of the procedure, including the positions of the clinician and client, the speed, distance, and various directions of the eye movements, and alternative forms of stimulation such as sounds and taps. It is important to do this initial demonstration prior to working with trauma material so that clients with boundary issues activated by the physical proximity of the therapist will have them identified.

The language used by the clinician during processing, such as "Go with that" and "Focus on that," is introduced and explained. Metaphors used to represent processing, such as new material being viewed like scenery from a train that clients should observe and report but not stop the train to hold onto, will be useful during processing.

A nonverbal stop signal that the client may use to halt processing when necessary is agreed upon. A nonverbal signal is important because war and terrorism trauma often involves the effort of clients to stop the experience at the time. A nonverbal signal reduces the possibility of confusion arising during abreaction.

SAFE PLACE DEVELOPMENT
AND ANXIETY MANAGEMENT

The safe place exercise is designed to provide the client with a resource for bringing down the intensity of an incomplete session during the closure phase and for dealing with any distress resulting from continued processing between sessions. It has the added benefit of acquainting the client with the eye movements while working on nonthreatening material. The client's reaction to the safe place exercise may also provide clinical feedback.

Unlike those who have experienced more circumscribed stressors, war survivors may have difficulty believing that any place is truly safe, so it may be preferable to use an imaginary safe place. One client identified a castle from a fairytale as his safe place with good results. Whether the image is real or imaginary, it is important to take the time to elaborate and enhance the imagery and associated sensations.

For some of these survivors, any safe place is simply unimaginable, even an unreal one. Such clients can be given training and practice in other tension and anxiety management techniques. The simpler techniques, such as progressive relaxation training, appear to be more successful than the more complex ones, such as self-hypnosis. Relaxation training is also useful at reducing levels of depression (Silver, Brooks, & Obenchain, 1995).

FRONT LOADING AND
RESOURCE INSTALLATION

Survivors suffering from long-term, chronic trauma reactions often feel helpless and hopeless. Ego strength may be so poor that clients are unable to withstand the stress of intense treatment. Given the chronicity of their condition, they may have difficulty believing in the possibility of improvement. Clients may also have some experiential deficits which contribute to the complexity of treatment.

In recent years, some EMDR therapists have become enthusiastic about a procedure called resource development and installation (Leeds, 1998). An early form of this tactic was described by Wildwind (1992, 1998). Noting clients' problems with attachment and parental deprivation problems, she proposed using eye movements as a way of installing needed resources. These "adopted" resources could then be utilized during the desensitization of traumas. Survivors of war and terrorism trauma may benefit from this approach. In effect, the resources needed to approach the trauma material are "front loaded." That is, they are provided before the trauma material is approached.

Indications that a client might benefit from front loading are usually discovered quickly. Such clients will consistently express their doubts about the possibility of change, focusing on their inability to function differently. Referring to the successes of other survivors only tends to make them feel even more helpless: "I can't even do what they can do." Their treatment history is often replete with failures, as therapists have given up in the face of their hopelessness.

If this problem is not identified prior to the beginning of desensitization, it rapidly becomes clear once processing begins. Movement stops and the client will use such phrases as "I can't do this" and "I don't have what it takes." Ordinarily, such blocking beliefs are targeted as irrational beliefs for continued processing; however, for some clients these beliefs show a recognition that they truly lack a needed skill or resource: self-discipline, endurance, faith in self, a sense of empowerment, an ability to handle emotions, and so forth. Such resources may need to be in place before processing.

The specific identification of the needed resource is done in cooperation with the client. The therapist engages the client and draws out information about what is needed. If the client shows some embarrassment about this deficit, one may speak in terms of a metaphor, such as a car needing fuel to make a journey. The lack of gas does not mean the car is worthless. It simply means there is a resource the car needs to use. The question is how to get the resource.

Once the resource has been identified (e.g., "I'm strong enough to do what I have to"), the desired state is developed into an image. This might be, for the resource of strength, seeing oneself participating successfully in a task requiring strength. Focusing on the image, the client is asked to identify any accompanying emotional and physical sensations. Linking the image to the sensations, the client is then taken through a series of eye movement sets. The number of repetitions in a set is generally low, usually in the neighborhood of 12 to 20. At the end of each set the client is asked what he is then aware of. The client's focus of attention is directed toward the changes in imagery or sensation reported and additional eye movements are done. The process continues as long as the client reports improvement. The needed resource can be buttressed by having the client identify additional images for installation.

CL: (*Describing a war trauma*) There's just no way I could go through that shit again.

TH: What leads you to say that?

CL: (*Pauses*) I'd break down. I don't have what it takes anymore. I'm not strong enough, not like the others (*referring to other veterans in the program*).

TH: You're saying you don't have any strength, any power?

CL: (*Nodding, eyes tearing*)

TH: Can you recall a time when you had that kind of strength?

CL: Sure. I felt I could do anything. Man, I could lick the world.

TH: Do you have a picture of yourself then? I mean mentally, an image of yourself as strong?

CL: Yeah.

TH: When you focus on that image, when you really get into it, how do you feel it in your body?

CL: Right through here (*gestures toward chest and shoulders*).

TH: Okay, here's what I want you to do. Focus on that image and that feeling and hold onto them for a second. (*Pauses*) How is it now?

CL: It's OK.

TH: Now focus on the picture of yourself strong and the feeling it gives you and follow my hand. (*A short set of eye movements follows.*)

TH: OK, let's pause, take a breath, and how is it now?

CL: (*Nodding his head*) Feel a little stronger.

TH: Go with that. Got it? Follow my hand.

The process is repeated until no further gains are made. Additional resources can be installed as well. Indeed, it appears that the installation of a relatively basic idea ("I am strong") then makes the installation of a somewhat more complex idea ("I'm quick to adapt") easier. As the therapist identifies the client's needs, arranging them in a hierarchical installation sequence may make the whole package easier to accept and utilize.

The key is the identification of the attribute that the client needs in order to address the trauma. Thus, the client might be able to get a sense of the attribute from sources other than his own history or experience. For example, if a client cannot identify himself as ever having been strong, the therapist might ask for whatever he would identify as being strong. This could be a memory of seeing someone else being strong. The therapist helps the client to identify the sensations aroused by that image. The image and sensations are the focus of the installation. The installation might be complete at this point, but the therapist may find that with the successful installation of this "indirect" resource the client spontaneously discovers an image of himself with the attribute. It may be worthwhile to install this new image and its accompanying sensations.

PHYSICAL AWARENESS PRACTICE

EMDR utilizes kinesthetic information in all phases of adaptive information-processing. Many clients are not particularly aware of physical sensations unless they are pronounced; in fact, during assessment the therapist may discover that the client cannot identify a physical response to the targeted trauma experience. The assessment phase is designed to catalyze the trauma experience and, through the use of a defined sequence, maximize an individual's reactivity to the experience. Given that the identification of physical sensations is the last step prior to the initiation of desensitization, it may be distracting to discover at that point that the client is unaware of his or her body and needs to be educated in that awareness. Consequently, it is preferable to assess the client's level of body awareness during the preparation phase. If practice is needed, it can be accomplished then, thereby avoiding disruption of the assessment phase and its catalyzing of the stored trauma experience information.

An easy approach to this is to ask the client to rate his or her current level of tension or anxiety with the SUD scale. This focuses the negative emotion most trauma survivors carry around with them relatively constantly. Then ask where in the body the distress is felt. The client is thus made aware of the link between emotions and physical responses, if he or she was not so already. If the client cannot identify a body sensation, then the therapist can coach him or her through a head-to-toe body scan. Then have the client relax, perhaps by using one of the tension management techniques taught earlier. Taking the client on a directed head-to-toe scan will generally allow him or her to discover what his or her body feels like in a generally relaxed state. It is not necessary to pursue changes or associations at this point. The goal is to simply have the client note the sensations accompanying the positive mental imagery or relaxation and to contrast these with the way he or she feels when anxious.

Client preparation might be viewed as an essentially educative part of the EMDR methodology. Certainly it should accomplish the task of ensuring that clients learn what they need to know about EMDR. As we have noted in this chapter, this phase also provides both therapist and client with clinical information on the relationships among past experiences, current reactions, and resources.

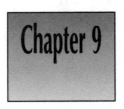

Chapter 9

ASSESSMENT

"On a scale up to ten? Maybe a fifteen . . . "

The primary focus of the assessment phase is the delineation of the specific experience to be targeted. This is done not simply to develop a jumping-off place but also to galvanize all the related components of the memory, including cognitive, emotional, and somatic aspects, as well as to gain an initial idea of how the client would like to think of himself or herself in the future. Unlike the exposure therapies, EMDR does not start at a point of relative calm. Instead, during the assessment process the therapist deliberately tries to stimulate a maximum level of intensity by using all the available components. Nevertheless, the clinician should realize that, whatever the level of intensity generated by the assessment phase, higher levels may be encountered during the desensitization, installation, and body scan phases, with the greatest probability of such encounters occurring during desensitization.

SELECTION BY CLUSTER

Since traumatic war experiences are typically several, it may be possible to select one as representative of a cluster. If the client is able to readily identify one representative experience, this should be the first target. It is often more useful to cluster memories that are similar in terms of meanings or feelings than to cluster memories that share similar physical details.

SELECTION BY SUD LEVEL

Typically, multiple traumatic experiences contribute to the reactions of survivors of war. If these experiences are not sufficiently similar in client-defined terms to permit the clustering approach, which memory should be approached first?

One approach is to start with the least distressing experience. This approach has several advantages. Clients find it less threatening, success on easier memories can build their confidence to take on more powerful experiences, and the treatment effect may generalize to more distressing memories prior to their being addressed directly. However, there is no guarantee that this will happen. Memories that appear to be minor may involve significant levels of distress once processing begins. Furthermore, clients may start with an easier memory and, by the process of association, find themselves confronting the very memory they had hoped to avoid. Clinicians opting to start with the least distressing memory should inform clients of this possibility in advance and develop a contingency plan.

Starting with the worst memory may be more efficient, since it tends to yield a more pronounced generalization of resolution; that is, resolution may spread to other memories, even those not identified earlier as part of an obvious cluster. For example, clients with survivor guilt are all wrestling with the problem of justifying their own survival or the action they took in order to survive. Resolution of this issue is likely to have a positive carryover to a wide range of experiences.

Selection of the most powerful experience does not mean that the clinician is committed to proceeding at full speed. As will be discussed in the next chapter, it is possible to pace the speed of movement with EMDR, thus allowing the client to work with very powerful experiences that they might ordinarily hesitate to approach out of fear of being swept away.

PICTURE

Whatever the initial experience selected, the standard EMDR protocol calls for starting with a picture that represents to the client the experience or the worst part of it. Ordinarily trauma survivors have little difficulty identifying such a picture, though visualizing it may be painful. (If the client reports several pictures from the same experience that are equal in intensity, it may indicate that the experience has not yet consolidated. A variation on the protocol for this situation is discussed in chapter 14.) Simply asking the client to identify the worst part of the experience can be useful in itself, since it keeps the therapist from relying on his or her own assumptions and may clarify the client's thinking abut the experience.

It is not necessary for the client to go into great detail describing the picture. Indeed, lengthy descriptions may serve to distance the client from the memory. The clinician should prevent this by keeping questions to a minimum. This also avoids the problem of requiring the client to put a lot of effort into verbalizing the experience, which is often difficult for individuals with PTSD. It is sufficient to ask if the client has a picture that represents the experience or the worst part of it. A nod from the client is really all that is needed. The clinician can then say that the picture the client now has will be called the "target scene" or the "picture of the experience." This approach also makes it easier for clients who do not want to disclose the details of the experience.

EMDR clinicians have found that for most clients a picture makes the rest of the information sought during the assessment phase more accessible. Given that human beings are highly visual animals, this makes sense. On the other hand, if the client is unable to provide a picture, assessment can continue. The therapist can simply ask the client to "bring up the experience" when eliciting the other information needed. This generic phrase is usually sufficient to stimulate the cognition, emotions and sensations.

NEGATIVE COGNITION

Negative evaluations of self are common among trauma survivors. This is particularly true of war survivors who have not resolved their experiences. Guilt for surviving and for actions taken in order to survive is quite common. Shapiro (1995) emphasizes the importance of identifying irrational beliefs that clients developed about themselves during the traumatic event that they retain in the present. In some cases it is easy to see how irrational the cognition is. For example, a survivor of Bangladesh's war of independence described leaving his university on foot and turning down a street only to find his way blocked by tanks. When asked to identify the words that went with this image he immediately said "I should have known better than to take that route." In other cases, the irrational quality of the cognition is more difficult to recognize. We once supervised a therapist who was working with the survivor of an air raid in WW II. When asked for the words that went with the image of the building being damaged during the bombing, the client said "I'm going to die." The therapist questioned whether this was an appropriate cognition to use in EMDR, since it wasn't irrational to think that way during the bombing. "Furthermore," he said, "we're all going to die someday." We clarified the issue for him by pointing out that the cognition was indeed irrational in the present when the client was safe in his office.

Having the client view the picture of the experience usually makes the accessing and identification of negative self-judgments and self-limiting beliefs relatively easy. Indeed, the more traumatic the experience, the easier it is for a client to identify the negative cognition. In fact, the client may provide more than a simple statement. Given the opportunity and the catalyzing effect of viewing the picture, the client may provide a relatively lengthy list of self-judgments and beliefs. The therapist should try to summarize such lengthy presentations with a short, succinct statement. This summary statement ("It sounds to me that what you are saying is, 'I'm no good.' Is that it?") provides the springboard to get to the next part of the assessment, the positive cognition.

Some clients have difficulty expressing a negative cognition for several reasons. First, they may believe that it is not acceptable for them to think negatively about themselves, an idea often conveyed in therapy. Related to this is the idea that, by now, they should have been able to put negative thoughts of self behind them. To admit to negative cognitions may be taken as a sign of failure in previous treatment or in personal efforts to resolve the experience.

If this is the case, the therapist should work to normalize the situation by providing the client with education on how people respond to traumatic events. Self-judgment, a naturally occurring process of the mind, can become "stuck" when an individual confronts powerful experiences. That these judgments have not readily changed with time or therapies is simply an indicator of their power and complexity.

Resolution of negative cognitions may be blocked by any of a number of variables heretofore unaddressed. EMDR permits the mind to access and deal with these blocks so that clients can go on to develop their own resolutions.

Second, the expression of the negative cognition is an act of self-revelation, which the client may find extremely difficult. An indicator that this might happen is the client statement that he would prefer not to explicitly identify the nature of his experience. It may be helpful to remind the client that an explicit statement identifying the particulars of an experience is not necessary. "I am no good" is sufficient; "I am no good because I was raped" provides more than is needed for purposes of assessment.

Some clients may have trouble understanding the instructions. It is important that they understand that the request is for a currently held belief rather than the thoughts they may have had about themselves during the experience. Alternative phrases may help in this situation. The therapist can explain, "Sometimes when people have a bad experience, they develop certain ideas about themselves that stay with them for a long time and which they take with them into new situations where they might not be useful. Does such an idea come to mind when you look at this picture?" Another alternative is to ask, "If someone else were looking at this scene, what's the worst conclusion that person could draw about you?"

We speculate that a broad negative cognition is more therapeutically useful than a tightly defined one. "I am no good" might encourage the elicitation of links to other experiences feeding into that negative self-appraisal, thereby increasing the efficiency of EMDR treatment during desensitization. In any case, if the client will not state the negative cognition, the therapist should understand that the client is aware of it on some level and its verbalization is of secondary importance. The therapist can move the client on to the development of the positive cognition.

POSITIVE COGNITION

The positive cognition is elicited by having the client hold the picture and the negative cognition together as the therapist asks what he would like to believe about himself. As with the negative cognition, what is sought is a belief about the self, in this case how the client would like to think about himself or herself in relation to the event.

Terrorism and war survivors may resist identifying positive cognitions about their experiences. Guilt about survival or, more commonly, about what was done in order to survive may lead the client to take the position that, "I do not deserve to think better about myself." Clarifying that the therapist is not asking the client to "think better" about himself but, instead, to identify how he would prefer to think *if it were possible* may be useful. Discussion around this proposition may reveal much of the heretofore unidentified elements of the experience. It can also be helpful to talk about "ideas that are *useful* to you now" rather than "positive ideas."*

The initial believability of the positive cognition is assessed by using the Validity of Cognition (VOC) Scale. The client is asked to hold the experience and the positive cognition together and to rate the felt believability of the positive cognition using a scale where one feels completely false and seven feels completely true.

Jeanne Varrasse, a clinical nurse specialist in psychiatry who works in our inpatient PTSD program, has encountered patients who are unable to identify a positive cognition. Finding that persisting in the formulation of an immediate positive cognition when the client has strong objections to the concept appears to be counterproductive, she sometimes goes ahead with desensitization without an identified positive cognition. This results in progress but the SUD, while decreasing, will not always go down to zero. When the client seems stuck, she reintroduces the idea of the positive cognition, suggesting one if the patient still cannot identify one. After this step, desensitization is resumed and processing usually continues normally and completely.

Desensitization and installation are really the same thing—information-processing—and are essentially two sides of the same coin. Anytime a client can identify a negative cognition, they have implicitly identified a positive cognition. The reverse is likewise true. Having said this, we recommend that therapists do not rush this part of the assessment. Taking the time with clients to develop the cognitions is worthwhile, since that effort in and of itself may be therapeutic, particularly those with chronic trauma reactions.

---

* Those who view themselves as perpetrators are a special case, and we discuss an approach to assisting them develop a positive cognition later in this book.

EMOTION

The client is asked to hold together the picture of the experience and the negative cognition and then to identify what emotion or emotions are felt now. Unless the emphasis is placed upon *current* feelings, the client is likely to identify how she or he felt, or believes he or she felt, at the time of the experience. The current level of intensity of the emotion is assessed utilizing the SUD scale.

Sometimes war and terrorism survivors respond with several emotions. It is not necessary to identify the primary one. Since this is just the jumping-off place, the clinician does not have to worry about neglected or overlooked emotions. If another emotion is a part of the targeted experience, it will be processed along with the rest of the information making up that memory. However, it is important to attach a label to the current emotional state, so that changes during processing can be identified as such. If the therapist simply relies on SUD levels, a shift from a SUD level of five for anger to a SUD level of five for grief, for example, may be missed.

The therapist should remember during life-threatening events an ability to mute emotional responsiveness contributes to survival. This mechanism is a superb defense in war. Therefore, when a client provides a very low SUD score for an experience that appears clinically powerful, the therapist may reasonably hypothesize that numbing is present.

PHYSICAL SENSATION

When the client identifies the level of emotional intensity, one asks them where in the body that intensity or disturbance is felt. For clients who do not usually attend to physical sensations, a directed body scan after putting aside the targeted experience may provide them a baseline from which to note any changes in physical sensations when they access the experience. However, war and terrorism survivors often have learned largely to ignore all but the most extreme physical sensations. Again, this is a prosurvival mechanism enabling attention to necessary tasks and responsibilities in life-threatening situations.

As described in chapter 8, physical awareness practice can be performed with such clients during preparation. This directed focusing of awareness on body sensations can be conducted whenever the client is not accessing stressful material, for instance, during the teaching of relaxation techniques. The therapist simply has the client sit quietly and verbally guides his attention from the top of his head to his toes. This can be repeated several times. The client then will have a baseline of physical sensations before getting into assessment so the catalyzing of the elements of the targeted experience will not be interrupted. By the time physical sensations are to be assessed in the EMDR protocol, it is often very difficult to put the experience to one side to do an initial body scan.

With assessment completed, the client is ready to begin the desensitization phase. Given that assessment is deliberately designed to galvanize as many elements of the memory of the targeted experience—the picture, the negative self-judgments, the desired but as yet unattained positive belief system, the emotions, and the related kinesthetic cues—it is important that desensitization commence in the same session.

DESENSITIZATION AND

BLOCKED RESPONSE

"You know, I just had a thought—a lot of those kids stayed alive because of me."

The word "desensitization" may be confusing to therapists familiar with cognitive-behavioral therapy, since it implies that EMDR is an exposure therapy that works by means of extinction. Indeed, this is what Shapiro assumed when she originally named the procedure Eye Movement Desensitization. EMDR did appear to decrease emotional distress by having clients focus on trauma memories. However, after noting the rapidity of change in EMDR, Shapiro began to question the idea that these results were a function of clients' habituating to conditioned stimuli. Instead, she proposed an information-processing model to explain the effects of EMDR. Despite this change in her thinking, much of EMDR terminology continues to show its initial behavioral theory roots. In the current EMDR model, the term "desensitization" simply refers to the phase of processing during which the client is focused primarily on negative material.

EMDR can be distinguished from exposure therapy by the fact that clients are permitted to associate freely between events or between features of a single event. No attempt is made to sustain clients' focus on any one element of the memory for a prolonged period of time. Instead, each reported change becomes the focus of the next set of eye movements. This principle comes into sharp focus when entering the desensitization phase of the EMDR methodology.

EMDR also has a considerable cognitive component, which has led some to speculate that it is a form of cognitive restructuring. Again, while there are some similarities, the cognitive changes that happen during EMDR often occur spontaneously, rather than as the result of the directive argumentation that characterizes cognitive therapy.

RETURNING TO THE
TARGET EXPERIENCE

One of the greatest challenges confronting therapists working with war survivors is knowing when to return to the target scene during processing. Certainly, it should be done when the channel of information appears resolved; however, individuals with multiple traumatic experiences may easily slide from one incident to another during desensitization. Therapists working with this population may observe their clients processing very long strings of association involving many different traumatic events. In some cases the client seems to get lost in a seemingly endless "pool of links." While it is clear that spontaneous associating is generally constructive, it can be experienced as overwhelming. It may also give the client the perception that he is not progressing, because the level of disturbance stays high while moving from experience to experience. It may also increase the amount of time needed for treatment.

When the client seems to be going from one event to another with little decrease in distress, therapists may occasionally have to decide whether to let the client continue or to interrupt the flow with an intervention. One intervention is to return to the original target experience. Returning to the original target before processing of a channel of information is complete should be regarded as a choice of last resort. This should be done infrequently, as the therapist may be preempting a useful string of associations that will have to be accessed again later. Nonetheless, there are times when the clinician may consider such a move useful:

1. Near the end of a session marked by a large number of links. The clinician may desire to have the client get a sense of progress on the original experience.

2. When the client has been progressing through a very large number of linked experiences with little decrease in disturbance. Returning to the original experience may show clients that change is taking place on that experience and reassure them that their processing is effective. This might be done several times in a treatment session.

3. When the circumstances require a crisis intervention orientation. For example, in a mass disaster situation the clinician might have to settle for a deliberate focusing on the present trauma, since time may not be available to process all linked experiences. In these unusual circumstances the clinician has to make judgments about which experiences are most critical in terms of the need for resolution.

Again, returning to the original target experience before processing of a channel is complete is a tactic of last resort. We much prefer to use the cognitive interweave (discussed below) when any of the above circumstances arise.

NUMBING

Emotional numbing is a common symptom of PTSD and can be confusing to the therapist if it comes up during the desensitization phase of EMDR. If, at the end of a set of eye movements, the client reports "nothing," it may indicate that he is at the end of a string of associations and so the therapist should return to the original experience. However, it may also indicate that the client has moved on to a part of the memory in which numbing was a feature. In this case, the numbing can become the focus of the next set of eye movements. Though it sounds odd, most clients understand the instruction to "focus on the numbing." One client, in his first EMDR session, responded to the first two sets of eye movements with "nothing," and "a different nothing." The therapist, noting that the client's language indicated change, decided that she needed no further information and kept processing. This strategy was successful. At the end of the session, when the memory was successfully resolved, she asked the client a few questions about the "nothings." The client confirmed that, while the first one was an absence of feeling not unlike the emotional numbing that he had experienced for years, the second one "felt more like normal relaxation."

Therapists should be alert when a client reports a SUD level of zero unexpectedly early during the processing of severe trauma. While it is possible for some clients to completely resolve a long-standing trauma very quickly, others may be engaging in numbing. A quick check of the validity of the negative and positive cognitions can settle the issue. If the client is numbing, the negative cognition will still seem to fit and the positive cognition will have a low validity rating. If this is the case, the therapist can have the client focus on the memory again and continue processing.

ABREACTION

The best way of handling abreaction is through adequate client preparation. Referring to the education provided during the preparation phase of the EMDR method and using the same terms and metaphors introduced then serves as a "here and now" anchor for the client. It also reminds the client of the explanations given earlier of the usefulness of continuing the processing.

The general guideline during abreaction is to keep the processing going to get the client through it as quickly as possible. To this end, therapists often end up doing longer sets of eye movements. If they find their arm getting tired, therapists can switch hands during a prolonged set by raising the free hand to overlap the first one, dropping the first hand while asking the client to "Just stay with my moving hand," and simultaneously changing positions to the other side of the client. The goal is to get the client past the most intense part of the emotion before pausing. It is usually fairly simple to identify a good time to pause by the expression on the client's face.

Since war survivors typically have multiple traumas and one may cascade into the next, the possibility exists the client may move from one abreaction to another. Certainly the client's right to stop processing should be respected. The handling of abreaction in multiple trauma cases is covered in greater detail in chapter 16.

BLOCKED PROCESSING

The techniques recommended by Shapiro for overcoming blocked processing are all generally effective for terrorism and war survivors. Nonetheless, several techniques are particularly useful and tend to be used more than others. It cannot be emphasized too strongly that therapists should use these techniques only when processing has stopped. Inappropriate use may result in a halting of processing. Even when processing continues, clients may lose their sense of empowerment because of the therapist's unnecessary intervention.

One of the fascinating aspects of EMDR is that it allows the therapist to observe clients' capacity for self-healing. Part of this is the emerging ability of clients to identify what keeps them from progressing. When encountering a blocked response, we first simply ask clients what is keeping things from moving. Though they may not have been consciously aware of such blocks at the start of treatment, typically they will be able to identify blocking belief systems after only a few sets of eye movements.

Blocking beliefs should be seen as part of the targeted trauma experience. Indeed, blocking beliefs may be the reason the individual has not been able to resolve the trauma reaction on his or her own. Where a blocking belief can be identified, it usually becomes the next focus of processing. Often little else needs to be done. Clinical skills may be needed to assist the client in identifying that belief, but most often it is readily accessible.

It is not uncommon to encounter multiple blocking beliefs. In most cases these beliefs originate in experiences subsequent to the trauma experience, while some, generally very few, may link to experiences prior to the trauma. In either case, the identification of one may lead to others. Once the client appears to have resolved that material, returning to the original target-experience often reveals a lower SUD rating. In a few cases, resolution of the blocking beliefs results in a complete resolution of the trauma experience itself.

Likewise, returning to the original experience and asking clients what they get now may show continued processing. A case example illustrates an encounter with blocking beliefs and a return to the original experience.

TH: So what is keeping things from moving?
CL: Well, the thing is, maybe I don't deserve to get better, maybe I . . . maybe it's like the thing that guy said at the VFW after I got back, maybe I'm a loser.
TH: I want you to just think about that statement, "I'm a loser," and follow my hand. Got it? *(Begins EMs)*

TH: What do you get now?

CL: I'm not a loser. I brought a lot of my guys back.

TH: Go with that. *(Begins EMs)*

CL: Oh, shit. I just realized. I didn't bring them *all* back.

TH: Stay with that. *(Begins EMs)*

CL: Nothing. It's stopped again.

TH: Same level of intensity?

CL: Yeah. *(Shakes head)*

TH: Let's try again. *(Begins EMs)*

CL: It's not going anywhere. Just like it was.

TH: What are you thinking?

CL: I know I should have done better. I was Regular Army, a "lifer." I knew what I was doing, I had the skills. I should have been able to get those guys through it. But I didn't.

TH: Just be aware of that thought, "I should have done better." Got it? Follow my hand. *(Begins EMs)*

CL: Well, you know, actually, I did get some of the guys through it.

TH: Go with that. *(Begins EMs)*

CL: I just thought about Franklin. He was a kid, didn't know squat, completely screwed up. I worked with him, tried to educate him, you know? Turned out to be a pretty good man. Got his act together. He was the one who got the ammo to us after we were dropped into that hot LZ I was telling you about the other day. Kept his cool. They gave him a Bronze Star for that. Guess I wasn't a complete failure.

TH: Go with that. *(Begins EMs)*

CL: Actually, I did a pretty good job. Some of my guys got hurt, but you know, realistically there wasn't much I could do about it that I didn't do.

TH: Go with that. *(Begins EMs)*

CL: Yeah *(nodding)*. I did a real good job. You can't control everything in a war, but what I could do, I did.

TH: Go with that. *(Begins EMs)*

CL: Yeah, I did what I could do.

TH: So let's go back to the original experience, back to when you guys hit the bunker complex. Just be aware of that and follow my hand. *(Begins EMs)*

TH: And what do you get now?

CL: Now? Well, it was a hell of a situation. I mean, you couldn't see the bunkers until you were standing on them. *(Pauses)* You know, I realized they were not only in front of us but on the right—that's what saved us, because I got everyone to keep from going any further into it. It was like being in a shoebox with no place to hide. I figured out what was happening, I was the first one. I began to pull everyone back. The captain was angry, he wanted us to press on, but I figured out it was a trap. *(Pauses)* He was really pissed. But he took my word for it. He trusted me. *(Pauses)* They all did. Because I had proven myself. You can't bullshit in combat. They respected my judgment because they knew I knew what I was doing, they had seen it. *(Pauses)* Seems stupid to think I was some kind of failure when I had all those guys respecting me when their lives were on the line. *(Smiles for the first time in treatment)*

TH: Go with that. *(Begins EMs)*

CL: *(Smiling)* I was a damned good soldier and I did some good work over there. Lot of guys are alive today who would not be if it wasn't for me. I was nobody's loser.

Continued eye movements showed the experience to be resolved.

As blocks are resolved, the client may continue processing between sets of eye movements and, to some extent, between treatment sessions. When either of these occurs, it is often useful to point it out to the client as a way of countering the sense of powerlessness that often pervades the lives of survivors of multiple traumas. The therapist can explain to clients that the eye movements serve to free up their abilities and assist in the progress they are making, and that it is their work, their brain, and their courage to continue that are resolving their experiences.

FEAR AS A BLOCK

Fear can serve as a powerful blocking force. In many cases a client's fears cannot be identified prior to beginning work. When they are, they may be targeted using EMDR. In all cases, adequate preparation requires teaching the client that the emergence of fears is a sign of processing. These fears generally fall into three broad categories relating to behavior, emotions, and meanings.

Fear of Losing Control

Many traumatized clients fear losing control of themselves during processing. They may be worried about being overwhelmed by feelings they have tried very hard to suppress. As one veteran put it, "If I ever start crying, the world will drown."

Clients' sense of their ability to withstand certain emotions may be accurate—their ego strength may be such that they cannot encounter powerful emotions such as shame or loneliness. In these exceptional cases the therapist needs to take the time to ensure that the client has developed the ability and resources needed for processing intense emotions. This is part of the history-gathering and client preparation work described earlier.

Clients' fear of their emotions—of rage or fear, for example—may lead them to underestimate their ability to process emotions. The therapist has several options at this point. Disputing clients' self-assessment should be avoided. Instead, the therapist might note that the clients have been through, and have lived with, the emotions associated with the experience for whatever time has elapsed since the experience. Clients may also fear a loss of behavioral control. They may be particularly concerned about becoming aggressive and hurting themselves or the therapist. These fears may be based on actual experience. The therapist can suggest continuing the eye movements while focusing specifically on the fear of acting out. Having encountered this fear regularly, we are able to reassure clients that we have yet to have anyone lose control during processing. If necessary, the therapist can make a "side trip" and process memories of previous incidents in which clients think they lost control. This is likely to lead back to the trauma eventually; when it does, the client will be able to proceed more comfortably.

Fear of Change

Survivors of major trauma often fear change. Essentially, they view the consequences of resolution as being negative in some way and so processing is blocked.

Clients may believe that by losing their trauma reaction they will also lose their ability to defend themselves and thus be vulnerable. They are aware, for example, that their hyperalertness enables them to respond to events in their environment that others may miss. They may also be aware that their PTSD keeps them in an aroused "fight or flight" state, a useful tool for someone who perceives the world as threatening.

Clients may also worry that resolving the memory is the same as forgetting it. Since they may see some value in aspects of the trauma, such as remembering the courage of another, they may approach desensitization with some resistance. Ideally, these concerns will have been identified and addressed during history-taking or preparation. Should they arise during processing, they can be targeted like any other blocking beliefs. It may be useful preliminarily to provide the client with information about therapy and what resolution actually means. Clients are often surprised to discover that resolution is not the same as forgetting, because the only way they have been able to conceive of not having the pain of remembrance is by not being able to remember.

Case history descriptions or publications can be powerful and effective ways of providing clients with alternative points of view that go beyond the statements of the therapist. Another way is through contact with other clients confronting similar issues. This "word of mouth" education often carries a level of legitimacy in the eyes of the client that may equal or surpass that of the therapist. In our inpatient PTSD program, much of this is accomplished informally among the patients and takes place well before any EMDR therapy actually begins. It can also be implemented formally by having the client talk to clients who have already been treated individually. We recommend using several sources to allow the client to discover the range of reactions and resolutions possible with EMDR.

Fear of Uncovering "Hidden" Material

A traumatic experience may have an array of potential meanings or interpretations for clients. They may not want to confront some of these, particularly self-judgments. Clients may be concerned that, if they try to resolve their experiences, these judgments will become validated and, in effect, made permanent. In a sense, clients believe they need to hide from an unpleasant "truth." "I am a monster," "I am worthless," and "I am unlovable" are examples of meanings clients may wish to avoid confronting. They may stop processing as they begin to sense the presence of these judgments. In effect, these are newly identified negative cognitions.

Directly targeting such beliefs is obviously desirable. However, this material may be primarily unconscious, with the client aware only of a desire to stop. At this point the therapist may be able to assist the client in identifying and verbalizing the negative meanings. If so, those beliefs can then be targeted with eye movements and resolved.

When the negative belief cannot be explicitly identified, the therapist might have the client "Think about the worst thing you could say or think about yourself. You don't have to tell me what it is. Got it? Now follow my hand." Given the context of the suggestion, it is highly likely that the negative meanings will be identified or linked to the client's starting point.

TOOLS FOR BLOCKS

Of the other tools commonly used for blocked processing, as noted earlier, all have shown themselves to be useful when working with war and terrorism survivors. These would include: identifying feeder memories, switching modalities, use of distancing techniques, and slowing the pace of processing.

Feeder Memories

Where the client history suggests it, the therapist might ask about other, usually earlier, experiences, or "feeder memories," that might have generated a similar emotion. It is important to do this in a way that does not imply that the client's inability to cope with the trauma was the result of preexisting pathology. It is simply a recognition of the mind's ability to link together a wide range of experiences.

Switching Modalities

It is a common practice among EMDR clinicians to respond to blocks, when other techniques have failed, by shifting the client's focus from one modality to another. For example, if processing has become blocked while the client has been focusing on cognitions, the therapist can ask her or him to focus on emotions. This movement from one information "flow" to another is minimally invasive and clearly leaves control with the client.

Michael Paterson (interviewed in chapter 4), drawing on his work with traumatized police officers in Northern Ireland, has reported an interesting variation on this shifting focus approach. When a client experiences a block while processing negative physical sensations, he makes use of the client's visual imagination while using bilateral aural tones. Alternating tones or alternating hand taps are alternatives to the eye movements we noted earlier. While alternating tones generally are used when clients cannot do eye movements or when the clinician wishes to slow processing, Michael combines them with a unique visualization procedure.

> I ask clients to notice the color of the area of discomfort, and then to identify an area of their body where they feel comfortable (even a small patch). I then ask them to identify the color of the comfortable area, then request they notice the two colors and be aware of what happens. Invariably the discomfort subsides, usually after three to four sets of tones, with the comfortable color having overcome the uncomfortable one. At this point I take the client back to target to open the next channel for reprocessing.

Distancing Techniques

In instances where the experience is so overwhelming that the client is not able to approach it, distancing techniques similar to those used with systematic desensitization are useful. One such technique is to have clients use a VCR metaphor to either "freeze frame" the experience or "fast forward" it to a place where they feel comfortable. The therapist should engage the client verbally and explain that the work will continue when the client is ready. Most clients, after a short break, resume where they left off. While such techniques emphasize a series of gradual steps, beginning from a point of no anxiety and then pausing to process any anxiety as it occurs, multiple trauma survivors often make a "leap" at some point and suddenly cover a great deal of distance in a short time. Whatever the distancing technique used—viewing the experience on the horizon, through bulletproof glass, or on a client controlled VCR—it is important to remember to remove the distancing device and have the client access the experience without it.

Slowing the Pace

Sometimes the clinician may wish to slow the pace of out of concern for the client's ego strength or physical health. This can be done by using shorter sets or slowing the speed of eye movements, or by using alternating hand taps or sounds. While this is ordinarily avoided, it may be necessary to enable the clients to discover that they can cope with the surfacing material. Typically, as they discover they can work through the emotions associated with the experience, they become increasingly willing to return to processing at their normal rate. We recommend allowing for this possibility by introducing the idea of moving slower with the statement that the therapist will check in periodically with the client, and anytime the client feels it is a good idea to pick up the pace, then the therapist will do so.

In recent years the number of older veterans coming forward requesting treatment for their reactions from World War II experiences has steadily increased. Some of these veterans' physical conditions are such that their tolerance for physical stress is limited. Monitoring breathing rates is a relatively simple way to judge the physical stress a client is going through. As intense material is approached, breathing may slow down and some clients tend to hold their breath. Doing this tends to increase carbon dioxide in the lungs, creating an unpleasant sensation often associated with being anxious. This sensation may have the effect of compounding whatever emotions are being processed. Reminding clients to continue breathing has the effect of alleviating this sensation while at the same time emphasizing their control and helping to orient them to the here and now. Briefing all clients during client preparation about the tendency to breathe slowly when processing intense material is a good idea; it is particularly important with individuals who the therapist suspects may have physical problems with intensive processing.

When working with clients for whom a technique for slowing processing might be utilized, it should be described during client preparation and phrased as "a way of taking a break if we need it." Care should be exercised that clients do not see its use as an indication that they have in some way failed.

Of course, clients may choose to stop processing at any point by using the stop signal discussed during the preparation phase. If properly presented, this is not likely to be interpreted as an indication that they have in some way failed. Indeed, it may reassure clients that the therapist is looking out for them.

CHECKING THE PROCESSING

War and terrorism experiences are often complex, multifaceted events that the client may perceive as a string of slightly or greatly different events. The request during assessment to bring up the picture of the "worst part" of the event may be insufficient for complete processing, since other parts of the experience may be compartmentalized. This may happen because of the nature of the meaning of those parts is separate from the identified "worst" part.

Gene Schwartz, a clinical social worker, suggests that, after targeting the worst part of the experience during desensitization, the therapist have the client run through the entire experience, start to finish, and stop when encountering any "twinge," a word he uses to indicate a disturbance. The client focuses on that disturbance and eye movements are done until it is gone. Then the client continues to run through the experience, looking for other disturbances. When all the "twinges" have gone, then the client runs through the entire event. Now the flow is expanded to include physical sensations—smells, sounds, and so forth. When the patient can get all the way through the entire event without stopping, he is done with desensitization and can move on to installation.

A case example illustrates this approach. A combat medic had his medical bag blown away by an exploding shell that killed several people. He pulled himself together, retrieved his bag, and began treating the wounded. When he was in therapy many years later, Gene worked with him using EMDR. They processed the event and, to check the work, the veteran was asked to run through the whole event. The veteran reported a level of anxiety when he recalled a "crack like the end of a whip." Gene asked him to focus on the sound and eye movements were resumed. The anxiety was eventually brought down to zero.

The veteran reported that for years he had been bothered by the screen door to his house. When it would bang, he would feel horrible anxiety, but he never understood why. With the resolution of his combat experience, he stated that he thought it was because the door's banging was a trigger to the crack of the explosion. In a subsequent visit he reported that the banging of the screen door no longer bothered him.

Checking the Body

Shapiro has increasingly emphasized the usefulness of checking the client's physical sensations as a way of getting around cognitive defenses and responding to blocks. The client history may have revealed indicators that the client tends to overintellectualize and otherwise distance himself from emotions. During desensitization, checking in with associated physical sensations ("And where do you feel that in your body?") may bypass that intellectualization before it becomes fully engaged. Likewise, when processing has stopped and the client appears to have emphasized intellectual distancing, a quick response that gets him focused on physical sensations may overcome the blocking and enable continued processing.

Most of the more powerfully traumatized individuals we have worked with, those with severe and frequently multiple traumas with reactions of a chronic nature, are unable to engage in intellectualization. They appear to lack the ability to remain focused long enough to use that defense. Moreover, it is important to differentiate intellectualization from cognitive (e.g., belief) blocks. Cognitive blocks, such as judgment statements like, "I am a failure," often respond best to cognitive interweaves rather than a refocusing on some other information flow like physical sensations. Of course, initially targeting the blocking belief is a good way to begin, as it may reveal a structure of blocking beliefs.

Checking for physical sensations is not just a way of heading off blocks and responding to defenses. Where the client becomes apprehensive about the amount of material needing processing, picking up on physical sensations is a quick way of responding requiring little additional preparation. For example, while this chapter was being written, I (SMS) was working with a multiply traumatized war veteran. In a pattern often typical of such veterans, as the targeted experience began to respond to desensitization with SUDs dropping from an initial ten to the range of "five or six," the veteran's rate of change began noticeably to slow. Fewer insights were reported, and changes in the picture and in emotions became less pronounced. The veteran spontaneously added to his report after a set of eye movements that he was aware he had "a lot of other things to work on" as well. I asked where he felt that in his body and he indicated his upper chest and shoulder. Focusing on those sensations resulted in a resumption of processing changes at his previous rate.

Similarly, returning to the body can refocus processing to an information "flow," which permits a speeding up of the work in time-limited situations, such as responding to mass casualty situations. In some cultures, reporting in terms of physical sensations may be more acceptable than describing emotions or thoughts.

COGNITIVE INTERWEAVE

The cognitive interweave (CI) is a brief statement or question introduced by the therapist during processing. Its purpose is to clear or identify blocks, to assist in the promotion of generalization of treatment effects, or to speed up processing. It is used for blocked processing only after the therapist has tried other less directive modifications. Because of the complexity of their trauma, war survivors may require CI more often than single trauma clients.

The CI should be a short, succinct statement or question that serves to shift the client's perspective and spark further processing. It is not an opportunity to enter into a dialogue with the client and should not be viewed as a back door to conventional talk therapy. The therapist offers the CI, notes the client's reaction, and returns to eye movements. The client's reaction may be positive or negative. A positive response may indicate that the therapist has succeeded in providing the client with new information that expands his or her understanding or shifts his or her perspective on the problem. A negative response may indicate that the client has a clearer focus on the blocking idea. Either one can be a useful prompt for further processing. The client is under no pressure to accept the therapist's suggestion, nor is the therapist attempting to solve the problem for the client with this intervention.

During processing the client will sometimes appear to be experiencing greater levels of distress. This can be an indication that the CI was inappropriate, and so the therapist should discuss with the client what is occurring. While the CI may have been inappropriate, the client may now be able to more clearly identify blocking beliefs or other issues that had originally stymied progress. These can then be directly targeted. On the other hand, the information the client is able to provide may be used to develop a new, more effective CI. Keeping the number of repetitions in a set of eye movements low will enable the therapist to make a faster response to an inappropriate CI. The following case illustrates the use of the CI.

The client was a Bosnian woman who was a witness to an atrocity. She was spared because the perpetrators needed her medical skills. The therapist was a Croatian psychiatrist learning EMDR. The Bosnian knew no English while the Croat was reasonably fluent. I (SMS) worked through a translator and supervised the session. The details of the experience have been deliberately obscured.

As the client began to abreact, one tear rolled down her cheek, the total extent of her emotional display. The therapist continued the eye movements and began to increase her verbal comments, encouraging the client to continue. This went on for several minutes until the client, still following the moving hand with her eyes, frowned, shook her head, and said something in her native language.

CL: *(Through translator)* It's not changing.
TH: *(Through translator)* Just keep going. *(In English to SMS)* What should I do?
SMS: Let's pause and ask her what is keeping things from moving.
TH: *(Through translator)* Please stop. Take a breath. What is keeping this from moving?
CL: *(Through translator)* I was helpless. I could not help them. All I could do was watch. *(Wipes eye, though no tears are visible)*
SMS: *(To TH)* Do you think she is stopped because she thinks she is helpless today, now? So she can't do therapy?
TH: *(To SMS):* Yes. The experience makes her think that. *(To CL through translator)* Are you saying you are helpless?
CL: *(Nods)*
SMS: *(To TH)* Try this. Ask her if her patients today think she is helpless. And do eye movements on whatever she says.
TH: *(To SMS)* I understand. *(To CL through translator)* Do your patients think you are helpless now?
CL: *(Through translator)* I don't know, I don't think they do.
TH: *(Through translator)* Think of that, please. Follow my hand. *(Begins EMs)*
TH: *(Through translator)* Please stop. Take a breath. What do you observe now?

CL: *(Through translator)* I had not thought of what my patients think of me.

TH: *(Through translator)* Think of that, please. Follow my hand. *(Begins EMs)*

TH: *(Through translator)* Please stop. Take a breath. What do you observe now?

CL: *(Slightly smiling; through translator)* This is very strange. I just realized that I am a very good doctor.

TH: *(Through translator)* Think of that, please. Follow my hand. *(Begins EMs)*

TH *(Through translator)* Please stop. Take a breath. What do you observe now?

CL: *(Through translator)* This is very strange. I am a good doctor, yes. I am not helpless. I did not hurt those people but I could do nothing for them. But that does not make me a bad person. The bad people were the men with the guns. I am a good doctor.

TH: *(Through translator)* Think of that, please. Follow my hand. *(Begins EMs)*

TH: *(Through translator)* Please stop. Take a breath. What do you observe now?

CL: *(Through translator)* I just realized that I have been a very good doctor because of what I saw. It is like I could not do anything then, but I can do something good now.

Processing continued normally. The client reported no further blocks and went on to attain a full resolution of the targeted experience. It should be noted that the use of the CI does not prevent abreaction. It may accelerate the already rapid processing of EMDR so that a client may get through abreaction faster, thus experiencing less overall distress.

"New" Information

In some instances, the CI may be based on providing new (or forgotten) information. A veteran became stuck while processing. His unit was badly hit and he found himself trying to get assistance over the radio, but he was unfamiliar with the proper procedures to call for help. He responded well to the CI: "Since they [the higher command] were monitoring your frequency, they knew who was calling even though your captain wasn't speaking and that you needed help even before you finished speaking. Think about that . . . " Of course, the veteran knew that information but had been unable to make use of it. Introducing it at this point took advantage of the information he had already processed during desensitization and he was finally able to link to it. Had he been unable to make use of this information the reason for its rejection would have been immediately targeted.

Unfair Self-blaming

If the therapist finds the client is engaging in a disproportionate amount of self-blame, it is possible to address this with a CI. A reference to someone they know is highly useful. "You mean if your buddy Bob had this kind of thing happen to him, you'd say he was to blame, too? Just think of that . . . "

Metaphors and Analogies

Some therapists are particularly adept at developing metaphors or analogies that have the purpose of introducing a new perspective to the client. These metaphors need not be long and complex; in fact, they are best when not. A client was stuck on grieving for a deceased friend. The therapist, suspecting that part of the issue was a fear of somehow betraying the friend by ceasing to grieve, said, "You're like a man who is trying to protect a candle flame by grasping it in his hand—all he does is burn himself and keep the flame from being seen by anyone else, including himself. Think about that . . . " This got the response, after a set of eye movements, of "He was too good a man to be wasted like that." More sets of eye movements, now that he was no longer blocked, resulted in a tearful abreaction, recall of several positive memories involving the other man, and the eventual resolution of, "I guess as long as I'm around, so is part of him."

Pretending

This approach is useful when encountering blocks around perpetrator issues, as it may open processing up in the direction of learning from the experience and making something useful out of the lessons learned.

Typically, it is posed as a simple question: "If you could do it differently now, what would you do?" The therapist does not have to wait for an answer—the eye movements can begin as the client considers the question. An alternative question, "What would you need to have done it differently?" leads clients to considered the limited perspective they may have had at the time and tends to correct the hindsight bias they may have developed since the event.

Appropriate Responsibility

It is not uncommon for trauma survivors to ascribe to themselves total responsibility for what took place. For war survivors whose actions may have resulted in the deaths or injuries of others, this problem can be even more severe. CIs in these situations often serve to reacquaint individuals with parts of the event they are not actively considering, such as, "I could not control the enemy." Likewise, clients might respond to a CI that emphasizes responsibility while at the same time providing a future orientation or plan of action: "I know more now than I did then and I learned something about myself."

"Weaving In" Information

Based on the client's history and self-report, it may be clear to the therapist that a particular cognitive interweave would be useful but is too great a leap for the client at this moment. Instead, the therapist gives the client an idea intermediate to the desired cognitive interweave. Then, during the eye movements, the therapist can introduce the CI when the client's verbal or nonverbal communication suggests that it might be possible for it to be considered. In effect, the CI is being woven into the processing of the intermediate cognitive interweave.

A client struggling with self-blame encountered a blocking belief that he did not deserve to get better because of his failure. Given the nature of the experience, I (SMS) understood that it was an impossible situation in which no one could have succeeded in producing better results. However, the nature of the blocking belief—"I'm getting what I deserve"—was such that any idea that would dispute it, however it was presented, would be unacceptable to the client. The initial statement of, "It sounds like it was a totally overwhelming situation" was offered and eye movements begun. While that statement was being processed, there was a change in the client's breathing. I asked, "Was anyone able to magically change what was going on? Just think on that."

The initial statement reflected the client's own evaluation of himself; the second was designed to expand the perspective of the client by pointing toward the behavior of others. In effect, his inability to change the situation was not a negative on his part, but normal and human.

Safety

It may be difficult for war survivors to develop a sense of safety. From their perspective, there may be no such thing. Bad things can happen to anyone, anytime. Therapists attempting to approach this issue with a CI should couch it in terms emphasizing relative safety and probable safety. Of course, survivors are correct—there is no absolute safety. So a CI posed as a question might be useful: "How likely is it that this office will be hit by gunfire?" The use of a question keeps the therapist out of the role of disputing various levels of probability with the client.

The key is the emphasis on the role of learning, not the idea that the circumstances might not ever come up again. A question for a client who is stuck might be, "What did you learn about yourself? Think about that." The client is likely to respond, "I'm no good" or "I'm a failure." As in the example above, this is an opportunity to use several linked statements. The therapist may offer, "How can you use what you learned to do better in the future? Just think of that." It is possible, of course, that the first question may be sufficient to link the client to the idea that we learn from our experiences and can become better people, a concept he already undoubtedly knows but is not accessing. If the first question does not complete the link, it clarifies the negative material. The second uses the response as a springboard to broaden the client's perspective. It does not dispute the judgment, even though the therapist may believe it to be incorrect. That decision is ultimately the client's.

Linking Perspectives

This CI attempts to deliberately link old and new perspectives. It can be quite useful in the area of self-blame, especially with perpetrator issues. A good indicator for this kind of CI is clients' comments about how they viewed themselves or what their expectations were of themselves prior to the experience. Unrealistic or naive expectations can lead to a sense of guilt, failure, and inadequacy. Using a more reality-based understanding of the situation and themselves, clients can be asked, when blocking on their failure, to focus on the knowledge they have now. The following illustrates this approach with a client whose progress has stopped. The therapist is asking the client to talk about what is keeping processing from occurring.

CL: I really wanted to do well, you know? I kind of wanted to be someone everyone would be proud of.

TH: So what happened?

CL: I screwed up. I was no John Wayne, man. When they sprung the ambush I froze. I couldn't even think to fall down. Someone had to drag me down. I lay there totally confused. The noise, the yelling, I had no idea what I was supposed to do. I almost peed myself I was so scared. I had no idea it was going to be like that.

TH: Which says what about you?

CL: I can't get it done, I'm a failure.

TH: How about later in your tour?

CL: *(Dismissive)* Oh, I did my job. *(The veteran went on to win several medals for valor under fire and was made a squad leader.)* But I never forgot how I fell apart in that ambush.

TH: Can you prepare someone for something like that? What does it take to be able to handle combat?

CL: *(Shakes his head negatively)* There is no way you can really be prepared for war. You got to be in it to know what it's like.

TH: So it takes some experience.

CL: Absolutely.

TH: Okay, I want you to hold those ideas together. The first one, "I'm a failure," and the other one, "It takes some experience." Got them? Follow my hand . . .

After the first set of eye movements the client paused for a moment and then began to describe how he had tried to slowly ease new men in his squad into combat by giving them different, low intensity tasks, such as perimeter guard, along with more experienced soldiers so as to lessen the shock of combat. "I didn't get that chance," he said, "my luck was bad, but I guess I learned from it, because I tried to make it better for my guys." The therapist simply responded with, "Go with that," and processing resumed. The point that he was not, in fact, a failure, did not have to be stated by the therapist.

Using the Positive Cognition

A useful intervention when the client encounters a block for which he is unable to identify a source and when the level of disturbance has largely been reduced to the equivalent of a SUD of two or less, is to introduce the positive cognition prematurely. Because of the lack of resolution the positive cognition will not be assimilated. However, in rejecting it the client may be able to clarify the blocking belief. The therapist has to use good clinical judgment about this particular CI, since it is designed to promote revelation by failure—the client may be at a point where one more perceived failure is difficult to bear and so a different approach would be better.

The procedure is to have the client focus on the positive cognition and the targeted experience together during a short set of eye movements. Then the clinician inquires as to what the client is aware of now. At this point the client may be able to identify a blocking belief or another experience, feeling, or sensation. Focus is then directed to this new material and processing continues.

Putting It in the Past

There is one CI that should be used infrequently with multiply traumatized war survivors. This is the idea that the experience is in the past, and they are therefore safe now. This CI is often useful with people dealing with a single traumatic event and/or overcoming blocks generated by anxiety and the need for safety. With war survivors, however, the greatest blocks to progress are reactions based not on fear but on self-judgments.

Gene Schwartz makes use of the conceptual framework of the "put it in the past" CI in his commentary while the client is processing. During processing he actively uses references to the here and now: "You are in my office. This is all old stuff. It is 2001." This both grounds the client in the present and helps the client to place the event in the past. Whether or not it aids in such chronological placement, it certainly is useful to remind clients working through particularly intense material that they are not actually reliving the event, no matter how powerful the current experience of remembering it.

In summary, the CI should be relatively short and succinct. Whatever it results in, such as emotions, cognitions, sensations, perceptual changes of the experience, or the emergence of new experiences, generally then becomes the target of continued processing. Elaborate discussion is usually unnecessary and may slow the client's progress. The CI may be used for blocked processing or, when circumstances require, to speed processing along. However, because it is an intervention, it is preferable to allow the client to process and progress at his or her own rate.

Desensitization proceeds with the therapist following the client's lead. The goal is to remain out of the client's way. The minimalist interventions used by the therapist increase the usefulness of EMDR by empowering the client, and usually at no time is this more dramatically accomplished than during desensitization. In many cases, these interventions are a matter of the therapist finding another way to access the client's existing resources.

Making use of client resources underlines the necessity of knowing your client. It is possible to form hypotheses about a client's orientation and belief system based on things like occupation. For example, emergency service workers tend to be, in the phrase of Roger Solomon, an EMDR clinician specializing in Critical Incident Stress work, "responsibility absorbers." Their calling virtually demands a powerful sense of responsibility and control. This may lead to an unrealistic expectation of what they could have done to control a situation, such as the aftermath of the terrorist bombing in Oklahoma City. During the rescue operations it was thought a second bomb was present, which necessitated the removal of the rescue teams. Leaving victims behind generated significant levels of guilt for these personnel. During processing with EMDR, clinicians found that resolution of this experience typically included the recognition both that these logical orders were necessary and had to be followed and that the teams did return to the victims.

Cognitive interweaves posed as questions are often highly useful at overcoming blocks because they take into account clients' need for control and require them to assess the situation: "What was under your control and what was beyond your control?" Where a mistake was made, seeing this as part of a process of learning to make better decisions in the future may provide resolutions responsive to the client's need for control.

Even if blocks to processing are encountered, it is important to always understand that EMDR is a very client-centered therapy. Where blocks are encountered, the therapist and client partnership is utilized to identify them and determine a course of action. This process is greatly aided by taking the time during the client preparation phase to address the possibility of blocks of various kinds, what their emergence might signify, and what can be done about them. Once the block is dealt with, the client should be guided back to the original targeted experience so that processing can resume.

Chapter 11

INSTALLATION

"All I can think of is, I did the best I could. And you know what? I really did. Why didn't I think of that before?"

Many clinicians, particularly those familiar with exposure therapy, see the desensitization phase as where the action of EMDR is, with installation as a brief cognitive "add-on." Though the installation phase was originally described by Shapiro as an opportunity to maximize the validity of a specific positive cognition (as shown by a VOC rating of seven), clinicians who rush this phase run the risk of truncating an important part of information-processing.

The experiences of war and terrorism often impact on multiple systems of belief. This has the effect of blocking clients' access to a large number of positive ideas needed to function normally. For these clients, installation can trigger a great unfolding of useful images and ideas.

The standard installation phase begins with the therapist asking if the original positive cognition is still the best one or if a better one has arisen. The chosen cognition is paired with the target event and eye movements are done until the strength of the positive cognition is maximized. As Shapiro (1995) notes, "The increase in validity may continue well past the arbitrary level of seven on the VOC Scale. . . . the guideline for the installation phase is that if the information continues to move further along the information-processing track, the sets should be repeated" (p. 138). Sometimes additional positive cognitions emerge rapidly. As they do, the therapist follows the client's lead with eye movements, as in the following case.

The client was a Vietnam War veteran whose PTSD was marked by intense feelings of guilt for failing to have done more when his unit was attacked. The primary reexperiencing symptoms were in the form of chronic nightmares of the incident. During the assessment phase he had identified, "I'm a complete screw-up" as the negative cognition; the positive cognition was "I did the best I could."

TH: So are the words, "I did the best I could," still the way you'd like to think about that experience, or is there a better idea?

CL: Well, I did do the best I could, but what I find myself thinking now is, "I was pretty good at my job." I don't know if that's the same thing or not.

TH: Neither do I. When you hold those words together with that experience of the battle, using our scale of one to seven, where one feels completely false and seven feels completely true, how true do they feel to you now?

CL: Five. An easy five. Maybe a six.

TH: Think about the original experience and those words, "I was pretty good at my job," and follow my hand. (Begins EMs)

TH: OK, let's pause, take a breath, and how do those words feel to you now using our scale?

CL: You know what? I just started thinking, "I was a good man."

TH: Go with that. (Begins EMs) How does that phrase feel?

CL: And you know, I *am* a good man.

TH: Go with that. (Begins EMs) What do you get now?

CL: Feels pretty good.

TH: When you think of that phrase, "I am a good man" and that battle, how true does it feel to you now using our one to seven scale?

CL: Hell, it's a seven, doc.

TH: Stay with it. (Begins EMs) How does it feel now?

CL: I just realized something.

TH: What's that?

CL: I've *always* been a good man. The only reason I haven't acted like one is because I wouldn't let me. And I don't have to do that anymore. (Pauses)

TH: So the . . .

CL: I don't have to do that anymore. I can just let myself be me.

TH: Go with that. Follow my hand. *(Begins EMs)* What do you get now?

CL: It wasn't anyone else, it was me. It's all right now. It's . . . I'm ready to come home, now. I'm ready to let myself come home.

TH: Go with that. *(Begins EMs)* How do those words feel to you now?

CL: It's kind of a surprise, you know? I mean, it's a surprise. Like I can, now I can let me be, and it's all right. Man . . . *(pauses)* it's always been about what I think of me and I just figured out that I can respect me.

TH: Is it, "I can respect myself"?

CL: Yes.

TH: Go with that. *(Begins EMs)* And what do you get now, how does it feel?

CL: You know, this is weird shit, you know? Damn. *(Pauses)* The thing is, there is a lot about me that should be respected, and it's like I'm seeing that. Why didn't I see it before? You know, this is like making a bunch of things OK, OK for me to do.

TH: Ah . . .

CL: Like, what I mean is, it's OK for me to care about someone. It's OK for me to love someone, like my family. It's right, because I am worthy of their respect, my respect, that makes it OK, you know?

TH: OK. Go with that. *(Begins EMs)* And what do you get now?

CL: *(Pauses)* I didn't let myself love anyone because I didn't believe I deserved it. But I did love people, I just wouldn't admit it to myself. Is that fucked up or what?

TH: And now?

CL: Now it's OK to admit it. I deserve it and they're not going to go away just because I love them. And I can give them something, like, something I couldn't before.

TH: What is that?

CL: A good man.

TH: Go with that.

In this example we see a client developing several empowering ideas corresponding to changes in his perspective of the relationship between himself and the world around him. He starts with a simple acknowledgment of his efforts, "I did the best I could," and can already see another positive cognition: "I was pretty good at my job." Note that the therapist did not try to rephrase this statement into the present tense. Given that his current negative cognition and its limiting effects were built on his perceived failure during the attack, the change in his judgment of his performance at that time affects his view of himself in the present. In effect, he is saying, *"My judgment today is,* I was pretty good at my job." This conceptualization is corroborated by his next sequence of positive self-appraisals, from "I was a good man" to "I *am* a good man." Clearly, processing is taking place in between sets of eye movements. His own information-processing system has been freed up and he is beginning consciously to identify links to the information he needs for full resolution.

He then moves on to identify his own role in holding himself back. His life since the war had been marked by a pattern of self-punishment and deprivation. It is not unusual for clients to report insights into their post-trauma behavior during this phase of treatment. This client is able to see that it is OK for him to love and be loved. Completing the circle, he notes that what he has to give is himself and that he—a good man—is a worthy gift.

Earlier we noted that the positive cognition is not always the literal opposite of the negative cognition. Some EMDR clinicians suggest that the positive cognition should specifically address the schema of the negative cognition: we have found that it invariably does, though not necessarily in ways immediately obvious to the clinician. After all, much of the meaning of any experience may exist in an unconscious form.

Clients may also produce strings of positive images, feelings, or sensations during installation. As with cognitions, the therapist should allow for the development of these themes even if the client has reached a seven on the VOC scale.

BLOCKS TO INSTALLATION

Blocking during installation is a halting of increased believability of the positive cognition prior to attaining seven VOC. Blocks will generally be manifested first as the emergence of a sensation, feeling, or thought experiences, if not encountered in their entirety.

Sometimes installation blocks are caused by the emergence of an experience, one discounted as less important or not previously identified. When a new experience is identified as the block, the therapist has the option of conducting a new assessment. We discuss this in the next chapter since this kind of block is more often encountered when conducting a body scan.

Most often a stalled installation is an indicator of a particular blocking belief that requires processing. It is not necessary to do a new assessment for a blocking belief. The therapist can simply continue in exactly the same manner as one would if a blocking belief came up during desensitization—have the client focus on the belief and begin processing.

Occasionally the installation process may stall at a point apparently near completion. Discussion with the client may reveal that the block has occurred because the client has begun to understand the implications of completing resolution, such as potentially changing his role in his social system. These changes may provoke blocking anxiety.

Blockage may also happen when acceptance of the positive cognition is dependent upon skills that the client does not have or when it requires testing to be fully validated. If this is the case, a more realistic positive cognition can be installed. It is perfectly acceptable for the client to "road test" a positive cognition. It is helpful to ask if the client has the resources and opportunity to test the cognition between sessions.

If the client reports anxiety or hesitation about trying the positive cognition, the therapist can attempt to process the "resistance" with further eye movements. While hesitation may be appropriate in particular circumstances, it may also be that the intensity of the response can be reduced. Also, additional eye movements may identify other issues needing attention.

As a practical issue when encountering a block during installation, the therapist may need to judge if time or other constraints permit continued processing or if the session has to be shut down. If shutting down, emphasis should be placed on a good briefing, during which the possibility of continued processing between sessions is carefully explained. If deciding to continue, after reaching resolution of the block, return to installation. The client may remain with the partially installed positive cognition or may now identify a better one. If a better one is identified, it should be installed.

Chapter 12

BODY SCAN AND CLOSURE

"It feels like a big rock on my chest has fallen off. Very odd feeling, because I don't think I realized before it was there."

In the standard EMDR trauma protocol, the success of processing is evaluated by having clients scan the body for any sensations while they pair the just-installed positive cognition with the target memory. Any reported sensations are focused on during eye movements, with the goal of dissipating negative sensations and reinforcing positive ones. The eye movements are continued until no further gains are made. Though the standard instructions for this phase require clients to close their eyes as they scan their bodies, many hypervigilant clients find that they are uncomfortable closing their eyes when someone else is in the room. Giving clients the choice to do the scan with their eyes open or closed eliminates the problem.

Therapists may want to inquire specifically about headaches during the body scan. Headaches come up surprisingly often in this population. Sometimes these are directly related to the material being processed: sometimes they are simply a manifestation of excess tension that can be triggered during processing. Headaches are fairly obvious when they come up during desensitization, but clients sometimes neglect to mention them if they come up later. These are usually resolved with a few more sets of eye movements focused on the point where the pain is most intense without connecting it to the trauma memory.

With multiply traumatized clients it is not uncommon to find that, with the resolution of the first experience, other experiences that had not previously been identified make themselves known during the body scan phase. This is not an indication that the previous work was incomplete; rather, it is a clear signal from the client's own mind that it is now prepared to deal with other experiences and issues. It is important that the client be educated about this phenomenon. After all, "uncovering," where other issues emerge as the presenting problems are dealt with, is fairly common in psychotherapy generally.

Time constraints often dictate whether the emerging experience will be immediately targeted or worked on in a subsequent session. Where time permits, it is preferable to focus on the new material immediately. This raises the question of whether or not a new assessment needs to be done. There are several advantages in doing a new assessment:

1. The assessment process helps to elicit the maximum content of the entire structure of the experience. Walking through the steps in an assessment brings up additional cognitive, emotional, and sensory details in a manner that often makes processing more efficient.

2. A new assessment clarifies negative as well as positive cognitions. These may be different from those associated with the previous experience. This kind of information has obvious relevance when considering cognitive interweaves or the selection of procedures to use if the client becomes blocked during processing.

3. The development of a new assessment is a good way to draw clients' attention to the progress they have made.

This assessment may be easier than the first one because clients are familiar with the procedure. The therapeutic relationship is likely to be stronger, and clients' confidence may make them more open in describing their thoughts and feelings.

It is important when discussing new material to be careful about the use of such terms "uncovering." This word is typically taken as indicating that what is being uncovered is deeper in the psyche and therefore more significant clinically than the first experience. This may or may not be the case. Sometimes the most significant event has already been processed. With that out of the way, other experiences and their issues are available for processing. Commonly, events identified during the body scan resolve much faster than the original experience. We think of life experiences as mutually interactive, as part of a structure, rather than one as key and the "real source of the problem." For clients who have been through a lot of therapy, especially with therapists who believe there is always a "core experience," this conceptualization may be new and difficult to accept.

CLOSURE

While it is certainly best to complete the processing of a memory before the session is ended, most therapists work under time constraints. This means having to keep an eye out for reasonable stopping places in processing. Sometimes it is possible to consult the client in making this decision.

With some clients we have developed an "interim positive cognition" by asking, "What's the most important thing you've learned about yourself from the work we've done today?" This gives them a sense of progress that makes residual distress that may come up between sessions more tolerable. The emotion reduction and management techniques originally taught during the preparation phase can also be used before the session is ended. We recommend using them even if clients are not experiencing residual negative emotion, since the supervised practice is useful for between sessions.

During the closure phase it is useful to repeat much of the information provided during preparation about continued processing between sessions and how this is an indication of the healing process. Clients should be encouraged to keep a log book or journal to ensure that any relevant clinical information is recorded, such as new memories, changes in old memories, identification of environmental triggers, sleep and dream patterns, and interactions with others, and to provide the client with a structure for dealing with any new experiences, cognitions, or feelings that might surface. Rather than simply having to endure any negative material, the client has a task to perform; this proactive position makes handling the material easier and increases the client's sense of empowerment.

The log book need not be elaborate. In fact, providing clients with a simplified form increases compliance. Table 12.1 shows a simple form that can be given to clients for this purpose. It serves as a reminder for entering information since it calls for daily entries. The log is reviewed by the therapist during following sessions. It is a good source of information on environmental triggers that the client had not previously reported. It can also give the first indication of changes in behavior resulting from resolution and any systemic responses to those changes.

Table 12.1
Weekly Log Book

Please record the following information day by day:

DAY & DATE	HRS. SLEEP	DREAMS
MON	_____	N Y (If Yes, summarize):
TUE	_____	N Y (If Yes, summarize):
WED	_____	N Y (If Yes, summarize):
THU	_____	N Y (If Yes, summarize):
FRI	_____	N Y (If Yes, summarize):
SAT	_____	N Y (If Yes, summarize):
SUN	_____	N Y (If Yes, summarize):

Did any changes in the target experience occur (pictures, feelings, etc.)?
Did any other experiences come into your memory?
Did you have any unusual interactions with anyone else?
Did you encounter anything that reminded you of your experiences?
Did you find yourself thinking differently about your experience?

We strongly recommend against using eye movements as a tension reduction method with this population, even for those clients who report that the movements themselves are relaxing. The reason for this is twofold. (1) Clients may tap into unresolved trauma material when the therapist is not available to help them and they may find it difficult to continue eye movements through an abreaction. (2) Unlike using the eye movements for safe place installation purposes during client preparation, clients may by this time have formed a link between the eye movements and trauma material. Trying to use eye movements for relaxation might quite readily remind the client of the trauma experiences previously worked on, thus defeating the purpose of their use for relaxation.

Closure should not be confused with termination of treatment, which will be discussed in the next chapter. Even very successful processing sessions require follow-up to determine whether any new issues have arisen and to evaluate the effects of the processing on the client's behavior outside the therapist's office.

Chapter 13

REEVALUATION AND

TERMINATION

"I don't think this finger waggling treatment is doing me much good, doc. By the way, it wasn't my fault those guys died."

The purpose of the reevaluation phase of the EMDR methodology is to check on the previous session's work. In its simplest form, reevaluation is done by asking the client to bring up the target scene and give a SUD rating. It is assumed that processing may have continued between sessions with continued resolution of old material or surfacing of new material.

Accessing the originally targeted material of the previous session will readily allow the therapist to identify any changes that have occurred since that session. Going back to the previous target is preferred over picking up at the point where processing ended, since it creates a greater probability of identifying related material now in awareness. It may also be difficult for clients to remember where they were at the end of the previous session, particularly if they had worked through intense material shortly before closure. Returning to the original target is a good way to draw clients' attention to the amount of progress they have made thus far, even if the experience has not yet been fully resolved.

If new material is identified, the therapist has to make a judgment call about whether to process the new material immediately or to do a new assessment. Since one of the purposes of the assessment phase is to activate as much of the trauma experience as possible, the question is not trivial. The key is whether the new experience is separate and distinct from the targeted one or related to it. We involve clients in answering this question, asking, "Does this experience seem like it is related to the one we already worked on?" If it is related (and in multiply traumatized war survivors it often is), then this material can be processed immediately, using the original target as the reference point. If the newly emerging experience is clearly distinct, then we do a full assessment to galvanize a maximum number of elements associated with the experience and identify current triggers and other features that will need to be treated before terminating treatment.

The client may or may not have mentioned the new experience during history-taking. We recommend discussing in the client preparation phase the possibility that previously forgotten material may arise during the course of treatment. When new memories surface, the therapist reviews how human memory works, so that the client understands that this is not a signal of decompensation. We also remind clients that this material may not be historically accurate.

The situation is somewhat more complicated when what emerges is not a clear experience but emotion, cognitions, imagery, or physical symptoms that the client is unable to attach to a specific experience. In this case, we recommend doing a complete assessment to bring forth additional information. The assessment questions may flesh out the experience so that processing will be more efficient. Taking a moment to explain this will help clients who are feeling somewhat frustrated by being unable to identify the source immediately. This explanation will also be useful with clients who are eager to process and concerned about any delay in getting to work.

Some clients report feeling reluctant to proceed with current material, perhaps because of the intensity of the previous processing. The therapist has to make a decision about the pacing of processing based on the client's fatigue and the amount of time available for treatment. Some clients respond well to several processing sessions in a row, followed by an opportunity to "come up for air" with a regular counseling session. If, on the other hand, the therapist senses some apprehension on the part of the client, this can be discussed and possibly used as another target for processing.

TERMINATION

Once all the identified traumas and associated material have been processed, it is time to start planning for termination. There are several issues to be considered before treatment can be considered complete, however. The resolution of trauma memories must be accompanied by evidence that the client has the skills and support to engage in new behaviors. The client history is crucial in checking on the work accomplished.

Target

As we have noted, war survivors and some terrorism survivors may undergo multiple traumatic events. Going back to the originally targeted experience is a useful way to review the work done. These "progressions" are discussed below, as is reviewing other members of the cluster of experiences that included the targeted experience. Returning to the original target, the client may identify additional experiences not reported during the development of the client history or encountered during processing. Clients should be reassured that their ability to be aware of these additional experiences is a very positive indicator of their progress—they have overcome their mind's previous repression of the experiences.

Triggers

The therapist will want to check on current and anticipated environmental triggers that have elicited the cognitions and emotions associated with the trauma experience. For example, if sirens have been identified as powerful triggers for emotions and thoughts relating to war experiences, we ask the client to mentally focus on them and report if any negative disturbance is still present. Such disturbances can generally be processed directly without an assessment. The previously installed positive cognition should be checked to ensure that it is still valid.

It is important to make a distinction between past reactions to triggers and *anticipated* reactions. This is the difference between the thoughts, "That reminds me of something bad that happened" and

"I am concerned with how I might react to that." Eye movements on triggers can be quite useful, but frequently clients will say they need to go and try it out before they feel that complete resolution has been achieved.

Clusters

It is likely that the therapist and client will have grouped or clustered several experiences of war or terrorism together. Though the client may have spontaneously linked to all of the related memories during processing, it is important to briefly focus on each memory making up the cluster while the client checks for any disturbance. If a member of a cluster has not resolved, it is probably because it contained some unique elements that have not, as yet, been addressed. The client will likely report that some portions of the experience have been resolved, as indicated by a lower initial SUD report. A common element of this sort is survivor guilt. This "thread," if encountered and pulled out of the targeted experience, will likely be removed from the weave of other experiences as well.

Progressions

War survivors often present a progressive journey of resolution, moving from experience to experience, including some that occurred before or after their combat exposure. It is important to review all of these experiences and ensure that they have been completely resolved. In all likelihood, all the experiences are resolved, but a particular experience may have included unique elements that need further processing.

One veteran began with an ambush his unit underwent, his first combat experience. After about ten minutes a second combat experience, that of an enemy ground attack, emerged and was followed. Two other combat-related experiences appeared in rapid succession and were followed, and then the ground attack memory returned. Shortly thereafter, apparently linked by the thought, "I didn't think we'd get out of it alive," a memory of his mother's reaction to his enlistment came into awareness. "She was really worried that I would get hurt," he noted. This was processed and thoughts reflecting resolution began to emerge: "I didn't get hurt," "I was OK," and "I am OK."

With the channel apparently resolved, the therapist directed the veteran back to the original memory, his first combat experience. He reported no disturbance. Installation of the positive cognition and a clear body scan followed.

In reviewing the memories the veteran had progressed through, he reported no disturbance associated with any of the combat experiences, including those that had only briefly been addressed. When going back to the memory of his mother's reaction to his enlistment, he reported some mild disturbance still present and was able to identify it as relating to his behavior since the war: "I haven't been much of a son to her." This cognition was targeted and was resolved in a subsequent session.

In-vivo Testing

It is important to give clients an opportunity to confirm progress outside of the therapy office. Clients often bring this up spontaneously, probably in response to the dramatic effects they often experience during EMDR. As in any form of therapy, this opportunity should be presented in a positive light; that is, the patient should be told that the next logical step is to try things out in the "real world" and that the focus is on identifying any disturbances still remaining. Bringing back a report of difficulties is helpful, since it gives the client and therapist an opportunity to clean out any remaining residual reactions.

The log book is ideal for identifying any remaining work. It provides a structured focus when disturbances are encountered and thereby places clients in a proactive position. They are not enduring the disturbance but implementing an already agreed upon plan. Indeed, this structure might also serve the therapeutic benefit of giving clients an opportunity to consider more fully what is taking place, rather than simply reacting and fleeing, and in so doing they may resolve the situation.

Typically, previously unidentified triggers, including those not encountered earlier due to the client's isolation and withdrawal, are noted at the end of treatment. Generally, simple triggers, such as sounds and smells, can be immediately targeted for processing with eye movements. More complex triggers that the clinician feels reflect unaddressed issues should be explored with the client; if needed, these can be fully worked up using the steps in the assessment phase.

Clients may also report that changes in memories of the targeted or related experiences continue to emerge over time. During client preparation and whenever the need arises, we educate clients on the nature of human memory, pointing out that memory is not "set in concrete," and that changes in perceptions of past experiences may reflect continued resolution, including the eventual linking of the target experience with other previously unreported memories. In effect, the client's mind is identifying what the client is now able to face.

In-vivo testing may also reveal the results of the client's new behaviors, as the system around a client reacts and resists change. The veteran, for example, who now is able to function appropriately as father and husband may find that other family members resist his attempt to appropriately assume his responsibilities and authority. A client may need coaching on how to deal with such situations, which may include EMDR processing for related anxieties and disappointments.

Significant Others

Relationships are often affected by the client's reactions to a traumatic event, even when the others in those relationships were not involved in the event itself. Numbing of responsiveness, withdrawal and isolation, increased irritability, and the other symptoms of PTSD have a generally negative impact on relationships; therefore, it is useful to have clients examine their current relationships before terminating treatment. Dealing with past damage that resulted from the hurt and confusion of traumatization can be facilitated by EMDR. Indeed, clients may discover insight into the reactions of others while using EMDR on relationships. This makes it easier to leave defenses to one side and tolerate the others' need to express their grievances.

It is often useful to have clients review their feelings toward others, specifically any negative feelings around the question, "Where were they when I needed them?" Disappointments should be addressed openly and clients educated that residual negative feelings can sometimes exist toward the people they care for, even love, and that these residual feelings are simply part of the reactive process. Rather than allowing negative feelings to continue to exist and hoping that time will take care of them or, worse, trying to ignore or bury them, it is more useful to resolve them quickly by using EMDR. This is particularly important when working with children. Their expectations of parents, siblings, and other meaningful people may be unrealistic but nonetheless result in conflicted feelings even after the trauma reaction itself is resolved.

Making EMDR available to significant others, those close to trauma survivors, serves the purpose of both resolving their wounds and, in many cases, gaining their support of the client's changes. It is a grim fact of war and terrorism that the ripples of trauma can be almost as powerful as the original trauma itself.

Reintegration

Survivors may have problems with integration into their families, culture, and society. Trauma from war and terrorism may have been a relatively unique experience, one not shared by their social system. It is common for such survivors to feel alone in their experiences, to be sure; even more profound may be an alteration in their belief and value systems resulting from the trauma experience. These alterations may make it difficult to fit in.

For example, a war veteran noted that getting back into the day-to-day routine that everyone else was in, even after the pathological symptoms of PTSD had been resolved, was extremely difficult. "I just don't seem to have the same priorities as everyone else anymore," she said. Trauma experiences, particularly those that are life-threatening, often result in a new appreciation for life and a discarding, to at least some extent, of the priorities of people who have not had to confront their own mortality. The perception of difference may, in fact, be an accurate observation—EMDR will not change that truth. However, where this perception has resulted in anxiety that the difference cannot be bridged, EMDR has application.

I (SMS) discovered this inadvertently while working with a war veteran early in my use of EMDR. The focus in the session was on a battlefield experience resulting in PTSD and, subsequently, isolation and withdrawal. The veteran had reported changes in his reaction to the experience suggesting desensitization was proceeding normally. After a set of eye movements, the veteran reported, "I just had a thought." During the next set the veteran suddenly smiled. The eye movements were continued for a brief period of time beyond that point and then I asked him what he was aware of.

"Well, before," he said, "when I said I had a thought, what had come into my mind was that there was no way anyone I knew could ever understand what I had been through. They had never had to deal with what I had to deal with, you know? Then we did the eyes some more and I suddenly realized that was OK. They didn't need to deal with it. No one should have to. But I had. And what I had dealt with didn't have to make me separate from them. What I've been through has made me better, maybe stronger, but whatever it was, that's what can make me valuable and they are going to pick up on that. It was funny—the thing I thought divided me from others is the very thing that other people are going to find draws them to me because it's given me stuff ordinary people don't have."

Resolutions like this go a long way toward answering the survivor's question, "How do I fit in now?" But sometimes this question is more practical and refers to the basic skills needed. After all, persons who have suffered from chronic PTSD may have been isolating themselves for years. With the trauma reaction resolved, going back into the mainstream of life may call for skills that have atrophied or never developed in the first place. While EMDR cannot provide clients with the information they do not have, it can be used on their anxiety about acquiring that information, enhancing their motivation to acquire social skills and move on with life.

Over and above anything else, the survivor has the gift of survival. That process teaches much and may impart wisdom, of which the survivor may not be consciously aware. Resolution assists reintegration, as the survivor puts aside negative self-judgments and comes to understand the truth behind a Winnebago elder's comment, "We honor our warriors because they are brave and because by seeing death on the battlefield they know the greatness of life."

Chapter 14

RECENT AND ONGOING EVENTS

"When we came by the second time, they were all dead. I felt bad that I had no reaction, but I have seen this before and will again. Death in Sarajevo is a part of life."

It was with mass civilian trauma that the need for an alteration in the basic EMDR protocol for trauma reactions was first identified. Following the 1989 San Francisco earthquake, EMDR clinicians volunteered their services to the survivors and relief workers. EMDR was seen as particularly relevant to the situation, since as its speed would permit therapists to work more effectively with a larger number of clients than conventional psychotherapies.

While performing the assessment phase of the methodology, clinicians immediately noticed that a large number of clients were responding differently than was typical for trauma survivors. In response to the request for an image representing the experience or the worst part of it, many of the California survivors reported there was not one picture that represented the experience but several. EMDR clinicians responded to the situation by developing variations of the EMDR procedure. Since then there have been numerous opportunities to try a number of variations, so that now the clinician responding to recent events can feel fairly confident that an appropriate resolution can be achieved in a brief period of time.

The EMDR clinicians in California were encountering individuals for whom the trauma experience had not yet consolidated. In effect, they were reporting a series of traumas. Clinical experience in other

147

situations suggests that this consolidation process is completed, on average, after ten weeks. However, there is a great deal of individual variation. Also, in some circumstances an "experience" may, in fact, be made up of a series of events extending even into the present and generating different issues and problems for the client.

IMMEDIATE REACTIONS

Therapists responding to recent events, whether terrorist bombings, school shootings, or ongoing war, need to deal with two possible immediate reactions before initiating a trauma treatment protocol. Numbing of responsiveness is a common immediate response to trauma. This reaction, because of its muting of overt display, tends to be overlooked by individuals doing psychological screenings within the first few hours and days following an incident. Those with more overt displays will get more attention. Those conducting screenings need to be educated on the nature of trauma reactions and the need to provide both immediate and follow-up education to survivors. In some situations—for example, in military units and relatively closed communities—it is possible for screenings to be conducted in an ongoing, repeated fashion so that emergent symptoms may be treated. Intervention with EMDR during the initial stage may accomplish little if the individual is emotionally numb. It may be better to wait a few days to see if the condition persists or if the individual complains of intrusive symptoms.

The opposite of numbing is, of course, is hysteria. Attempts at psychotherapy, including EMDR, may accomplish little when the person is out of control with grief, fear, and anxiety. What is needed is support and an opportunity for the individual to release the overwhelming tension and anxiety until he or she can focus sufficiently to benefit from treatment.

USING EMDR FOR
CRISIS INTERVENTION

A clinician responding to very recent or ongoing situations—crisis intervention—may find that making clinical judgments about the degree of numbing or hysteria and the appropriateness of the client for therapeutic intervention is difficult. The basic guideline for whether or not to use EMDR is rather simple: if the client can follow directions and communicate consent, try it. Under these circumstances we recommend simply having clients focus on their feelings and begin desensitization without an elaborate assessment. If clients are unable to focus because of their apparent state of shock or hysteria, discontinue the procedure and identify them for follow-up evaluation. In the meantime, provide supportive services, which can also provide the monitoring of the individual.

It is common to encounter clients, still in the initial shock of an experience, who do not have negative or positive cognitions to report or have great difficulty focusing on cognitions. In some cases the clinician may find that an initial processing of the numbing of responsiveness or intense emotion is highly effective. Under crisis intervention circumstances, processing tends to remain very specific without a great deal of linking to other experiences. Even though the procedure is begun without the identification of negative or positive cognitions, when desensitization progresses to resolution, the clinician should ask for a positive cognition to install. The simple question, "How would you like to think of yourself now when you think of what happened?" is usually enough to bring forth a positive cognition. Following installation a body scan should be conducted in the usual way.

RECENT EVENTS PROTOCOL

The recent events protocol is a relatively straightforward way of organizing the targeted experience and giving the clinician guideposts of what portion to work with and in what sequence.

The first step is to teach the safe place relaxation technique or another tension reduction technique appropriate for a particular client. Given that war and terrorism survivors often have difficulty identifying even imaginary safe places, the clinician should have other techniques available. If time permits, the client should be given the opportunity to become comfortable and familiar with whatever techniques are taught.

The next step is to develop a chronological narrative of the experience. The narrative should include everything the client remembers—the elicitation of thoughts, feelings, sights, sounds, smells, and so forth helps to catalyze the trauma material and bring more of it into conscious awareness, with the apparent effect of making processing more efficient. It is particularly important when dealing with war and terrorism survivors to extend the narrative beyond the immediately identified experience because of the possibility of additional contributory events occurring in the aftermath.

For example, we treated terrorism survivors whose experience essentially lasted all day and included the bombing, what they did and what they saw immediately following the explosion, and their evacuation to a hospital and the situation there. Extending the narrative to the following day uncovered the experience of leaving the hospital and encountering relatives of the more seriously injured survivors, as well as those arriving to identify the dead, and the resultant generation of survivor guilt.

The extension of the narrative beyond the immediate chronology of the experience can be accomplished simply by asking if anything happened after the event that in any way related to it. Keeping the question relatively open-ended increases the likelihood client input.

Fragments of the narrative become targets for processing. Each fragment should be subjected to its own assessment, including the identification of a picture, negative and positive cognitions, emotions, and the location of any physical sensations. VOC and SUD scale measurements or their appropriate equivalents are used. Each fragment is then processed with desensitization and the installation of its positive cognition. A body scan check is not utilized, since the entirety of the experience has not as yet been addressed and it is common to find that there is some residual physical disturbance that will not lift until all the fragments are treated as a whole.

After all fragments have been processed, clients mentally review the whole experience with their eyes closed. If any distress is encountered, they focus on that distress and eye movements are begun. There is no need to do a new assessment or a formal installation at this point—this chronological visualization aids the joining of the fragments into a coherent whole and identifies any resistance to that process. It also sets the stage for the installation of a positive cognition.

Next the client visualizes the entire experience while a positive cognition is installed. To do this requires, of course, that the eyes are open. It is likely that several if not all of the various fragments have had the same positive cognition. But whether there has been one in common or not, the therapist does not presume to know what the final positive cognition will be. The client selects a positive cognition for this final installation. With the installation of this final positive cognition, the stage is set for a body scan to ascertain if all processing has been completed. The body scan is conducted as usual.

Questions arise when using this protocol with war and terrorism survivors. Below we consider some of the most common questions.

1. When new material not associated with the targeted experience emerges, should the therapist follow it or not? Ordinarily, the answer is yes. However, in some situations time is a constraint. The therapist may only have a limited number of sessions to spend with a client because of the sheer number of people to be seen or because the therapist will be leaving the area. The possibility that the normal development of the therapeutic relationship has been truncated, the client history may have been perfunctory, and the opportunity to learn how the client responds to EMDR may have been limited may further hamper the therapist.

We have found a technique, though not formally researched, that appears clinically to be useful. The role of the therapist with this new material will be deliberately more active for the sake of efficiency. As a link emerges to new material, the therapist performs a set of eye movements on the material. If resolution is not immediate, then a cognitive interweave is utilized to accelerate processing. What takes place after the introduction of the cognitive interweave is a "checkerboard" approach. After a set of eye movements on the cognitive interweave, the client is directed to focus on whatever comes up. If there is no major therapeutic movement, then another cognitive interweave is introduced. This pattern is repeated until the client is returned to the original targeted experience.

2. Should EMDR or any other effective psychotherapy be used in situations where the threat is ongoing? Clinicians have expressed concern based in part on the recognition that anxiety in such situations is normal and that once the crisis passes it may resolve without the need for intervention. Further, many clinicians prefer to have clients in a stable environment before starting psychotherapy—for some clinicians this stability is a necessary prerequisite. Since such conditions may not be available in an ongoing situation, their preference is to defer treatment.

For this question we cite the EMDR concept of "ecological resolution." Because EMDR does not work by suggestion from the therapist, the resolutions produced are those of the client and are appropriate for her or him. What clients need to hold on to, they will. Learned skills are not pathological and are retained for future use as needed.

It has been established that EMDR does not inhibit rational fear. This was first observed in Shapiro's 1989 study. One of the subjects of that study was a rape victim whose anxiety had decreased to a zero SUD during treatment. This anxiety was later reported to be at a four when she was queried during the follow-up. After treatment she had learned that her assailant had been released from jail and was living in her neighborhood. This case contributed to Shapiro's "ecological resolution" theory.

Since the introduction of EMDR numerous examples of clients retaining what they need have been noted. For example, survivors of traffic accidents that took place while they were driving their cars had their traumas resolved but did not lose their knowledge of how to drive. That which is useful is retained. The dysfunctional portion of the reaction is all that is discarded.

There seems to be an assumption by some therapists that all anxiety during ongoing events is normal and useful. However, in situations where danger is still present, the resolution of past traumatic reactions permits more effective utilization of existing survival skills. Clients' ability to deal with a present situation is no longer hindered by a past one and their useful skills learned from the previous experience are retained. For example, an Israeli clinician working during the period of upheaval in the autumn of 2000 reported on a client who sought help for panic attacks. These were based not only on the current situation in her neighborhood—frequent gunshots, the sound of helicopters overhead, and bullets hitting people's apartments—but also on the domestic violence she had witnessed as a child. It was suggested that treatment targeted on the earlier experiences might reduce her anxiety to the degree where her response to the current situation would be more appropriate. This suggestion was followed and the results were as predicted.

3. *How does one select a positive cognition in an ongoing situation?* Clinicians working in ongoing situations should be careful about the positive cognitions selected for installation. Cognitions such as "It's

safe now" are clearly untrue and are unlikely to be successful. It is generally more effective to focus on internally oriented cognitions, such as ones that emphasize the individual's resources for responding effectively to danger, rather than on those about the external environment.

4. *When should the therapist stop processing?* Since it is not possible for the therapist to identify the appropriate resolution in advance, it is not always easy to know when to stop the processing. The general guideline for desensitization is to continue until the client stops reporting change. But if the client reports a SUD level greater than one for several sets of eye movements, the therapist must make a decision about whether to proceed or not. If therapists stop too soon, useful processing may be preempted. If they persist too long, they may create a demand situation that may unduly influence clients' behavior. Therapists in this situation should be sensitive to signs of resistance or restlessness and be willing to discuss these with the client to determine their meaning.

In anticipation of the possibility of incomplete processing, therapists should educate their clients during the preparation phase about the possibility that additional material will surface in the future and inform them about the usefulness of making use of assistance. This education is also part of the closure phase and may need emphasis in situations where the decision has been made to stop before reaching full resolution.

5. *How can one work with clients whose psychological strength has been depleted by ongoing trauma?* People in ongoing situations may be functioning in deprived personal conditions, which means they may not have the psychological strength to undergo intensive psychotherapy, particularly one that zeroes in on powerful material. Fortunately, there are ways of using EMDR that decrease the intensity of processing.

The key is to slow down the rate of processing. Continued processing accomplishes two things. First, it demonstrates to clients that they do have the ability to begin their own healing. This restores self-confidence and strength. Second, as incremental resolution takes place, it frees up mental energy previously used to suppress traumatic material and makes it available for resolution work. It is possible to slow down the pace of processing by using shorter sets, taking more time between sets, using more frequent cognitive interweaves, and using taps or sounds in place of eye movements—we cover these techniques in more detail in chapter 16.

Slowing down an individual's processing may seem unrealistic when the therapist is responding to mass casualties. However, rather than choosing not to see clients who appear to be severely traumatized because they may require too much time, we suggest using these modifications to begin. Our experience has been that those who appear too fragile to move at normal EMDR speeds begin to accelerate in their own processing as gains are made. Additionally, resolving even one experience may make a dramatic difference in an individual's life and give them the strength to take on other experiences. Finally, resolution of the issues associated with one experience, particularly one associated with war and terrorism, may quite readily generalize to other experiences from the same source. This is particularly true of survivor guilt.

PROTOCOL DECISION-MAKING

It is possible to construct a "branching tree" approach when trying to determine whether to use the recent events protocol or the standard EMDR procedure. The key in this process is to remain clinically attuned to the client and to take the time to discover how the experience exists for the client, rather than mechanically applying this process of decision-making. This discussion, then, should be viewed as taking place within the context of exploration of the client's reaction to the experience.

The first decision point is to determine if one image or several represent the experience. One image suggests consolidation and the standard protocol is probably going to be the best approach.

Where the client reports multiple images, the second decision point is to determine if one is worse than the others. If a "worst" image is identified, then the standard protocol should be used with it. After that portion of the experience is resolved, two things must be checked. First, see if the body scan is clear of negative sensations. If not, the other images or memory fragments may not be resolved and should be processed using the recent events protocol. Second, whether or not the body scan is clear of any negative response, the other remembered images related to the event should be accessed and gone through in a chronological fashion to see if any disturbance remains. The procedure described below as part of the recent events protocol is a good way of doing this.

If the client reports multiple images of equivalent intensity or reports no images but the remembered fragments of the experience have equivalent intensity, then the recent events protocol is the method of choice.

Remember that the fragmentation of a memory can be due to the recency of the trauma or the complexity of the event itself; in effect, there was more than one moment of significance within the entire experience. The recent events protocol may be useful even for old memories that are complex enough to produce several issues or conflicts for the client. War and terrorism traumas are particularly likely to produce this multiplicity of issues with the resulting fragmenting of the event. Thus, familiarity with the recent events protocol is very useful for any clinician working with war or terrorism trauma, regardless of the length of time since the specific events.

DEBRIEFING AND EMDR

Rapid responses to traumatic situations has led to the use of debriefing procedures originally developed for emergency service workers. Participants are given an opportunity to describe their experiences, thoughts, and emotional reactions. These debriefings, like those carried out under the Critical Incident Stress Management Program, attempt to normalize reactions, provide education on reactions, and let traumatized individuals know about services available. While not treatment, these debriefings may be useful when directed carefully toward their intended goals. They are also useful in giving participating mental health professionals an opportunity to observe and evaluate individuals who may require treatment.

Roger Solomon has had extensive experience with EMDR, emergency service workers, and Critical Incident Stress Management. He has found that EMDR can be very effective for individuals with good support systems who have suffered single traumas if delivered in a "one-two punch" arrangement of debriefing in a group followed by an EMDR session for the individual. For individuals with complex PTSD due to multiple traumatic events, more thorough preparation is needed before initiating treatment. Peer support personnel may play an important role by providing education about EMDR prior to treatment, debriefing after EMDR sessions, and supportive follow-up between sessions. These peer support personnel are generally part of the debriefing team.

Such debriefings should be organized carefully. It is possible to inflict vicarious traumatization on the participants by exposing them to aspects of the experience that they had been spared or which resonate with their own unresolved issues. This is a particularly salient issue when responding to instances of terrorism involving children. While there may be institutional pressures to respond rapidly to as many survivors as possible, the typical group debriefing format is often inappropriate for children for reasons we will discuss in chapter 15.

Because reactions may emerge some time after the trauma, part of the immediate response should include the development of resources able to respond whenever reactions do show up.

As with much of the EMDR approach, the client determines, by presentation, whether the recent events protocol is needed. The clinician's role is to ensure that the experience and its triggers, including those that can be anticipated, are resolved. A thorough client history will identify many triggers and reevaluation will help to ensure that all have been addressed.

CHILDREN

"Then they came with guns and we had to leave because they hated us. I don't know why."

Early experience in providing treatment for traumatized children led to the development of modifications of the EMDR protocol (Greenwald, 1999), which we briefly review. Over the years, from Dunblane to Columbine, from Bangladesh to Israel, additional issues in the treatment of children surviving war and terrorism have been identified, along with ways of approaching those issues.

CHILDREN'S PROTOCOL REVIEW

There are several recommended alterations in the basic protocol when the client is a child. Children generally have shorter attention spans than adults, especially when they have been traumatized. The EMDR clinician will need to be more active to maintain their attention and will likely find that shorter sessions will work better.

The complexity of the assessment phase may pose problems for children, particularly in the identification of cognitions. The emphasis should be on simplicity, and, especially with younger children, the therapist may need to suggest negative or positive cognitions after discussing how the child has been dealing with things. With some children, the specific statement of cognitions may be waived.

The SUD and VOC scales may be too confusing and more informal ways of indicating the levels of disturbance or acceptance, such using a yardstick or having the child spread his or her arms (or the therapist's) to indicate the magnitude of any disturbance, may be much more useful.

Drawings are a good way for a child to describe an experience. They are particularly useful when children are afraid of divulging details of their experiences, since the pictures can be hidden from the view of the clinician. Drawings are useful when returning a child to the targeted experience, whether or not they were used for confidentiality.

Desensitization generally moves faster with children than adults. Shorter sets of eye movements are appropriate. While very young children are less likely to link to other experiences, as children's ages increase, the possibility of linking grows.

Explorations of the future should be conducted if they do not occur naturally in the course of processing. Children may have some anticipatory anxiety about entering certain situations—starting school, returning home, moving to a different refugee camp—that needs to be addressed.

Before terminating treatment, the therapist should explore children's reactions to the significant people in their lives to ensure no negative reaction remains. Children may feel people allowed them to be harmed and this can corrode relationships unless resolved.

BUTTERFLY HUG

Lucy Artigas of Mexico developed this variation of the EMDR protocol while working with young children affected by Hurricane Paulina in 1997, and it has been used with good effect with children in a variety of settings since. As an alternative to eye movements, children are asked to cross their arms as if they were hugging themselves and tap alternate shoulders while thinking about the traumatic event or while visualizing a positive resource. The butterfly hug can also be taught as a simple self-soothing technique. In some situations the butterfly hug has been used along with the children's drawings of life before and during the trauma, as well as drawings of current and future situations. This allows for a gradual approach to the trauma memory and gives the therapist an opportunity to ask the child questions about various aspects of the event. This method was used successfully with Kosovar children in a refugee camp in Germany (Wilson, Tinker, Hoffman, Becker, & Kleiner, 2000). Children can also be asked to sit behind each other in a circle and tap each other's shoulders. The butterfly hug is a flexible technique and can be taught to an individual child or to a group of children. Because it seems like a game, it may break the ice and lighten the mood when working on trauma memories.

SECURING THE ENVIRONMENT

Alan Cohen has noted, based on his work with EMDR-HAP in Turkey and Bangladesh as well as in his nation of Israel, that the critical first step in treating children is ensuring that they have trust in their environment. Securing the environment, then, is not just a concrete task but also a matter of children's perception. While the adult clinician may have complete faith that the current setting is safe, children, with their limited perspective, may not share that perspective. In addition, traumatized children are not likely to be engaged in a great deal of environmental exploration. Their tendency to isolate may prevent them from gaining access to accurate information about their surroundings and leave their fears unchallenged. Indeed, some children's level of fear may actually increase as their imaginations run rampant without anything to dispute them.

Being with the child as she or he explores the current setting is one tactic offering several positives. First, of course, the child may discover that the environment is free of threats—"There are no bad men with guns in the hall." Second, it may enhance the therapeutic relationship, as the child is given an opportunity to be with the therapist outside of the context of formal therapy. Third, the child's reactions to elements in the environment may help the therapist identify triggers and trauma sources needing processing. Fourth, venturing forth to explore the environment helps to break down the pattern of isolation and withdrawal common among child survivors of war and terrorism.

Accompanying children returning to a school where a shooting has taken place and permitting them to explore the entire area is possible and would accomplish these goals. However, in some situations the current environment is simply not safe or stable. A child in a refugee camp, for example, may not have any idea where he or she is going for permanent settlement, or may fear going to some place totally unfamiliar, such as a foreign country. They may be in a safe country, but only there temporarily, with the return to their own country and an uncertain future looming. Under these circumstances, the focus of treatment should be on the child's current safety. In other situations the area may still be a target of terrorism or subject to the impact of war. Even a refugee camp, as recent history has shown repeatedly, may not be beyond the range of attack.

PRESENTING AND INITIAL
FOCUS OF TREATMENT

The presentation of treatment should be tailored to the child, of course, and some exploration may be needed before deciding on which approach to take. Some children accept therapy focused on their trauma experiences; other children are more readily engaged by an approach oriented toward their expressed goals. Following their lead empowers children and may offset the possibility that it was not their idea to enter treatment. Having children identify their problems and goals gives the therapist a point of engagement. Sometimes these problems are immediately related to trauma, such as sleep disturbances or nightmares; other times, they are more general, such as a desire to have friends or not get in so much trouble.

With some children it is best to focus initially on nontrauma material, such as the safe place installation and enhancing positive attributes and characteristics, such as strength. Emphasizing positives strengthens children's confidence before moving on to more general problem areas and eventually to specific trauma experiences. It also gives them some experience with EMDR and permits development of the therapeutic relationship before getting into the most critical material. The clinician might have the child focus on the potential for developmental change, pointing out that as children grow, they have more abilities, freedom, and strength. Helping the child to acquire this perspective may make dealing with immediate problems easier, especially if these current difficulties can be perceived as part of the developmental strengthening process.

CHILDREN'S INDICATORS OF
TRAUMATIC REACTIONS

Obviously, children can be exposed to all aspects of war and can have many of the same reactions as adults. It is commonly observed that children are more likely to manifest their distress behaviorally than are adults. Severely traumatized children may repeatedly act out aspects of the traumatic experience rather than talking about them. Sleep disturbance and nightmares are common occurrences. Poor concentration can affect school performance, while irritability and withdrawal may affect peer relationships.

Children's ability to comprehend what they have witnessed is limited by their intellectual development, leading to extreme, even superstitious, beliefs about cause and effect. Just as they do in peacetime, children in war situations may develop irrational beliefs that their behavior plays a role in negative events that are actually beyond their control. For example, children may believe that they caused someone's death because they had an argument earlier that day or because they were playing when or where they shouldn't have been.

Therapists should be alert to children who are responding to the war situation by "over functioning." Under the circumstances of war and terrorism, children may begin to hold themselves inappropriately responsible. They may believe their good behavior will comfort their parents, which may be true, and prevent bad things from happening, which is not true. If the family has had to flee the country, this belief can become strengthened, as the children may be best able to adapt to the new situation and learn a new language. In these situations the children's adaptability may result in their serving as spokespersons for the family with relief and other agencies. This position of responsibility can reinforce children's belief that suffering in the family is a result of mistakes on their part.

FAMILIES AND CHILDREN

Therapists working with children surviving war and terrorism often find families are a critical part of the situation. Families may identify problems children experience and are a rich source of information about the children, particularly for children whose ability to describe their experiences is limited. On the other hand, families may be contributors to children's difficulties.

Children may suffer from the secondary effects of their parents' traumatization. Parents may be unable to provide their children with their usual level of attention because of their own symptoms. Children may take parents' irritability and social withdrawal personally.

Children can be helped by the providing of EMDR to other family members. This is true especially for parents, whose ability to function effectively in their family roles is impaired by their own traumatic stress reactions. No matter how successfully a family coped with the war situation, parents tend to engage in self-blame about failing to protect their loved ones. This may result in negative cognitions concerning their unworthiness in assuming their appropriate parental role.

EMDR may serve to establish a "circle of healing" that is important for children and the people around them. As the individuals making up a family resolve their traumatic stress reactions individually, they are ready to take on their appropriate roles. This stabilizes the family system, which can then be more supportive of its members. EMDR can assist them individually as any new blocking material is identified.

A clinician should be alert for three broad issue areas for children whose parents are lost, either killed or separated because of the war. These include grief for the loss, anger toward parents for being gone, and anger at the world for depriving them of their parents. These issues are fairly familiar to EMDR clinicians working with children in a variety of settings, such as adoption and foster home placement.

These issues may be at the root of behavioral problems and the focus of the people making the referral to the therapist, overlooking the underlying traumatic separation from the parent. Underlying these issues is children's loyalty to their parents, an extremely powerful dynamic.

Identification of this dynamic may provide an EMDR clinician with a very powerful intervention, perhaps used in the form of a cognitive interweave presented for processing prior to directly addressing the trauma material itself. This intervention consists of having the child focus on what the missing parent might want the child to do. The specific terms of the intervention will vary, but the gist is: "What would your father say to you now if he could speak to you?" "What could you be doing that would make your mother proud of you?" Such interventions may result in a change in behavior, as the child begins to evaluate his or her actions on the basis of loyalty toward the absent parent.

"HOMEWORK" AND EDUCATION

EMDR is about processing information. The emphasis on bilateral stimulation that makes up so much of the discussion of EMDR should not lead us to forget that information must be present in order to be processed. A careful selection of "homework" tasks may be useful in helping the child gain exposure to new information or become reacquainted with old. Bilateral stimulation can then be used to process blocks to this information as needed.

New information might include the relative safety of the environment, as discussed earlier in this chapter. Older, overlooked information could be the competency of parents and the availability of age-appropriate activities such as school or play. This information helps children in understanding that their lives can continue. Discovering this information means entering the world, which children may be reluctant to do. EMDR, as Ricky Greenwald noted concerning refugee children, can be useful in overcoming this reluctance.

Education for the parents, guardians, or caregivers of children is often useful. Children who have been traumatized may exhibit a variety of negative behaviors and difficulty with bonding and attachment. People who do not understand trauma may ignore such children and instead respond to children who are not problematic. This, of course, deprives the traumatized children of the structure needed to promote security, which generally means that the problems will worsen. Education may also help adults understand their own reactions and increase their willingness to ask for assistance. An example of this approach utilized cross-culturally by Howard Lipke is discussed in chapter 21.

Group debriefings often are regarded as educational, since they provide participants with information concerning trauma reactions and the event itself. However, for children such debriefings are often inappropriate. Children may find that hearing the experiences of other children compounds their own anxieties. In addition, the length of time needed to do the group debriefing may exceed children's attention spans.

THE FUTURE TEMPLATE

It is not uncommon for trauma survivors using EMDR spontaneously to focus on their actions in the future. This is more common following single rather than multiple traumas and with adults rather than children. Clinical experience suggests that children who have survived war are the least likely to bring up the future. The therapist should be prepared to have children focus on the future and identify any negative reactions toward it they may have. A future template—a positive view of the self in the future—should be installed with eye movements.

Because the child's situation during or following war or acts of terror may be highly fluid and uncertain, the future template should have an internal focus to it—that is, how the child wants to be, feel, or think, rather than how things are going to be in the environment around the child. It is best if the child brings forth the future template. It may be a measure of the success of the resolution of the trauma material that a child is able to do this. This is generally identifiable in response to the question, "How do you want to be?" "I can take care of myself," "I will be OK," "I will live so my parents would be proud of me," and "I will be a good person" are all positive future templates.

The therapist may reflect the child's statement to form it into a succinct, preferably "I" statement. When the child agrees that the statement is correct, the therapist asks the child to focus on the template while short sets of eye movements are done. After each set, the child is asked how he or she feels. Blocking beliefs that arise can be targeted in the usual EMDR fashion.

If better future templates arise, they are treated like evolving and emerging positive cognitions. The child focuses on each in turn and the processing continues as long as the child is describing improved acceptance of the template.

RESOLUTION OF TRIGGERS

The therapist using EMDR is always trying to ensure that all potential triggers of the trauma reactions have been identified and resolved. While children may or may not be able to identify these triggers, parents and others are usually able to tell the therapist what kind of situations have been tapping into a child's trauma. Unresolved triggers are targeted for bilateral stimulation after the primary material has been finished.

Searching for the triggers begins during the client history phase, though a child may not provide the kind of detail that an adult would. In some cases, a clinician might build a list of possible triggers. This list should include triggers a child cannot anticipate but the clinician, with a more objective understanding of the experience and the child's present and future environment, can begin to identify.

For example, shootings or violence in schools with deaths and injuries to the children might leave a variety of triggers. While the bullet holes in the hallway walls can be plastered and repainted, the fresh paint itself may remind a child of what took place. Consider a child returning to a classroom where a shooting took place. What in that room might serve as a trigger? Beyond the damage to the physical space of the room, what will be the effect of the absence of injured or dead children? An unoccupied desk may be a very powerful trigger, as Alan Cohen found in the aftermath of a shooting at Bet Shemesh, Israel. Children on an outing in a school bus were fired on and several were killed or wounded. Several children had unresolved grief triggered by the sight of unoccupied school desks. Cohen's experience rinds us that triggers are not tightly linked to the place where the trauma took place. A clinician must look at the totality of children's environments. Where might they encounter reminders not just of what happened, but of the disruption to their social system? Where do they go to play and socialize and will any of those places now be different because of the impact of war or terrorism?

In summary, EMDR requires the therapist to be more active to hold and maintain the attention of children and to be attentive to the special needs of children who survive war and terrorism. In return, EMDR offers the therapist responding to traumatized children several advantages: the therapy is comparatively fast; it can accommodate children's possible need for secrecy around an event; it is thorough, helping to resolve experiences holistically and readily addressing anticipatory issues; and, as experience in the field has shown, EMDR can be used across cultural boundaries.

Chapter 16

ABREACTION

"My heart would break to talk about it if I still had a heart."

THERAPIST ISSUES

Working with trauma survivors always carries with it the chance of encountering abreaction. Because incorrect handling of abreaction may not only interfere with a client's processing but actually result in unnecessary suffering and potential withdrawal from treatment, it is important for all therapists considering working with survivors to be thoroughly prepared. This preparation may include personal preparation as well as familiarity with the EMDR methodology and procedures. It is important to remember that, while it is not evident that abreaction occurs more frequently during EMDR than it does in other therapies, it may arise more suddenly.

Abreaction may be defined in a variety of ways. For the purposes of this discussion it refers to a reexperiencing of a memory at high levels of emotion. It should be noted that the simple expression of emotion does almost nothing toward promoting resolution for individuals suffering from the severe PTSD typical of war and terrorism survivors. Many survivors have experienced powerful emotional reactions, often triggered by an unexpected encounter with a reminder of the trauma, but without gaining any mastery over the event. Undergoing these emotions without resolution promotes a desire to avoid all emotions for fear of opening the floodgates to pain and suffering. The negative consequences of such avoidance are clear—those around

166

the individual find little in the way of emotional responsiveness or grow to fear the consequences of inadvertently triggering the tsunami of grief, guilt, or despair, and so they withdraw. And the individual, trying to avoid embarrassment, to keep from being swept away by the pain, and to protect others from the feelings he or she believes are uncontrollable, also withdraws.

Some therapists go to great lengths to keep their clients from abreacting. There are some approaches to therapy that are based on the idea of minimizing the stimulation of the autonomic nervous system (Rothschild, 1997). It is true that some clients do not have the strength to endure a major abreaction, but in our experience these clients are relatively rare. When exposure therapies were first introduced as trauma treatments, the concern was that the treatments were unsafe because they involved prolonged periods of anxiety. However, treatment outcome research shows a very low incidence of adverse outcome and reasonably low rates of dropout. In some direct comparative studies, the dropout rate for exposure therapy was actually lower than that for such low-anxiety methods as supportive counseling or stress inoculation training (Foa, Rothbaum, Riggs, & Murdock, 1991). EMDR has been found to have lower dropout rates than exposure therapy, possibly because clients get through the distressing part of treatment faster (Ironson et al., in press; Lee et al., in press; Powell et al., 2000; Rogers et al., 1999).

Another reason therapists may avoid abreaction is that they are simply uncomfortable with their clients' distress. Proper training may reduce this discomfort. We believe it is useful to experience any therapeutic intervention that we might use with patients; in some circumstances, it may be vital. In typical EMDR training, for example, and trainings sanctioned by the EMDR International Association, participants work with each other in small groups under the supervision of experienced facilitators. While the intent is educative, the practicum sessions make use of the actual experiences of an individual participant when that person is in the role of client. Besides increasing familiarity with the EMDR methodology, this format gives participants an opportunity to sample firsthand what the experience may be like as a client. Occasionally, selected targeted experiences link to more intense material and an abreaction occurs. The participant in the role of therapist has an opportunity to put into practice the procedures for responding to abreaction, which are reviewed below. The participant, as therapist, observer, or client, discovers how rapidly EMDR processing enables a client to get through the abreaction and achieve resolution of the targeted material.

Of course, not all therapists can or should be working with trauma survivors. Therapists uncomfortable with high levels of client emotion or with unresolved experiences of their own may be inappropriate candidates for such work. Some therapists, after having witnessed abreaction in an EMDR training, opt not to work with trauma survivors. It is better that they learn of their aversion in a training environment, rather than in the middle of a therapy session with a client. If therapists in training discover issues needing resolution before working with trauma survivors, both the therapists and their future clients benefit. The advantage of formal training is that it assists therapists in understanding themselves as well as learning the methodology.

Another way to decrease the discomfort a therapist might have is to use consultation and supervision. This is a good principle whenever beginning to work with war and terrorism survivors. If the therapist's aversion is due to unresolved personal issues, therapy focused on those issues may be helpful.

CLIENT ISSUES

Part of the client preparation phase is spent discussing the possibility of abreaction and the appropriate response to it. For war and terrorism survivors, encountering powerful emotion when inadequately prepared for it will generally result in blocked processing.

Clients need to hear repeatedly that any emotions that come up are a sign of processing; that is, their mind is focusing on the emotions associated with the experiences, just as it might with the thoughts, physical sensations, or links to other experiences and memories. Simply telling the client that this may happen, however, is not enough. It is important to explain *why* these encounters with feelings are signs of progress. Remember, to war and terrorism survivors, powerful emotion may be perceived as disabling, and therefore dangerous, or chaotic, and therefore resembling the trauma experience. Clients may have invested much in the way of personal resources in suppressing emotions and dread encountering them.

The EMDR model of memory nodes may serve as a useful basis for explaining the role of any encountered emotion. We are looking to develop connections between a trauma experience encoded into the brain and the information needed for its resolution. To give clients the idea that something is needed for reality-based understanding to affect how they feel, we describe how clients are able to state their understanding of the reality of a situation ("I did all I could do") or their present state ("I know I am safe now") even though this may be far different from how they feel.

It is assumed that the information being processed in EMDR is a "package deal," so that as the client observes changes in the image, feelings, thoughts, or sensations associated with the target memory, the rest of the package is changing as well. It is also assumed that movement is always in the direction of resolution. Therefore, changes in the feeling, even increases in its intensity, are usually signs of progress

Preparation also involved the use of a metaphor that serves to orient clients during abreaction by reminding them of the importance of movement. Noticing scenery from a train window, keeping the foot on the accelerator of a car when entering a dark tunnel, and similar metaphors help encourage the client to stay with the material long enough to achieve resolution.

The stop signal provides clients with the assurance that they are in control and can stop processing if they so choose. We have found two elements useful when discussing the stop signal. First, it is best to offer it with an emphasis on, "If you need to." To describe its use in terms of, "If you feel you are going to be swept away," may result in clients' using it in anticipation of the abreaction when, if they would permit themselves, they might be able to handle far more of it than they currently imagine. Second, describing the stop signal as a "time-out" helps clients to understand that engaging it does not mean that they have failed and that therapy is over. To the contrary, if they need to pause and gather themselves before pressing on, that is perfectly in keeping with the client-centered nature of EMDR.

Therapists should never sugarcoat the issue of abreaction. Clients should be told that negative feelings may get more intense before they resolve. With combat veterans it has been helpful to predict aloud that they will reach a point where they may want to "bail out" and stop the procedure. While it is important that clients be assured that the stop signal will be respected, they can also be given a rationale for continuing past this point. If they stop in the middle of an abreaction, it is like taking their foot off the gas pedal. They are still in the middle of the feelings and it may take them quite some time to get through it. They may know from experience that when a memory is stimulated accidentally, it can take hours or even days before it subsides. It is far better to continue processing so as to get through it faster and get some resolution of the experience if possible.

War and terrorism survivors often have a powerful need to reassure themselves of their own ability to control what is happening with and to them. Describing the feelings associated with abreaction as theirs, as stored up within, and as released by their own mind, as opposed to a reaction to something the therapist is doing to them, speaks to this need.

There are circumstances where clients need to encounter powerful feelings more slowly. Proper education and preparation of clients should take place to prepare them for slowing down and directing processing using a variety of procedures. One of these is to use alternative bilateral stimulations, such as hand taps or sounds, rather than the eye movements. While processing continues, it appears to do so at a slower rate than with the eye movements. This can give clients greater forewarning of approaching abreaction and a more gradual introduction of intense emotion.

Another alternative is to reduce the number of repetitions in a set of eye movements. If a typical set of eye movements would run for 20–30 seconds, the therapist can use five-second sets. Clients may eventually request that a greater number of repetitions be used. Discussions with clients after treatment sessions reveal that they begin to realize that their capacity for dealing with their feelings is greater than they thought and they may note changes toward resolution that they wish to accelerate. These requests should be respected.

A third alternative procedure is to increase the time between sets of eye movements. Where ordinarily brevity is the key, with some clients the focus is on making processing more gradual. Allowing clients more opportunity to discuss what they are experiencing will slow down processing by distancing them from the targeted experience and its associated material as well as by perhaps giving them the opportunity to engage defenses. These obstacles will be overcome with processing, albeit at a slower rate. In the meantime, clients have a chance to gather their strength before taking on the next set of eye movements.

Once in an abreaction, the general principles for all EMDR clients hold true. It is important to keep the processing going, to keep clients in contact with the here and now through the use of the therapist's voice and hand movements, to remind them of what they know about abreaction through reference to the metaphors introduced earlier, and to look for a plateau of resolution where the processing can stop so the client (and the therapist) can rest.

Because war survivors often have multiple traumas, the therapist should be prepared to assume a more active role in directing abreaction. The possibility of emotional linking to other experiences can result in clients' feeling like they have been caught in an avalanche, as each experience piles on top of the preceding one. Clients may wish to make use of the stop signal to catch their breath and perhaps to be reminded by the therapist that the accessing of these linked experiences, while stressful, is a sign of their own healing.

In the rare circumstance when a client encounters a block while abreacting, the same tools would be used as in normal processing during desensitization. An excellent tool in this circumstance is the cognitive interweave.

One of the great strengths of EMDR is its ability not only to get a client through abreactive material rapidly but also to promote the resolution of that material. In other words, rather than the repeated exposure-abreaction-exposure cycle typical of other therapies, EMDR offers the high probability of resolution. Thus, the elicitation of abreactive material during treatment, if it occurs, is a natural part of the curative process. Clients are engaged in self-healing. Whether their awareness at any given moment encompasses physical sensations, cognitions, or even emotions of an intense nature, the therapist's role is to facilitate that healing process.

Chapter 17

GRIEF AND LOSS

"If I ever cry, the world will drown."

Chronic unresolved grief and grief so severe as to cause dysfunction in life are unfortunately common results of war and terrorism. Grief seldom walks alone; rather, it is accompanied by anger, guilt, and abreaction. These issues are discussed in more detail in the preceding and other chapters.

TRAUMATIC GRIEF

There are several characteristics that distinguish traumatic war grief from normal grief. First, deaths that are violent and unexpected have a shocking impact that tends to keep the individual stuck in the re-experiencing phase of symptoms. The individual may have sustained several losses without sufficient time to grieve any of them. Individuals who were under stress for a prolonged period may have developed emotional numbing, which complicates the grieving process. The individual may lack emotional support because the immediate social system has been directly impacted by the war. Conversely, those close to the individual may not have shared the war experience and may find it difficult to empathize.

Grief often has some irrational component to it, though this is usually of limited scope. These components can include, but are not limited to, guilt, anger, and other feelings. Traumatic grief may em-

172

phasize such components. For example, there can be guilt at failing to save another, guilt at contributing to the death of another, and guilt at surviving when others did not. There can be guilt about the relief felt when the client survived and others did not.

Traumatic grief tends to freeze the client in the past. With the past unresolved, there is little joy in the present orientation. Further, there may be a sense that to let go of the grief would be in some way disloyal to the dead and that a focusing on life and not on the past is an act of betrayal.

EXISTENTIAL ELEMENTS IN GRIEF

Traumatic loss can trigger an existential crisis. Though this can be expressed in a variety of ways, such as, "Why did God let this happen?" or "Nothing means anything anymore," the central issue is one of meaning. Because these issues often tap into religious themes, some clinicians feel uncomfortable addressing them. However, it is worth taking the time to understand these critical issues from the client's perspective. Indeed, even for the nonbeliever, existential issues can be addressed directly with EMDR. It is not necessary that the therapist share the client's belief system, nor is any interpretation of those beliefs needed.

Aspects of existential grief may be presented at almost any point in therapy. Sometimes during history taking clients refer to posttraumatic changes in behavior that suggest existential issues, e.g., an inability to rejoin their church since the war or difficulties in finding meaning in their current activities. These issues may also arise spontaneously during desensitization or installation, or during discussions as termination is approached.

When encountering existential issues during history taking, the therapist may provide information that assists in processing. Some clients are unaware of alternatives to their current perspective. Taking into account their cultural value systems, the therapist might provide exposure to alternative points of view. We do not take a cognitive therapy approach of trying to get clients to accept the alternative. There is no need for homework, rehearsal, and other techniques. Instead, we simply provide clients with the information without elaboration. If even marginally acceptable, the information may then serve the function of a "preemptive cognitive interweave"; that is, it is a piece of information clients can utilize for resolution during processing with eye movements.

After examination, clients may find the alternative point of view totally unacceptable. Nonetheless, the process of examination may have the positive result of enabling clients to clarify or rediscover resources useful for resolution (e.g., "I read that book and I don't believe in a Higher Power but I've always thought we need to believe in ourselves"). This, in turn, may make resources more readily accessible during processing. The process of examining another perspective may help define the issues more precisely and completely, which assists in the identification of a starting point for processing. The therapist is not arguing for a point of view; indeed, with a collection of readings or other material, the therapist might provide a range of views, increasing the information available to the client.

Let us emphasize that this providing of information or of alternative perspectives is similar to the procedure used in EMDR when encountering a client who simply lacks the knowledge that would permit resolution. It can be used with other issues and reactions, such as guilt and anger. This is not additional therapy. We would also stress that this intervention must take into account the cultural values of the client. For example, Viktor Frankl's books might be recommended to someone with Western values; other sources might be better for a client in Asia.

THERAPIST ISSUES

When dealing with grief issues, therapists are often very clear about what they think clients' positive cognition *ought* to be. Naturally, therapists want what is best for their clients. It is very hard to keep this desire out of the way of processing, but it is critical that clients be permitted to discover their own resolution. Empowerment of the client is paramount in EMDR, even during the development of the positive cognition. Therapists have to walk a fine line. On the one hand, they work to develop the therapeutic relationship; on the other, they need to avoid imposing their interpretation of the experience. Timing in such things as the expression of empathic understand is important in this regard. Preemptive empathic expressions, such as, "I know how you must be feeling," often fall flat in these situations because of the overwhelming power of the experience to the client.

The therapist's understanding may be incomplete or inaccurate. This can cause uncertainty or irritation and loss of the therapist's credibility. In circumstances where it becomes important to have clients elaborate on their reactions, such as when they are having trouble identifying the information for some part of the assessment, it is far better to wait patiently and to assist clients in their expression of feelings and thoughts.

EMDR ISSUES

Careful client preparation is the key to success in processing grief reactions. Clients may have unrealistically high expectations for EMDR. They may have the idea that it will eliminate their pain completely. It helps to explain the issue of ecological resolution—that their resolution will be appropriate for them at this time of their life—rather than allow clients to set themselves up for further upset. It is helpful to take some time to talk about what EMDR can help them accomplish, such as resolve the dysfunctional aspects of the grief and integrate the loss into their life. This discussion will typically involve clients in identifying what is currently not working in their life, such as important relationships that are suffering from neglect.

This discussion may very well reveal what will become the negative cognition. With perceptions of self as failing in other areas of their lives, it is not uncommon to hear negative cognitions of "I am a failure" or "I am inadequate." In any case, discussion of the impact of unresolved grief assists clients in beginning to see the relationship between this unresolved past experience of loss and their current situation.

On the other hand, it is equally important to talk about what EMDR cannot do. Clients are sometimes apprehensive about the possibility of reducing their intrusive symptoms because they have come to see them as their only connection to the deceased. Clients should be told that EMDR cannot cause them to forget the loss, nor can it erase all the feelings associated with that loss if there is a need to retain some of them. Making this point may require educating clients about the role of loss in life and about an appropriate level of resolution. There are several different approaches to this which may also have the effect of stimulating the development of a positive cognition.

One approach is to simply point out that the structure of the brain is such that they cannot be compelled to forget—human beings are made up of their experiences and these experiences are stored in the brain. Thus, a goal of forgetting is contradictory to what the brain is designed to do and may even deprive them of the opportunity to grow as a person. Modeling is a good way of explaining what is meant by such growth. When the therapist points out how others have come to grips with loss and used it as the basis for positive change in their lives, clients may be able to see that resolution is more than simply stopping the pain. In any case, the point is to help clients understand that forgetting is not a viable goal. It may be too soon for them to see what resolution will ultimately mean to them, but letting them know that resolution might include a wide range of possibilities prepares them for what may be the surprising nature of their own resolution.

It also helps to talk about the range of reactions people have to loss and to describe the kinds of feelings—grief, guilt, anger, relief—and the kinds of thinking people may be left with after the loss. This broad discussion often permits clients to identify their negative cognition, as well as issues accompanying the grief.

Another approach is to ask clients about losses they experienced before the war. This discussion will be an opportunity to raise the idea that the end result of EMDR will be the same as normal resolution of grief. The memory will become less intrusive, the negative feelings will become more diffuse, and the client may have greater access to positive memories of the deceased. One client said that EMDR resulted in his having a whole table full of pictures of his friend to choose from, where prior to treatment he had had only the image of his friend's death.

When selecting the first target for processing grief experiences, it is useful to ask clients about the last time they saw the deceased. This often helps to focus on sources of unfinished business, such as the need to say goodbye or guilt about not preventing the death, as well as grief.

Some clients process loss in a series of visual images, first of the event as it occurred and then later with positive reworkings of these images. One veteran with PTSD and a history of alcohol dependence resolved a 30-year-old memory in one very brief session. The target image was of the look of panic on his friend's face as he died. The negative cognition was "I can't do anything." At the beginning of treatment, his most acceptable positive cognition was "It happened in the past." The SUD level was six.

CL: We shouldn't have been there that day. A new lieutenant walked us down the middle of the road.

TH: Go with that. *(Begins EMs)*

CL: Either way, I couldn't keep him from dying. I've blamed the lieutenant, but he didn't know.

TH: Go with that. *(Begins EMs)*

CL: Everything, the whole thing. I feel full.

TH: Go with that. *(Begins EMs)*

CL: I'm feeling something good in my body, I can't explain it.

TH: Go back to the scene we started with. What do you get now?

CL: The feeling in my chest is almost gone. *(Reports SUD of three)*

TH: Go with that. *(Begins EMs)*

CL: A whole bunch of feelings. It happens to everybody. It could have been me. It was a war zone. I've got to accept it . . . it's a relief.

TH: Just focus on that. *(Begins EMs)*

CL: We had some good times.

TH: Stay with that. *(Begins EMs)*

CL: It's time to let him rest and continue with my life, time to stop worrying and being upset. I want to remember the happy times.

TH: Now put the idea "It's in the past" with the scene. What happens?

CL: It's harder to get. It's like he's talking to me with his eyes, that it's OK for me to go on.

TH: Go with that. *(Begins EMs)*

CL: He's smiling, not saying anything, saying with his eyes, "I love you, thank you for what you did for me. You were a good friend."

TH: Focus on that. *(Begins EMs)*

CL: It's over.

TH: On a scale of zero to ten, how distressing is the memory now?

CL: I'm more relaxed. *(SUD was at zero, while the VOC was at seven)*

The client and therapist were both aware that this new image was a distortion, yet it seemed to be an accurate symbolic representation of the emotional resolution he was experiencing at the time. Reevaluation the next week showed continued resolution. At a one year follow-up the veteran reported that he had not had a drink since he left the program and was feeling "great."

Traumatized clients have usually been so focused on the past that they have had little time to think about the future. A stronger future orientation often arises spontaneously during processing. When processing of the trauma is complete, clients can be engaged in a discussion of what they have learned and how they intend to use this new information. We want to see if the resolution of the past trauma now permits a future orientation. This will provide a fairly clear indication of the alterations and modifications in the client's cognitive structures and the current degree of resolution. Since one of the features of traumatic grief is its ability to essentially freeze the client in the past, we are looking for the orientation to shift to the present/future. Installation of a future template based on the desired behavior may be useful.

CASE HISTORY

The client was a World War II veteran who had served in France and the Battle of the Bulge. An intermittent excessive drinker, he came into treatment after his wife finally left him. A substance abuse treatment program had identified probable trauma reactions and referred him to our inpatient PTSD program. He was skeptical of EMDR but was willing to try it, saying, "What have I got to lose?"

When asked about his involvement in a 12-step program for his alcoholism, he reported, "It was all right, but I have no Higher Power anymore." The particular experience he described as most disturbing was when he had been wounded by artillery fire and was moved to the rear. Shortly afterwards his unit was overrun and few survived, with a number massacred after surrendering. He had a clear image, unfaded with time, of looking from his stretcher as it was loaded onto a truck and seeing his friends standing around the farm buildings they were holding. His report of his negative cognition included, "I left them alone to die. I never came back. I never went back. I never even cried for them. I wanted to but I wouldn't let myself, like I'm some kind of bastard who doesn't care. That's what I think. I'm a bastard."

His positive cognition was, "I did all I could. It was out of my hands." He rated the believability of that statement at only a two on the seven-point VOC scale. The primary emotions he said he felt were grief, guilt, and anger. The disturbance of these emotions was initially assigned a SUD of ten. The location of the felt disturbance was his stomach and face.

After about five minutes of processing he began to report recalling the faces of the men he had known in the unit. Each set of eye movements seemed to surface another remembered friend. His commentary included remarks like "I had forgotten him" or some detail about the man, such as, "He was from New Jersey and we were going to get together after the war." Emotion remained relatively unchanging through most of this.

During a set of eye movements he suddenly became very teary-eyed. Eye movements were continued but nothing further seemed to happen. When the eye movements were stopped, he reported that he had recalled yet another friend, Mike, and reported, "I just remembered that he was one of the guys who helped move my stretcher." Asking him to stay with that and resuming the eye movements led to remembering each of the other three men who had carried him in his stretcher to the evacuation truck.

He paused after identifying the fourth man and then said, "None of them made it." He was asked to stay with that thought and eye movements were resumed.

TH: *(Halting eye movements)* And what do you get now?
CL: *(Shaking head)* All those guys. I never said goodbye. And they all died alone. *(Begins to cry)*
TH: Go with that. Follow my hand. *(Begins EMs)*

(Client struggles to follow therapist's hand with his eyes. Tears flow heavily for about a half minute and then stop. Eye movements become smoother and his eyebrows lift as if in surprise. Eye movements are continued briefly with no other overt signal.)

TH: All right, let's pause. Take a breath. What are you aware of now?
CL: *(Wipes eyes)* I just thought of something. Those guys didn't die

alone. They had each other. I wasn't there, but they were there
with each other. *(Sighs)* I guess I wish I was still with them.
TH: Stay with that thought, Okay? *(Begins EMs)*

*(Client begins to abreact again after just a few repetitions. He again begins
to cry. Tracking becomes difficult but with encouragement he persists. Eventually the tears stop and tracking becomes smooth. He nods his head slightly
and shortly after that the eye movements are halted. It is a long set, close to
two minutes.)*

TH: What do you get now?
CL: Well, you know, we were a pretty tight group. Knew each
other pretty well. And they knew that we were all friends and
they knew how I felt about them. They felt the same way about
me. They knew if I could have been there I would have. But
none of them would have wanted me to be killed. I figured
that out, I guess I always knew it, when I remembered their
faces as they carried me on the stretcher. They were all very
worried about me, I could see it. After they got me on board,
Mike gave me a thumbs up. I always felt I let them down by
not being there. I guess I was ashamed. But that's why I never
cried for them. The shame scared me off. I'm not a bastard. I
loved those guys. But I have nothing to be ashamed of. That's
just how it is in war sometimes. You have to play the cards you
are dealt.
TH: Go with that. *(Begins EMs)*

Additional sets of eye movements proceeded with continued resolution. No further abreaction occurred. His thinking became
more and more positive. He reported a SUD of zero. Prior to beginning installation, the therapist decided to check on the range of the
resolution.

Recalling the remark made about his experience with the 12-step
program, he asked the client, "And how do you think about a Higher
Power now?" The client responded by stating that he had been raised
with strong religious beliefs in his family but what had happened to
his friends had convinced him that God did not care. He had felt that
God was no longer in his life. Now he realized God was always with

him, just as He had been with his friends. The therapist asked him to think about that idea and resumed eye movements.

After the eye movements were concluded he smiled and said, "It's kind of funny, since I spent so much time in Sunday School, but I forgot that God is always with you, especially in the bad times. Even when you feel alone, you never really are." Further eye movements corroborated this thought and treatment moved on to installation.

Shortly before discharge the therapist conducted a review of the work accomplished by the veteran and again returned to his relationship to his God. The veteran was able to identify that the block to the relationship had been his view of himself as a terrible person for never having mourned for the men he had shared so much with, but "I guess that changed in this office." He said he noticed that the grief he now let himself feel was helped by the strength he drew from understanding how he had come to think of himself as a "bastard"—"I felt like I was letting them down because of things I couldn't control, which sounds crazy"—and from the relationship he was reestablishing with his religious beliefs.

When asked what he would be doing with this knowledge about himself and God, the veteran replied in both generalities and specifics. Getting back in touch with his religious beliefs would be a source of strength for him and keep him on the right track. More specifically, "I think that 12-step business makes more sense to me now." Though reconciliation with his wife did not take place, he handled the separation well.

Traumatic grief often brings to the therapeutic hour a rich array of additional issues and concerns. A therapist, whether using EMDR or another treatment methodology, needs to keep as broad a field of view as possible to assist the client in identifying and resolving these additional issues.

Chapter 18

GUILT

"I did something wrong. I don't know what it is but I've always known I did something wrong. Maybe just for making it."

CLIENT ISSUES

PTSD has been classified as an anxiety disorder and many of the current treatments were developed from those used for anxiety disorders, such as flooding for phobias. Anxiety is certainly present among trauma survivors, but we have found that when war survivors are asked to identify the emotion most closely associated with their traumatic memories, they select guilt with far greater frequency than they do anxiety.

Guilt is not only more common but also more disabling than anxiety. Survivors tend to cope with guilt by isolating and engaging in self-destructive behavior. They may be vulnerable to suicide. In addition, guilt has a negative impact on those close to the survivor.

War offers a multitude of opportunities for the development of guilt. Besides experiencing events that threaten their own lives, survivors have often witnessed the death or injury of others, may have had to make critical decisions under pressure on the basis of limited information, and may have caused the deaths or injuries of others. The combination of a high level of responsibility and low control is likely to leave individuals with some negative appraisals of themselves.

The result is that the experiences the individual finds most disturbing are the ones he or she is least likely to talk about afterwards.

In many cases, the therapist will be the first person to hear the story. The correct handling of guilt may be critical to the success of treatment.

The power of guilt can be immense. Prior to coming to Sarajevo, I (SR) thought the primary trauma of most of the people I would encounter would be the threats and dangers to their lives. What I found was that many people had adapted, to a greater or lesser extent, to those threats and dangers but had far greater difficulty with danger to others. This was particularly true of parents who had felt unable to protect their children and often had to agonize over the decision to send them out of the country.

In his work with combat veterans, Kubany (1994) has developed one of the most comprehensive summaries of the sources of war-related guilt. These sources include survivor guilt, unrealistic expectations of knowledge or skill, forced choice situations with no good options, negligence or incompetence, insufficient performance, pleasure in violence, commission of atrocities, and guilt about numbing of responsiveness at the time of the experience. These self-defined sources are logically driven, though the logic may be based on incomplete or erroneous information. In other words, the cognitive elements are paramount. There may even be a tendency for guilt to become worse over time as the individual continues to see that he or she has failed to develop an adequate corrective response and continues to engage in self-punishing behavior.

Resolution of guilt, therefore, requires either a reinterpretation of the traumatic event or the development of a corrective plan of action that will satisfy the individual's moral sense. Kubany's approach, while based on the correction of flaws in logic common to many cognitive therapies, is also firmly linked to specific traumatic events. This is an advantage because attempts to introduce positive self-appraisals without consideration of the meaning of the event tend to be rejected by clients.

THERAPIST ISSUES

Clients who feel guilty about their experiences often have difficulty articulating those feelings. They are extremely sensitive to the reactions of others, sometimes to the point of developing quasi-paranoid beliefs about what people can see in them, a "mark of Cain," so to speak. The response of the therapist to these issues can assist the client in resolving them or it can be counterproductive, resulting in the client's shutting down or avoiding further treatment.

The first mistake a therapist can make is to miss the issue of guilt completely. This is easy to do because clients sometimes present the issue in veiled form. They may focus on events that, however traumatic they may sound to the therapist, are a less threatening focus for the client. If therapists settle into working on these events, they may miss the ones that are most disturbing and the effectiveness of treatment will be compromised.

Clients, especially those who have had negative therapeutic experiences in the past, may try to "sound out" the therapist by making an indirect reference to feelings of guilt and waiting for a response. They may refer to "things I'm not ready to talk about," or "things I'm not comfortable with," or even simply "things I've done." These innocuous sounding comments may come up at the very end of a session. It is important that the therapist respond to these messages immediately, even if only to say that she or he is willing to return to this topic when the client is ready. While this is a critical treatment issue, consideration must be given to the client's sense of control. A receptive, rather than eager, attitude works well.

Guilt can be an uncomfortable topic for therapists as well as clients. While most clinicians approach problems like anxiety and depression with confidence, they may have doubts about their ability to address guilt successfully. They may also be uncomfortable addressing moral issues, seeing this as something that is more properly addressed by the clergy. As a result they may end up steering clients away from discussion of guilt toward more familiar problems. Highly structured psychoeducational approaches to trauma treatment may have the effect of preempting discussion of complex issues of guilt altogether.

Who Am I to Offer Resolution?

Therapists may also struggle with the determination of the appropriate resolution for their clients—usually far more than the clients know. Mental health professionals often feel unqualified to grapple with religious questions, existential issues, relationships with God, forgiveness and its attainment, and questions about the meaning of suffering. On a personal level they may feel uncomfortable occupying a position of authority and speaking to these and related issues. To avoid the discomfort, they may sidestep the client's issues.

Blaming the Victim

Instead of shutting the issue down or steering the client away from it, some therapists place the blame for the experience on the client. This happens because these therapists find the occurrence of such events disturbing and want to protect themselves from the implication that such awful things might happen to anyone. Rather than face the invalidation of the perspective that the universe is a just place where one's fate is under one's control, these therapists will convince themselves that the client did something to cause the traumatic event. This position leads them to try to move the client's thinking in a particular direction, that is, to admit that what happened was the result of the client's actions, which others, such as the therapist, would be unlikely to commit.

Rushing the Resolution

Another common mistake therapists make is to rush when they encounter the problem of guilt. It is natural for helpers to want their clients to feel better quickly, but the tendency to push for a quick resolution can lead to some problems.

First, clients may resist if they get the impression that the therapist is trying to "whitewash" their experience by minimizing their sense of responsibility. Blanket statements like "It wasn't your fault" or "You couldn't have known," if delivered prematurely, almost always fail because clients know the statements are based on a limited knowledge of the event. They may also resist because they see the therapist as someone who is attempting to reassure them by overriding their sense of right and wrong. It can be helpful for the therapist to inform clients that this is not their intent.

It is possible to talk about guilt in metaphorical terms. We might liken the feeling of guilt to a smoke or burglar alarm, which serves the purpose of protecting people from harm. Alarms are often placed in areas of greatest risk. If one is a heavy sleeper, it may be important to set the alarm so it is very loud. If one is a light sleeper, it may be possible to decrease the volume. Once the sleeper is awake and aware of the problem, an alarm that is too loud may have a paralyzing effect, keeping the person from responding appropriately to the crisis. It would be foolish to disable such a useful device, but it makes good sense to calibrate it so that it leads to a correct course of action. Hearing this, clients are reassured that we are not going to try to exonerate them of a sense of responsibility for their actions, but will help them review the issue in detail if necessary.

Therapists are often advocates for their clients. They care about them both in terms of how they cope with the problems they bring to therapy and how the rest of the world regards them. Given the tendency of many to blame the victim, some therapists may take the position that their clients are never guilty and should never feel guilty. While it is true that blaming is not helpful for resolution, what a client feels is what a client feels. The therapist's view of the inappropriateness of that emotional reaction and the internal judgment behind it will, in and of itself, do little to change the client's view. Indeed, insisting that the client only view herself or himself as, for example, a victim rather than a perpetrator, may exacerbate guilt.

It may be, of course, that the client, because of decisions made at the time of the trauma experience, did contribute to it and perhaps was an actual perpetrator. Efforts to talk such clients into believing something else will conflict with their fundamental moral and value systems. Challenging their sense of right and wrong is likely not only to fail but also to alienate clients from the therapist. If the therapist is particularly adamant or strident in presenting his or her position, clients may eventually feel coerced into stating what they believe the therapist wants to hear.

On the other hand, let us assume that a client had absolutely no responsibility for what took place yet still believes that he or she was at fault in some way. Most therapists are familiar with the difficulty of convincing clients that they should not feel a particular way. Guilt is one of the more difficult emotions to change. Clients will often admit that they are wrong to consider themselves guilty for the actions of others or situations in which they had no control, but, nonetheless, that is how they feel. This is sometimes related to their need for a sense of control during the event or series of events. While an unrealistic sense of control may help reduce a person's anxiety during a traumatic event, that individual pays a price for it later in terms of a deep-seated sense of responsibility and guilt. Encountering such situations, the therapist may feel frustrated. Inherent in this frustration is the belief, often unconscious, that the therapist knows what is best for the client, including the nature and kind of resolution.

Overestimating One's Objectivity

Therapists, being human, have moral perspectives of their own. When encountering clients whose behavior violates that morality, they are challenged to put aside judgments in order to work effectively. For some therapists this is extremely difficult. One VA psychologist stated that she admired others' work with Vietnam War veterans, then made a point of stating that she refused to work with any because, "My sympathy is with the victims." Her self-awareness was unusual. Listening to discussions of such matters among mental health professionals makes it clear that most view themselves as morally objective and not at all influenced by their moral systems, much less countertransference in general, in their work with clients. It is better to acknowledge one's limitations and avoid working with such a population than to work without awareness of the problems that could be created.

This lack of self-awareness is dangerous to the therapeutic relationship. However successful a therapist thinks she or he is at presenting an objective countenance, the reality is that trauma survivors are extremely sensitive to the reactions of others. It will not take long for the client to understand the actual perspective of the therapist. Even if this does not occur, the subtle influence of the therapist's own reactions to the client, especially those coming from moral judgments, may lead the client to resolutions acceptable to the therapist but inappropriate for the client.

On a societal level war and terrorism events are distinct when compared to other trauma sources. A car crash, a robbery, or a natural disaster can be terrible experiences. Whether accidental or deliberate, such experiences are not aimed at an entire society. But war is between societies, and terrorism is always aimed at the society beyond the targeted individuals. Consequently, when treating survivors of war and terrorism, therapists are hearing about events most likely not experienced firsthand, but that involve them as members of the affected society. A good example of this is the Vietnam War. Having observed the reactions of Americans who never set foot in Southeast Asia, we contend that all Americans who lived through the period 1965–1975, and perhaps beyond, were veterans of that war. Society in general responded to those terrible years as though a traumatized individual does, with responses that included feelings of guilt. Such feelings can result in denial, avoidance, and other reactions which negatively affect the therapeutic relationship.

Therapist Resolution

Self-awareness is important for any therapist working with trauma survivors. Personal reactions must be understood, not so they can be eliminated but so they can be directed and, if necessary, kept out of the way.

It does not matter whether one has undergone the experiences of the client. While it is true that the client's perception of such sharing may result in a slightly more open door initially, in the long run it makes little difference. As we have discussed, what does matter is competence, commitment, and compassion. With those everything is possible; without them, nothing will take place. The presence of the last two will make up for deficits in the first, for they are the most critical and the ones the client will most immediately recognize as real or false. But commitment and compassion, regardless of the therapy method being used, require self-awareness on the part of the therapist. Serious self-examination, perhaps even engaging in personal therapy, should be a prerequisite for working with these survivors.

Role of Education

Often the client may be operating with misperceptions or inadequate or erroneous information. Providing that information from authoritative sources may permit some resolution and a more realistic appraisal of the individual's personal role.

It is not uncommon for survivors to focus on social or political issues only peripherally related to their individual experience. Anger toward the government and society may be based on legitimate grievances, but often is used as a cover for underlying issues such as guilt. Again, EMDR is effective in cutting through this emotional camouflage, but the process is more efficient if the client is able to access clarifying information. There is, however, a risk in this approach: clarifying information may make the survivor more legitimately angry and provide an even more effective distraction from their other issues. A more useful approach is to simply pose the question of what it means to the client that the government or society may have been wrong in its actions. Steering thinking back to self is more useful than engaging in debates about social or governmental policy.

Using Group Therapy

Part of the difficulty in discussing, even approaching, guilt is that many clients see themselves as totally unique in their experience—not just that the experience has never happened to anyone else, but that their behavior at the time and their reactions since are dissimilar from those of other survivors. Here involvement in group therapy is useful. It is one thing to have information provided by the therapist or through bibliotherapy—these sources are helpful, to be sure, but personal contact with other survivors provides the same information more powerfully.

ATONEMENT AS AN ALTERNATIVE TO PUNISHMENT

Clients are often hampered in their struggle to identify a different perspective, a positive cognition, because they do not see any alternative to either ignoring the experience, impossible and morally unacceptable, or self-punishment, dysfunctional and nonproductive. But there is an alternative path, one of atonement. Introducing the concept to a client takes careful timing, as will be made clear below, but it offers the possibility of expanding the client's perspective so that new ideas and new information may be made available for processing. I (SMS) used this approach before training in EMDR, as shown in this case history.

The client was a Vietnam War veteran who had been working on a combat trauma. At about the time he had reached eleven months in the field, his unit was ordered to sweep through a village and search for enemy arms and supply caches. When they approached the village, several snipers opened fire on his squad and pinned them down behind the dikes of several dry rice paddies. For several hours they lay in the sun until other parts of their unit forced the snipers to withdraw. At this point his unit went into a line formation. He was on the extreme right side of the line. as it moved forward into the village.

The villagers were being very careful. All were in their doorways, keeping in sight and making no sudden movements. The Americans carefully checked for hidden supplies, and the soldier was aware that other GIs had found some buried rice near the other side of the line. Suddenly, out of the corner of his right eye, he saw a figure rushing toward him. Instinctively he fired and hit the ground. When there was no return fire, he got to his feet and discovered he had killed a young girl whose age he put at about 11. The child was not carrying a weapon of any kind. Why she was running under those dangerous circumstances was a mystery. He had little emotional response at the time. He recalled one of the other men uttering an expletive when they discovered it was a girl, but no one blamed him.

He said he had no reaction to the incident until his own little girl reached the age of 11. His now-surfaced self-judgment had resulted in prolonged self-punishing behavior in his life, including high-risk behavior, the loss of employment opportunities, and termination of positive relationships.

Using primarily a cognitive approach, I had explored with the veteran the various other elements influencing the event in an effort to gain a realistic self-appraisal. We used a circular diagram that represented the total responsibility for the killing and the veteran marked various pie shaped wedges representing the other elements. These had included the orders he was operating under, the nature of the war in Vietnam, his own psychological and physical fatigue, the necessity of having quick reflexes in combat, and even the girl's family who let her loose while the sweep was going on. The largest "piece" was still his. While he understood cognitively that it was not his fault, he nonetheless continued to blame himself. As he put it, "It was my finger on the trigger."

At one point the veteran remarked, "I wish there was something I could do about it." This comment, almost textbook for war and terrorism survivors, reminded me of something from my previous vocation of historian. I told the veteran the following.

The knights of history were their societies' warriors; their equivalent can be found in all cultures. Because they were skilled with weapons and fighting, they functioned under several moral codes, all designed to serve as brakes on their potential for violence. There was, of course, the personal morality they had learned growing up in their families. Additionally there was formal church law. On top of all that there were the various formal strictures on their behavior that came out of their training as knights, such as the Code of Chivalry. But they were still men and they still erred. Perhaps they would lose their tempers or get drunk or whatever and commit an act of violence. Afterwards they would be particularly distraught, because the strength of their moral systems (and remember, they had three) would be fully felt. Absolution became paramount. Some never found it and spent the rest of their lives wandering the world, disconnected from home, trying to end their agony by finding death in combat.

More often the knights would turn to their local priests. The priests realized these warriors were different from ordinary people. When an ordinary person did something wrong, the priest would prescribe some act of contrition—say some prayers, that sort of thing. If the sin was serious, the priest might prescribe some punishment, ranging from a fine to physical punishment, such as flogging.

The priests recognized that such an approach would not work with these warriors. They had been trained to endure, to suffer, and so pain and punishment would be essentially meaningless to them. After years of training, for example, their designation as a knight included praying all night on their knees clad in iron armor in a stone chapel. They could hold a broadsword, three feet of iron blade, at arm's length for 45 minutes—try holding this book in the same manner. They fought in deserts in armor and typically continued to battle even after receiving multiple wounds.

So punishment would provide no relief to knights. Pain was their profession, in effect, for they had been taught to endure suffering for their people. That is, in fact, what distinguishes a warrior from others—they endure not for themselves but for their people.

What the priests did was to give the knights a task. Instead of punishment, they offered atonement, payback. In some situations this was direct. If the knight had torn up a tavern, he was to go and rebuild it. But the most serious issues could not be addressed directly. It is not possible to go back in time and undo a rape or murder.

However, the priests recognized that the moral scales of the knight were internal and not time-dependent. A scale out of balance remains out of balance until it is rectified, regardless of the time since the unequal weights were applied. One way to rebalance the scales is to take some weight out of the negative side, as in the case of rebuilding the tavern. But where that is not possible the other way to rebalance a scale is to put some weight on the positive side.

And that was the principle behind atonement. The task given by the priests would require the knight to perform some act that would add weight to the positive side of the scales. For example, he might perform six months of guarding the road between the village and the castle of the king, protecting all travelers on it from outlaws, bandits, highwaymen, Robin Hood, and all the other evildoers. So for the next six months the knight would be out there, day and night, in all kinds of weather, and at the end of that time he would know that travelers were still alive and their property safe because of his efforts.

The veteran's reaction to the story was to say he thought it was great and then to ask what was his task. I had no idea and said so, but added that finding the task (and here I borrowed from work with Native American veterans) is part of the quest for atonement. And so it was up to the veteran to find his proper task.

A few months later I ran into the veteran in Philadelphia while doing some liaison work with a local Vet Center. We traveled into North Philadelphia, a pretty beat-up section of town, and he took me for a walk into some of the grimmer areas. He finally stopped at an intersection. I could see the usual row homes, a few of which were boarded-up crack houses, some small stores, a weathered church with one of those inner-city playgrounds attached, and not much else. The veteran turned to me with a big smile and asked, "Well, doc, what do you think?"

At first I had no idea what he was referring to, until the veteran went on to explain that on Saturdays he was a volunteer supervisor for that playground. While he was there no drug dealer, no child molester, no gang recruiter got anywhere near those kids. And at the end of each Saturday, a little more weight got added to the positive side of his scales.

When using this approach, it is important to first address and de-molish the role of self-punishment. We concede that self-punishment, for a given individual and transgression, might work. The way to tell is to see if the level of guilt has risen or declined over time. If it has declined then we can say that they have not done enough and need to do more. If it has increased, then whatever they are doing about the experience is not only failing to resolve it but making things worse. Yes, they undoubtedly have done more of the same in a steady escalation, but it cannot work because the self-punishment, like their original act, is violating their moral code, so the guilt continues to increase.

The three principles of tasks of atonement are:

1. Sacrifice. It should place a demand on the client that would not ordinarily be there.
2. Look outward. It should be something that benefits others.
3. Make use of client abilities. It should be something the client can realistically do, or rapidly obtain the skills to do.

Identifying the proper atonement is part of the task. Clients must search. With the therapist's help they may be able to get a sense of what would be appropriate. The key is that the right task can be identified by clients' reaction to doing it. If it feels appropriate, they are on the right track. Typical tasks have included working for Habitat for Humanity, volunteering in a hospital, volunteering in an animal shelter, helping hospitalized veterans, and many others.

EMDR AND GUILT

Guilt does not end when the experience is over since it is the result of ongoing judgments of self. Until those judgments are resolved, until the emotional system has something different to react to, the feelings of guilt will continue and worsen. So far we have focused on the issues that might impede addressing guilt and developing a context of information to supplement what clients already know. Often clients have sufficient information and need only to process it.

A good example of this is the police officer in Northern Ireland whose colleague was injured by a motorist at a check point. He blamed himself for the accident. Because of the guilt, he had become largely dysfunctional in his relationships and occupation, as he feared making decisions that might result in negative consequences for other people. While using EMDR, he suddenly remembered the first comment of the injured officer: "Forget the doctor; get me a barrister!" The remembered humorous statement came with the realization that the accident was just that, an accident, and he was not to blame. The resolution resulted in changes throughout his life. His wife later remarked, "I have my husband back."

Identifying the Positive Cognition

When doing EMDR, developing a future orientation in the form of a positive cognition may be challenging. Regardless of the source of the guilt, clients may view themselves as undeserving of ever thinking positively of themselves. It often helps to emphasize that the positive cognition is a *desired* way of thinking. The therapist is not asking clients to accept the positive cognition now; he is simply using it to get a sense of where they are at present and as a device to measure their movement.

When the client is struggling to identify a positive cognition, using the negative cognition, with its emphasis on their current negative beliefs about themselves, will often clarify the issue, as in this case example. The client was a Vietnam War veteran whose squad's position had been overrun by the enemy. While he had succeeded in rallying the survivors and forming a defensive position that saved their lives, several men were found the next morning dead, their bodies terribly mutilated. He felt he had failed the dead men and had the additional fear that they were not dead when the Viet Cong got to them and were alive when the atrocities were committed.

TH: So when you think of that experience, what words go with it that express your negative belief about yourself now?
CL: I was a complete fuck-up. A total failure.
TH: Is that how you think now, "I am a total failure"?
CL: Yeah, I guess that's it.
TH: So when you think of that battle, how would you like to think of yourself now?
CL: "Like to think"? I don't even like thinking about it. What do you mean?
TH: What would you prefer to be thinking about yourself, now, when you think about it?

CL: You mean like thinking I did a good job or something?

TH: Yes. A more positive view of yourself.

CL: That's impossible. I fucked up. Nothing positive about the whole thing.

TH: So you are left with, "I am a total failure." But if you could, how would like to be able to think of yourself now?

CL: How would I like to think? I'd like to think I didn't fail, I'm not a failure.

TH: Something like, "I'm OK" or "I do all right"?

CL: Yeah, I do OK.

TH: When you think of that battle and hold that with the words, "I do OK," using the scale where one equals feeling totally false and seven equals feeling totally true, on that scale, how true do those words feel to you, now?

CL: Maybe a two.

If the client has been introduced to the concept of atonement it may facilitate the formation of the positive cognition. Typical positive cognitions coming out of this include:

- I can balance my scales.
- I can help others.
- I can repair the damage I have caused.

Nondisclosure

What can sometimes be a critical advantage of EMDR processing is the fact that the client does not need to disclose the details of the event. Processing is essentially internal. In some instances, particular experiences with resultant guilt or shame have been treated without the clients' providing specific details.

We caution against utilizing this approach too quickly, however. It is important to ascertain the reasons for the lack of disclosure, as they may have relevance later during treatment. For example, if the reason is the lack of a strong therapeutic relationship, this may have an impact if the client abreacts during processing. The therapist will naturally encourage the client to continue, but if sufficient trust in the relationship is lacking, the client will stop processing.

It is usually best to approach this subject directly. Inform clients that they control how much they will tell the therapist. Explain that the therapist understands that clients may fear repercussions about disclosing the specifics of particular experiences, or that clients may fear the reactions of others toward them because of surviving some kinds of events. Therapists may point out that their relationship with the client requires that they be nonjudgmental, but they recognize that is easier said than done and so the client's caution is understood and respected. Finally, therapists need to explain that, whatever the reason for withholding information, however legitimate, their primary concern is that the client trusts their advice concerning EMDR processing. If the client accepts this last point, then processing may continue.

Clients who have been in therapy previously may find this stance unusual. Typical therapy requires self-disclosure. EMDR does as well, but the audience is narrowed to only one—the client. The client is sometimes reassured to hear that the therapist is essentially a coach, not a judge. Helping clients understand this important concept provides protection and empowerment.

The issue of nondisclosure comes up more commonly among terrorism survivors than among war survivors, because of the potential for retribution. Terrorism works because it recognizes no front lines. Its covert nature often means that anyone, a relative, friend, neighbor, or even therapist, may have some kind of link to the other side. The danger of secrets becoming known in some environments can be very real. In this sort of situation, it may be advantageous for the therapist to be able to provide treatment without knowing the specifics.

The same principle of continued processing without disclosure may come into play if new material surfaces that the client feels cannot be shared. This will usually appear as a block to processing, but discussion with the client should rapidly make clear the concern. Again, the guidelines described above about how to present the therapist's position should be followed.

Cognitive Interweave and Guilt

When actual blocks to processing occur, the therapist has a variety of ways to respond. There is no substitute for the clinical skills of the therapist in identifying the block. Often it takes careful phrasing, a solid therapeutic relationship, and an awareness of the client's verbal and nonverbal communication to identify the block. Its identification and articulation may help the client.

The basic EMDR protocols for blocked responses should be the first response, because they are the least intrusive techniques. Their successful utilization leaves the client with a better sense of personal empowerment. However, because of the severity and complexity of war and terrorism trauma reactions, the basic responses to blocked processing may be insufficient. Also, in some instances of ongoing situations, particularly in mass situations, increased efficiency and speed may require a more active role by the therapist. This means using the cognitive interweave.

The introduction of the cognitive interweave may be preceded by some discussion and information-gathering. While the general style in EMDR work is to be as minimally intrusive as possible, preparation for the intervention may require some time, particularly when new information is being presented. For instance, one veteran was feeling deep guilt because, during a situation in which he killed a large number of enemy soldiers, he felt not just excited but actually happy. During processing he had blocked on the thought "I must be a monster for feeling good about all that death." The therapist provided information on the biology of reactions in combat, including the role of endorphins and adrenaline, as well as the psychological and emotional relief at surviving and removing a danger, the reinforcements in the military for that behavior, and how these things make use of and impact on our evolutionarily developed brains. The presentation was summarized with the comment, "So your emotions are just how you feel, not who you are." When the client indicated that this idea might be acceptable, he was asked to focus on it and eye movements resumed. Processing continued normally after that. While the overt cognitive interweave was the summary comment, clearly the intervention was dependent upon the entire presentation.

Again, the goal is to provide the impetus for continued processing by offering information or perspective in a short presentation. Initial total acceptance of the new idea is not necessary; minimal acknowledgment that it may be possible is enough. Likewise, an elaborate debate is both unnecessary and potentially counterproductive. The time spent in debate works against processing by permitting a gathering of defenses. If the therapist "wins" the debate, the client loses not just his view but his sense of empowerment. Finally, a debating approach presumes that the offered intervention is the final goal. All it is designed to do is to initiate processing when it is blocked or to accelerate processing when circumstances require.

It is probably unnecessary to state that the goal is not the eradication of appropriate guilt. From an EMDR perspective, that is impossible. We cannot remove that which is appropriate for a client. Moreover, the resolution of guilt is brought about not by the erasing of the events but rather by the discovery of an appropriate level of responsibility and the development of an appropriate response to that responsibility. Often, it is true, trauma survivors, especially those surviving war and terrorism, judge themselves guilty completely inappropriately by any objective criteria. EMDR may help these clients come to understand this. But there are clients who have committed real acts that violated their own senses of correct behavior. Their problem is not their moral sense but their difficulty in finding a coherent and positive way of responding to it. EMDR will help these clients take on the appropriate level of responsibility and response. It is not the therapist's job to offer absolution or condemnation— the first is impossible and the second inappropriate. The therapist assists clients in discovering their own unique, and sometimes startling, resolutions.

A way of organizing cognitive interweaves pertaining to guilt is to use the model of guilt types proposed by Kubany (1994). This may permit the EMDR clinician to better tailor the cognitive interweave. Below we offer some possible cognitive interweaves for Kubany's types of guilt. The reader will note that we tend to use questions. While this is somewhat a reflection of our personal styles, it is also a recognition of survivors' need to be in control—developing an answer is more empowering than having one supplied.

1. *Survivor guilt.* Being a survivor may be a source of guilt for several different reasons. There is the negative self-judgment coming out of relief at not being the one killed. Such feelings may be viewed as unworthy, even unacceptable. A successful cognitive interweave for blocks of this type will enables clients to see themselves as they were then from their current perspective. "Bring up your picture of that person you were then, right after it all happened. What could you tell him that would help him understand what he's feeling?"

Of course, often the most powerful issue for survivors is the justification for surviving. In effect, an existential crisis is blocking processing, because clients cannot identify a meaning for their life. Changing perspective, always a powerful tool of cognitive interweaves, can be introduced in this fashion: "Suppose you had been the one to die, while your friend had lived, and he ended up in the chair you are now sitting in with the same questions you are struggling with. What would you say to your friend about what he should be doing with his life?"

2. "*I should have known better*." Despite having made a reasonable decision at the time, the outcome was bad. There may have been no chance of a positive outcome, but clients may not be able to see that and be stuck on the idea that they should have known the unknowable and somehow made a better choice. It is a prosurvival perspective, especially in combat, to believe one can at least accurately predict and at best control events. To think otherwise might result in a fatalism that could be disastrous. This perspective may carry over long after the experience itself and result in resistance to the idea that, in war and terrorism situations, very little is either predictable or controllable. A cognitive interweave might be aimed at linking them to a broader, more realistic appraisal of themselves and forgo any direct confrontation of their perspective on the experience: "What other choices could you have made? How could you have known their consequences?"

3. *Impossible choices*. In situations where the individual was "damned if you do, damned if you don't," the block may be a reflection of the powerlessness such situations can breed. Whatever they are confronting therapeutically becomes blocked by their fear that whatever they do will be wrong. The cognitive interweave suggested for the situation described above might be useful in this situation as well; however, because the individual knows that the alternative choices would have had bad results, another cognitive interweave might be more useful, one that focuses on the situation rather than the individual. The goal is to widen the perspective of the experience so the client can see that what once was is no longer. One of the best ways to accomplish this is to let the client do it: "So what are the differences between the experience and today?"

4. *Error*. The client did something wrong because of incompetence or an error in judgment. The negative self-judgment resulting from

this can result in a block that simply holds that the client does not deserve to get better. Sometimes the error results largely from circumstances, such as physical and psychological state, as well as inadequate preparation or insufficient knowledge. A Socratic line of questioning is often a useful cognitive interweave: "What didn't you have that would have allowed you to make the correct decision?" (Client responds.) "What kept you from getting it?" (Client responds.) "And how would have known you would need it?"

On the other hand, information, training, and other deficits may not be contributors to the erroneous decision. Instead, clients may have known what to do but did not do it. Their perspective may be that they were too scared or too lazy or too irresponsible to function adequately. A two-phase approach is often useful. First, we link to a broader perspective by using the cognitive interweave, "What were the outcomes of the decisions you made in other situations?" This is followed by a cognitive interweave aimed at gaining a broader perspective of the situation: "So what caused the difference between how you were in those decisions and how you were for this decision?"

5. "*I should have done more.*" Most often this perspective arises from situations in which the individual did all that was humanly possible. Hostages literally held at gunpoint, medics treating fatally wounded soldiers, and survivors of a school shooting are typical candidates for this kind of judgment and resultant feelings of guilt. Clients may be unable to recognize what they actually accomplished: the school shooting survivors got themselves and others out of the building, the medics successfully treated other soldiers, and the hostages managed to stay alive by not provoking the terrorists. For these survivors, there is sometimes an underlying belief that the only way they could ever be sure they had done enough was to have died.

The demands such survivors have placed on themselves might appear to be almost magical in nature, requiring skills and abilities they could not be expected to possess. These demands are, to a large extent, a reflection of a need to control events. This need can be pronounced in war and terrorism survivors because of those experiences. The idea of living in an uncontrolled world is so threatening after going through those experiences they would rather, in an unconscious manner, live with the feelings of guilt for not having done enough.

Cognitive interweaves addressing blocks caused by such thinking seek to broaden the perspectives of self and the experience. Another approach is aimed at the unrealistic demand the client may have engaged by using the "I'm confused" cognitive interweave: "I'm confused. Are you saying that, even though you were an unarmed school teacher with no combat training, you were supposed to take down two heavily armed gunmen?"

6. *The pleasure of violence.* In situations where the survivors had the opportunity to fight back against the enemy and even kill, their positive reaction to doing so may leave them with a conflict. One should not feel good about taking lives. Their pleasure brands them as psychopathic monsters.

An educational approach is often useful for this type of guilt. Clients may not be aware that their emotional reaction at the time was affected by the sheer relief of surviving the experience, and they may not be aware of the effects of physiological changes the body undergoes during its preparation for "fight or flight." These hormonal surges are generally experienced as positive sensations. Once the information is provided, a good cognitive interweave might make use of the client's here and now judgment: "Is a real monster bothered by what they did in the past?"

7. *Participation in atrocity.* Those who have never been in an experience of war or terrorism may be convinced that they will never be involved in an atrocity. Such people have not discovered that the most terrible thing about these experiences is finding that few people are immune to the brutalization of the spirit by war and terrorism. Nonetheless, clients who have participated in an atrocity often view themselves as fundamentally flawed and outside the mainstream. After all, normal people would not do such things.

Prior to learning EMDR we found this kind of guilt exceptionally difficult to treat. Instead of making a direct assault on the formidable nature of this kind of judgment, we often introduce the concept of atonement when a block around this theme occurs. This naturally progresses to cognitive interweaves that make use of the experience as a way of furthering growth: "Now that you know what can happen to people in those kinds of circumstances, what do you want to do with that knowledge?"

8. *"I should have felt worse."* This judgment is made in response to the muting or numbing of reaction during an experience. This muted responsiveness may persist for years, until some life event serves as a

trigger for the surfacing of the experience. This type of guilt that benefit from some education on the prosurvival usefulness of muting emotional reactions while in the trauma environment. Clients may know of others who were unable to restrain their reactions, which resulted in negative consequences. An empowering approach builds on this information and introduces a cognitive interweave with positive implications for how they are dealing with life today: "So maybe this was just you taking care of yourself?"

"USING THE BAD FOR GOOD"

Survivors often need to formulate some sort of a response to their experiences and resulting guilt feelings, that is, to incorporate a behavioral response into their cognitive restructuring. Certainly atonement speaks to this change in behavior and may be applicable to many of the types of guilt presented above.

Conceptually, resolution of guilt is found in learning about oneself, life, and the world, and putting that learning to use. After clients resolve guilt associated with trauma, it is helpful to ask what they are going to do with that resolution. Has it resulted in changes in how they are going to treat others or themselves? The goal is to have clients consider more thoroughly where they want to go with their lives now. Resolution of guilt does not have to be a purely retrospective event; it can be the basis for future growth. People who have survived the worst of life and who have powerful moral systems at the heart of judgments and guilt are a valuable resource for themselves, the people around them, and the world in general. Helping them understand that the experiences they have been through, while painful, may be the foundation on which they build lives of integrity can be a useful avenue of exploration using EMDR. We recommend making this an element to be explored prior to terminating treatment for individuals for whom guilt has been a major component of their reaction.

"Using the bad for good," as one survivor of a terrorist bombing put it, may be an initially difficult concept for clients to grasp if they have not gotten to it spontaneously. A good example of this was a client who had been a career soldier. He joined the Army during Vietnam and stayed in, retiring shortly after his participation in the Persian Gulf War. While in Vietnam he had been involved in an incident he later came to regret and, after his release from active duty and the structure that had provided, the array of symptoms associated with PTSD had emerged, most painfully guilt.

While in the Gulf an incident occurred that illustrates the concept of using the bad for good, of the trauma experience being transformed into a learning experience. He was overseeing a group of young GIs, part of an infantry unit that was gathering Iraqi soldiers who were emerging from trenches and bunkers to surrender. The Iraqis, many of whom were in shock from the bombing and shelling and deprived of sleep, food, and water, were very fearful of falling into American hands.

One of the Iraqi soldiers stepped out of the column, which was being shepherded to the rear, and approached an American private. In his cupped hands he carried a small book, which later turned out to be a soldier's copy of the Koran.

Those who were not there tend to remember the Gulf War as fast, efficient, successful, and not terribly difficult. We forget what life was like for the allied troops prior to the launching of the ground war. Iraq, it was said at the time, had the world's fourth largest army, which was combat experienced and not above using chemical weapons against external and internal enemies. News commentators said that it would be a bloody and prolonged conflict, with as many as ten thousand Americans returning home in body bags. For the troops on the ground, including the young American private, it was a time of waiting and anxiety in the hostile environment of the desert. When the ground war began, the troops experienced a myriad of feelings.

Many of those feelings were undoubtedly swirling in that private the Iraqi approached. So when the Iraqi came up to him with his hands extended, the GI, impatient and pent-up, used his rifle to knock the book into the sand and to push the Iraqi back toward the column of prisoners.

The veteran sergeant saw what he did. Quickly he went to the young private and ordered him to pick up the book and give it back to the Iraqi. Discipline held. Muttering under his breath, the GI picked up the book, dusted it off, and walked over and gave it to the Iraqi. During treatment the veteran sergeant was able to integrate the experiences of Vietnam and the intervention with the young GI and tell the therapist, "I saved that young man thirty years of grief." The sergeant understood, because of his own experiences on the battle-field, how quickly behavior can escalate and lead to unnecessary brutality. He used that understanding to help someone else.

This is the principle of using the bad for good and serves the function of atonement. It is common for war and terrorism survivors spontaneously to discover this concept during EMDR processing. When they do not, the therapist may find it useful to introduce it. Once it is introduced, then eye movements can be done to help develop it. Occasionally, going into the future like this will reveal other material for resolution, which is, of course, all to the good.

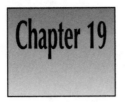

Chapter 19

ANGER

"I sometimes think the only thing I can feel is how angry I am."

SOURCES OF ANGER

In the *DSM-IV*, poorly controlled anger is listed, along with hyper-vigilance, decreased concentration, startle response, and sleep distur-bance, as a symptom related to persistent physiological hyperarousal. In this conceptualization, posttraumatic anger is regarded as a form of residual "survivor mode" functioning. There is some empirical support for this view, since individuals with PTSD are more attentive to trauma-related stimuli and have a greater tendency to see neutral stimuli as threatening (McNally, Kaspi, Riemann, & Zeitlin, 1990; Trandel & McNally, 1987). It could be argued that treatment should be focused on teaching clients skills to offset this defensive cognitive bias and to reduce arousal.

While this conceptualization is certainly accurate as far as it goes, it is incomplete. We suggest that clinicians working with war survi-vors approach posttraumatic anger on three levels: anger as a defense against physical threat, anger as a defense against other incapacitating emotions, and anger as a rational response to man-made catastrophe.

Anger can easily serve as a means of physical self-protection. The "fight or flight" response has long been recognized as an adaptive response that mobilizes mental and physical resources toward neu-tralizing a threat. Shapiro's basic EMDR model views clients' current problems, including the tendency to respond to current situations with inappropriately high levels of emotion, as the result of information dysfunctionally stored in the nervous system. It assumes that processing the trauma memory will in itself eliminate the threat appraisal cognitive bias. In some cases this seems to be exactly what happens. One veteran, during an EMDR session that was focused on a recent confrontation with a supervisor, found himself recalling an incident in Vietnam when he almost shot a civilian to avenge the death of a friend. Once he processed the earlier incident he reported a powerful sense of confidence and was able to resolve workplace disputes without having to resort to physical intimidation.

It is easy to see how anger is an advantage to someone who is physically threatened, but it is not unusual to encounter clients who use anger to protect themselves from other emotions, such as fear, grief, and guilt. For example, many individuals exposed to repeated life threats find they are able to override their fear by becoming angry. This is probably not a conscious decision. As one client said, "It's like hitting a switch, the fear just shuts off." Once discovered, this effect is not forgotten and may be relied on whenever the individual feels threatened. This response is rapid and automatic, which is why standard anger management interventions often fail with this population.

Just as fear can be incapacitating, so can grief. Taking time to grieve in a war situation can be dangerous. Instead, survivors may fix their attention on anger, which may encourage revenge behavior. This allows them to feel less helpless temporarily, but in the long run it inhibits the grieving process.

For some clients, anger is the outward projection of the negative feelings they have about themselves. Such feelings can be intolerable. Anger at oneself, guilt, may result in suicidal behaviors or subtler forms of self-destructive behavior, such as substance abuse. Because of its strong physiological component, anger can serve as an excellent distraction from the underlying guilt. Survivors may also find that they can reduce their sense of guilt by focusing on the shortcomings of others.

None of these observations should blind the therapist to the possibility that clients may have some legitimate anger about their experiences. We have defined a trauma as an experience that violates an individual's basic assumptions about oneself and the world. Just as a violation of one's beliefs about safety can lead to anxiety, violations of one's beliefs about power and fairness can lead to anger. Since the traumas of war are man-made, it is reasonable to expect a certain amount of anger in response. These reactions often center on betrayal, mistreatment by those in authority, and actions of perpetrators. Clients are living with the knowledge that their world view has been violated and that they may not have responded coherently or adequately. Such clients may perceive the therapist's attempt to alleviate their symptoms as an attempt to "make nice" with aspects of human behavior that are unacceptable.

There may also be an existential aspect to survivors' anger. Existential anger is anger toward the universe or toward the clients' God or Higher Power. The challenge to clients' moral sense is such they may be unable to make use of perspectives and understandings that helped them in the past. They may find, for example, that it is impossible to call on God for assistance when their anger is directed at that God.

The issues generating the anger may, of course, be out of conscious awareness. Rage reactions in response to otherwise nonthreatening triggers may be present, as Frances Yoeli has noted in her work with trauma survivors who have often attempted to suppress those reactions with substance abuse. Focusing on these triggers when the particulars of the initiating experience are unknown typically results in clarification of the role of anger for a client.

CLINICAL CHALLENGES

Working on anger poses numerous challenges to the clinician. It is not always easy to recognize anger in traumatized clients. Many of them have had at least one incident where they have overreacted and lost control of themselves. This can be a deeply disturbing experience. As a result, they may have gotten into a pattern of suppressing their anger. It may come out in indirect ways that the therapist doesn't identify. They may have lost relationships because of poorly regulated anger and fear its expression toward the therapist. Some clients are even afraid that they might hurt the therapist physically. Even when clients are aware of being angry, they may be quite apprehensive about expressing it or even admitting to its existence for fear of losing control. Just talking about it, they fear, may be enough to permit it to explode.

The potential for the therapist to become uneasy with clients' anger should not be overlooked. It is a natural impulse to become defensive or placating. Therapists may also be apprehensive about opening up the anger because they are afraid it will escalate outside the office. Unfortunately, these reactions preempt the exploration of the anger.

In order for the therapist and client to feel confident in approaching anger, it is necessary to spend some time discussing goals. If clients get the impression that the therapist is afraid or is trying to take away a necessary defense, they may shut down or become resistant. Many clients are concerned that their justifiable grievances will be dismissed as entirely symptomatic. Before starting EMDR it is important to discuss the positive and negative aspects of anger and to define a reasonable goal as gaining control of anger rather than eliminating it. Along with this can come training in anger management techniques that clients can use between sessions.

EMDR requires clients to "go with" feelings they may usually try to suppress. The therapist can help the client feel safer by doing some preliminary exploration using some questions from the EMDR protocol. For example, when the client is describing a recent episode of anger, the therapist can ask, "When have you felt this way before?" or "When were you angriest during the war?" or "Where do you feel that in your body?" and follow these questions with some discussion of the responses. The therapist's willingness to discuss anger helps to reassure the client that the therapist is not going to back away from it or them.

Gender and cultural variables may influence the presentation of anger. Among male war veterans, for example, we have observed that anger often appears as an surface presentation, with other emotions encountered beneath it. Among women veterans, on the other hand, anger and the other emotions may be presented essentially side by side, with the client moving between them quite readily. This probably reflects the cultural influence that makes anger a more acceptable emotion for men and the emotions of grief and loss more acceptable for women. We see all of these emotions as reactions to the issues of meaning.

EMDR TREATMENT RESPONSES

Exploring anger and the issues it comes from illustrates some general principles of trauma treatment. We can see why desensitization is insufficient, since the issues of meaning are not addressed. Behavior therapies for PTSD are based on repeatedly exposing the client to the trauma memory. While this is effective at reducing anxiety, it has been found to be less effective at reducing posttraumatic anger. Clinicians using exposure therapy are not advised to explore clients' reports of anger; instead they are encouraged to redirect clients back to the anxiety-provoking aspect of the trauma memory.

Cognitive therapists treating PTSD have also found anger to be challenging. In cognitive therapy, clients are usually trained to monitor their reactions to current situations, identify distortions in their thinking, and to practice counteracting these distortions with corrective ideas supplied to them by the therapist. Clients may also be trained in relaxation. We found this approach effective, but it is a slow and effortful process for clients. While cognitive therapy directly addresses the issue of meaning, it does not always do so in the context of specific traumatic experiences.

One of EMDR's strengths is that it is an "inside out" therapy. That is, clients discover new meaning from within their own experiences. Because EMDR allows (indeed, requires) the resolution of the trauma experience to be discovered and generated from within the client, issues of control are greatly reduced. While we stress this throughout our review of the EMDR protocol with clients, it is particularly important, when dealing with war and terrorism survivors struggling with anger and rage, to emphasize that the goal is to allow them to do their own healing and to reach a resolution that is appropriate for them.

If clients express a fear that if they work on that anger they may lose control, it may be reassuring to reacquaint them with the stop signal and its function. Likewise, education in tension reduction techniques as a way of dealing with clients' fear of anger can be useful and reassuring. Education in EMDR for clients should emphasize the comparative speed of getting through their anger and the underlying, additional emotions, including ones perceived as dangerous.

The therapist should avoid going into processing with a preconceived end point in mind. For example, forgiveness may be an appropriate resolution for some clients, but it will not be appropriate for all. Therapists should be careful not to stop processing prematurely because they believe clients need to hang onto some of their anger. Therapists should also be prepared to encounter a strong somatic component when processing anger memories.

Anger is likely to come up first during the assessment phase, as clients develop the negative and positive cognitions. Individuals who are stuck in anger are usually externally focused; that is, they are likely to come up with negative cognitions about the behavior of other people. On the other hand, the EMDR protocol calls for a negative cognition about oneself. This request in itself may prompt a shift in clients' perspective and allow for an exploration of other feelings. Even when negative cognitions are readily accessible, problems may arise with the positive cognition. If anger has served the function of self-protection, a future-oriented positive cognition might be perceived as a threat. After all, clients may believe the therapist is making them vulnerable by asking them to drop the shield of anger. From clients' perspective, anger that is appropriate must be maintained. To lose it would mean abandoning the righteous issue and giving in to the perpetrators or otherwise engaging in an act of betrayal. For some, righteous anger may be so strong that identification of a negative cognition may be problematic. The client might perceive the negative cognition as an admission of culpability; therefore, the therapist must be prepared to take his or her time in explaining and developing the negative and positive cognitions and may have to settle for less-than-optimal cognitions at the beginning of desensitization.

The following cases illustrate the influence of anger on the identification of negative and positive cognitions and some typical interventions.

In the first case, the client was a war veteran. His squad had been assigned a soldier who apparently was borderline mentally retarded, a very unusual circumstance. The other members of the squad had been together for some time and were fairly closely knit. One of the other soldiers continually harassed the new man, who was clearly confused and fearful. Though he was tempted to intervene, finding the harassment offensive, the client elected to do nothing about the situation because he did not wish to offend the other soldier, to whom he felt loyalty.

When a sudden firefight began, the new soldier froze and did not know what to do. The soldier who had been harassing him yelled for him to take cover behind a fallen tree, but he was so terrified of the situation and distrustful of the soldier that he could not decide what to do and remained standing in the open. Before anyone could get to him, enemy fire killed him. The client remembered the expression on the new man's face as he looked at the soldier who had harassed him and felt that the man had not known whether or not to trust the soldier. The client thought, that if he had intervened, the harassment could have been stopped and the new man would have learned to trust the soldier instead of hesitating and dying.

He sought admission to an inpatient PTSD program with the primary goal of reducing the anger he carried around inside of himself. Evaluations had found the usual constellation of symptoms present, including nightmares, sleep disturbances, and hyperalertness. His behavior over the years was marked by ever increasing isolation and withdrawal from others. He was aware of this behavior and described it as resulting from his fear that "I'm going to blow up on someone and hurt them." In point of fact, in the thirty years since the war he had physically assaulted other men twice and two or three times a year would have a violent verbal explosion.

He initially stated that he did not understand where his anger was coming from or why it had persisted through all the years since the war. He also said he was not aware of any pattern to his acts of physical or verbal violence, though during the development of his history it appeared to his therapist that the anger was usually elicited in circumstances where someone other than the client had been threatened.

He identified the killing of the new man as the most traumatic event in his war experiences and, after discussion of the pros and cons, elected to work on that experience first.

TH: What picture do you get that represents that incident?

CL: I can see that poor guy just standing there, out in the open, kind of bent over, a look of terror on his face. He doesn't know what to do. I'm yelling at him but he can't hear me, I'm not close enough.

TH: When you hold that picture in your mind, what kind of statement or judgment about yourself do you make now?

CL: I let him down. I was the sergeant. I was supposed to be in charge. I could have prevented the whole thing if I'd done something in the beginning.

TH: You said you let him down—so how does that lead you to think about yourself now?

CL: I'm no good. I might as well have shot him myself. *(Hands clench into fists, jaw tightens)*

TH: When you focus on the picture, how would you like to think about yourself?

CL: *(Pauses)* There is no way I can think differently about myself.

TH: I understand what you are saying, but if you *could* think differently, how would you like it to be?

CL: *(Pauses)* You know, I think what it is, is that I don't believe I deserve to think differently about myself. I mean, he got killed because I didn't do my job as a sergeant.

TH: You mentioned earlier that you didn't understand why you were so full of anger, why you got angry so quickly. Do you think it might be because you are angry with yourself because you didn't do what you think you should have?

CL: Well, yes, sure.

TH: And when you think back on those times you blew up on people, did any of those situations have anything in common?

CL: No, it was just me going nuts.

TH: Well, when you beat up that guy at work, you said he was pushing around a smaller guy, and when you were arrested for attacking your brother-in-law, it was after he had hit your sister, I guess a couple of times. And on that other job, when you blew up on that supervisor who was ordering the line crew to work on those cables without securing the area or the electricity, that was a lot like the other job where you got into a shouting match with the crew boss who got into a hurry and . . .

CL: Yeah, he wouldn't put out road guards.

TH: I don't know, but it sounds like there's a pattern in your explosions.

CL: I can't get along with authority?

TH: Well, I don't know if that's it. Have you ever blown up on someone who threatened you?

CL: Well, no. You mean, threatening me? No.

TH: Seems to be mostly on behalf of other people.

CL: Well, yeah, I suppose so. Never thought of it that way.

TH: Kind of like you're trying to protect them.

CL: Yeah.

TH: That's important to you?

CL: Yeah, well, I guess, since the war. I guess I've been trying to make up for things without realizing it.

TH: Wanting to take care of people needing help isn't a bad thing, most people would agree.

CL: Yeah, but I've been really screwing up trying it.

TH: So how would you like to do it?

CL: Without blowing up on people. You know, just deal with things.

TH: When I asked you about your negative thoughts about yourself when you remembered that incident, you said, "I'm no good."

CL: Right.

TH: So when you think about that incident, how would you like to think about yourself now, today?

CL: That I can do the right thing without hurting anyone.

TH: I can do the right thing?

CL: Yeah.

The client's negative judgment about himself was one source of his anger; the other was his sense of right and wrong and a need to live up to a moral standard. Getting him to recognize that a major value for him was taking care of others enabled the formulation of a positive cognition.

Recognition of the pattern of defending others in the client's history gave the therapist an understanding going into the assessment phase. The client's long history of angry explosions and his own repeatedly stated concern with his anger and the danger it posed suggested that he might have trouble with the positive cognition. Going into the assessment, the therapist had several plans in mind for responding to this potential difficulty.

The next case illustrates anger as a defense. The client was a 48-year-old war veteran who was referred for inpatient treatment from a substance abuse treatment unit. Although he had not used hard drugs while in the military, he began to use heroin shortly after his discharge from an Army hospital, to which he had been evacuated after being badly wounded in combat.

While in Vietnam this man's platoon commander had led his platoon up a hill. Although they were supposed to wait for the rest of the company, their commander had insisted that they go ahead so as to secure a landing zone for helicopters to take out the company. It appeared to the soldier that the platoon commander was trying to look good to his superior. In any case, they were almost at the top of the hill when they came under fire by enemy soldiers in several concealed bunkers.

Though hit in the leg in two places, the client managed to get his machine gun into action. His assistant began bandaging his wounds while he operated the gun. His machine gun attracted the attention of the enemy, which enabled most of the rest of the platoon to slide partway back down the hill. But his assistant was hit and killed and he was wounded again.

When the rest of the company arrived, the enemy was forced to withdraw and the top of the hill was secured as a landing zone. He and a number of other men were evacuated by helicopter. Before he was airlifted from the hospital back to the United States, he was told that he had been put in for a medal, along with the platoon commander.

When the veteran was asked about his assistant gunner and whether they had been friends, he became angry and began talking about how much he hated the platoon commander. He also described himself as being "totally unable to trust anyone." This had led to many failed relationships. He stated that he had known another veteran who had been treated with EMDR and said he knew it could work, but that the other veteran had described "all kinds of feelings coming up." He said he was afraid to use it, because the only feeling he had was anger and if it came up he might lose control.

I (SMS) did not dispute this possibility initially, since, short of experiencing EMDR, there was no way for the client to know how he actually would respond to treatment. Instead, I noted that there were many therapeutic tools we might use and, if anger was a concern for him, we might start by helping him manage it.

While teaching the veteran several tension reduction and anger management techniques, I also educated him about EMDR and how it worked. I gave him several articles showing research findings. The primary focus was on reassuring the client that the processing was under his, the client's, control and that if it felt overwhelming he could stop the therapy and take a "time out" until he felt ready to go again. I also pointed out that there were things that could be done to slow down processing; however, his own mind might decide that it was appropriate to move more quickly so there could be no guarantee that things would move slowly.

After a couple of weeks of practicing anger management techniques he agreed to try EMDR. The assessment phase went relatively smoothly, with a good picture readily available, and the negative cognition of "I'm not safe anywhere," and the positive cognition of "I can take care of myself." The primary emotion was anger and he placed it at a nine on the SUD. He described a feeling of tension in his stomach and chest.

Initial eye movement sets were deliberately held to six to eight repetitions and the time between sets was allowed to be longer than usual. He described his focus in terms of the pictorial unfolding of the firefight, beginning with the first burst of fire from the enemy and proceeding through the moment when he was wounded. Then processing began to bounce back and forth between the picture and his emotions. At this point a block emerged.

TH: And what do you get now?

CL: Oh, shit, I can see Bob has been hit.

TH: Go with that. *(Begins EMs)* OK, let's pause, and what do you get now?

CL: That son of a bitch. He got Bob and all those other guys killed. They gave him a fucking medal. I wouldn't take mine, but they gave it to me anyway.

TH: Is that what you see now?

CL: All I see is Bob. He was kneeling over my legs trying to patch me up. I didn't even know he was hit until he fell on me.

TH: OK, stay with that. *(Begins EMs)*

(The client's self report loops between a very high state of unchanging anger and the image of his assistant gunner sprawled across his legs.)

CL: This isn't getting any better, doc. I feel like I could kill someone.

TH: Yeah, I can hear it in your voice. Listen, let's try something. Can you pull up a picture of Bob from a different time? You know, just a picture of him in your mind without anything going on?

CL: You mean like when we were in the rear or on R&R?

TH: Yes, like that.

CL: *(Shrugs)* Well, sure.

TH: OK, hold that picture in your mind, and follow my hand. *(Begins EMs)* OK, let's pause and take a breath. What do you get now?

CL: Well, I can see him when we went to Bangkok together.

TH: OK, stay with that. *(Begins EMs)* OK, let's pause and take a breath. What are you aware of now?

CL: *(Long pause)* He was a good man.

TH. Go with that. *(Begins EMs. The client becomes teary-eyed and eye movements are continued until after the client lets out a deep sigh.)* Let's pause here. Take a breath. What are you aware of now?

CL: I was just thinking that I really miss him. You know, he saved my life.

TH: Let's stay with that. *(Begins EMs. The client begins to abreact and eye movements are continued for approximately a minute until the client appears to calm down.)* OK. Take a breath. What do you get now?

CL: You know, I never cried for him. All these years. I was just pissed off. I didn't feel anything else. Like I had forgotten that we were friends. I mean we were really tight. But all I thought about was that platoon commander, never about him.

TH: And what are you thinking now?

CL: Like I'm getting back in touch with him after thirty years.

TH: Go with that . . .

My hypothesis was the anger was defensive, given how it was manifested in relationships. Certainly part of that defense might be protection against being hurt by others as he had been hurt by his platoon commander. But the defensive nature of the anger might also have been about protecting the client from other emotions. Considering that the block occurred on an image involving his assistant, it seemed possible that those other emotions might be about Bob. This was almost immediately confirmed by the client's response. His reference to being on R&R with Bob was the first time he mentioned doing anything enjoyable with him specifically, though he had described several enjoyable times with his platoon when they were out of the field. His comments about Bob prior to this battle had been very limited.

The identification of an internally focused negative cognition can make use of the client's presentation of anger directed externally. A question like, "How do you think about yourself now for not having done anything effective about the things for which you are so angry?" takes the focus internally. When the client struggles with the concept of the positive cognition, taking the time to explain it thoroughly is important.

Anger can be frightening, both for the therapist and for the client. Yet it is another part of the structure of the traumatic experience and offers an opportunity for engagement and processing in the same way that other emotions, cognitions, sensations, and images do. Considering the nature of war and terrorism, with the damage inflicted by other humans and often in a repeated manner, anger may be manifested in a number of ways. Its root is always meaning: the meaning of one's life, of survival, of one's relationship to the world. Its presentation, though admittedly frightening, is also hopeful, for an understanding of it offers the key to unlocking the client's trauma.

Chapter 20

RELIEF WORK

"Many of the people who said they came to Sarajevo to help us were on 'emotional safari.'"

Therapists get involved with relief work through any number of ways. While many agencies, such as UNICEF, Catholic Relief Services, and U.S. AID, have made use of EMDR clinicians in relief work, the agency specializing in this is the EMDR Humanitarian Assistance Programs (EMDR-HAP). This involvement by the EMDR community has evolved over the past dozen years or so. The first large volunteer effort of EMDR clinicians to respond to a major disaster was in California following major earthquakes. Volunteers responded again following Hurricane Andrew's devastation in Florida. Those efforts resulted in the initial work on the recent events protocol. Paralleling the work in the civilian sector was the early work of VA clinicians with war veterans and of Israeli mental health professionals working with both veterans and terrorism survivors. One of the first trainings Francine Shapiro did was in Israel. But it was the wars in the former Yugoslavia and an act of terrorism in America that began to bring various threads of EMDR relief work together.

The first organized response to an ongoing war was in Croatia. Dr. Geoffrey White, deeply moved by the unfolding tragedy in the Balkans, sought a way to bring EMDR to that region. A team consisting of himself, Dr. Gerry Puk, and Steve Silver was invited to Croatia, where a training in EMDR was provided through an educational program developed by U.S. AID, Catholic Relief Services, and Dru-stvo za Psiholosku Pomoc (Society for Psychological Assistance), with the support of NGO Ruke, the latter two organizations based in Croatia and responding to the needs of refugees. The training team was then invited to Sarajevo, Bosnia-Herzegovina, to provide train-ings there. Adding Dr. Rogers to the team, it arrived as the Dayton Peace Accords were implemented (Puk & Silver, 1997; Silver & Rog-ers, 1996a, 1996b).

In the United States, the bombing in Oklahoma City resulted in a response organized at the grass roots level. In addition to providing over 300 hours of EMDR treatment to those affected by the bomb-ing, three trainings were provided so that local clinicians could pro-vide ongoing and follow-up treatment. At the same time, the Critical Incident Stress Foundation provided a familiarization course to the EMDR Institute facilitators who were assisting at the trainings.

Since a growing number of requests were being received for train-ing assistance, a group of clinicians interested in providing pro bono assistance met informally at the 1996 EMDR International Associa-tion conference and formed what would eventually be EMDR-HAP.

The ongoing training program in EMDR for VA clinicians devel-oped parallel to these events. These trainings, conducted in VA medi-cal centers across the country and open to hospital and Vet Center staff with occasional participants from local community mental health programs, trained over 350 people before the end of the '90s. These trainings were focused on the treatment of combat trauma.

The VA training program became a part of the EMDR-HAP ef-fort. While EMDR-HAP was capable of providing crisis intervention services, the bulk of its work was made up of trainings. HAP volun-teers gained a great deal of experience working cross-culturally, eval-uating training programs, and forming and educating teams.

There are several advantages to this model. By teaching EMDR to local therapists, we are essentially "dropping a tool into their tool-box." The professionals who are already part of the affected commu-nity are not being replaced by outsiders; they are simply being given one more resource to be used when and how they think best. Because trauma reactions are sometimes delayed, and because individuals often try to resolve problems on their own before they seek profes-sional intervention, these trainings ensure that EMDR is one of the available treatment options when people decide they need therapy. It also makes EMDR an enduring community resource extending beyond the parameters of a single event.

I (SMS) worked for several years as the program chair for EMDR-HAP, which involved coordinating relief efforts and team formation and preparation. I (SR) organized an EMDR-HAP training program for Bangladesh, which was funded by UNICEF. The recommendations below are based on our experiences, as well as those of others who organized responses to such situations as the bombing in Oklahoma City.

CLINICIAN SELECTION

An ideal situation would be to have a large pool of experienced mental health professionals to respond to the needs of survivors of war and terrorism. The reality is that the pool of clinicians available for the selection process is often largely made up of individuals with little experience with this population. This is not an insurmountable obstacle but it is a factor to take into account during education.

It is understood that in some circumstances an individual clinician may be asked or may volunteer to help in a relief setting. Operating alone is a difficult undertaking but may be the only option. Formalized clinician selection as described here may still be utilized by the agency responsible and can be incorporated, with some modifications, by a clinician as an internal, self-evaluative process.

The first step in clinician selection is a determination of the needs of the group to be helped. Whether the clinicians will supply training or direct services or both, the selection process should be tailored to provide the most appropriate response possible to the identified needs. For example, the project for Bangladesh noted earlier included an assessment developed "on the ground" by EMDR-HAP members and their Bangladeshi counterparts. During this assessment they found that one of the problem areas faced by Bangladeshi mental health professionals was that many people were still suffering from reactions to their war of independence in 1970–71. In response to this, each of the six teams sent to Bangladesh had at least one member with expertise in chronic psychological reactions to war trauma. The assessment was also responsible for ensuring that experts in the treatment of children, abused women, and mass disaster survivors were included. If there are no clinicians available with the needed skills, consultation should be arranged.

Clinicians should also be screened for personal appropriateness. There are several issues to be considered. First there is the obvious, but seldom addressed, issue of team compatibility. Succinctly put, is the clinician under consideration willing to pull his or her own weight and work as a member of a team? Mental health professionals are often loath to make judgments of this kind about their peers, but team morale and performance can be compromised when members are not oriented to the mission, are not prepared to carry their share of the load, or have needs that conflict with the completion of the mission.

Past participation in relief efforts, along with some evaluation of performance in those situations, is desirable, but often lacking. After all, everyone has to have a "first time." It may be possible to get a sense of clinicians' capacity to do this work by observing interactions in other settings. For example, an individual with a rapier-like wit used to tease coworkers may be amusing on an academic committee, but not so on the third or fourth day of relief work, when people have been driving themselves through the cold and wet, without showers or hot food, while dealing with all the pressures associated with trying to provide teaching and therapy cross-culturally. A good way to judge people is to see contributions they have made in the past. Have they volunteered to work, for example, in a supportive role of some sort during relief efforts? Or have they shown up on your doorstep wanting to participate in what they view as the "exciting part" with no evidence of prior commitment to the effort?

In an agency where such efforts are frequent, making use of people who are willing to help out in any way they can in various supportive roles is desirable. It gets more people involved in the efforts of the agency, which means greater public awareness of those efforts. It also lifts some of the burdens that the core staff typically carry. It gives volunteers a chance to learn the basics of relief work and increases their awareness of such issues as leadership, team selection, and cultural differences. It enables the agency to get to know a range of individuals and see how they perform. It is in the agency's interest, then, to find work for anyone who wants to participate. Obviously, there is a point where efficiency can be impaired by having too many people involved, but the nature of relief agencies is that most of the time the problem is not one of too many hands but of too few.

Assessment of volunteers includes examining their cultural values. It is not necessary that relief workers agree with the values of another culture or regard all cultures as equal. However, they must be aware of their own values so as to keep them from interfering with the mission. Western values and attitudes are not shared universally. A classic example of this is the perception of the role of women. Team members may find it difficult to avoid commenting on apparent inequities in the status of men and women in some countries. They may find it even more difficult to adjust their personal conduct and day-to-day behavior toward other team members. Familiar social rules with regards to touching, personal space, and manner of dress may need to be put aside "for the duration."

CLINICIAN EDUCATION

The process of educating team members may serve as a filtering process, since it should acquaint the prospective participants with the challenges they will face. It is not uncommon for volunteers to reconsider when they begin to learn of the specifics of the effort.

Education should be aimed at three areas:

1. Required clinical skills for the mission
2. Information about the specifics of where the effort is to take place, including the culture, politics, social structure, and current situation
3. Information and training needed to function on a relief team

The immediate mission of the relief team defines the clinical skills. While therapists can be presumed to have clinical skills, the uniqueness of a particular situation may necessitate some additional clinical training so that they will be able to respond more effectively to the situation on the ground. Cross-training can be conducted within the team to meet these needs and build team cohesion. Training in the approaches being used by other relief agencies may have the benefit of upgrading clinical skills, improving knowledge of the specific situation, and increasing interagency cooperation.

For example, therapists working in relief work often are unable to obtain comprehensive client histories because of the numbers of people to be seen, cultural issues, or language difficulties. When having to work in an abbreviated fashion, we have found the critical question to be, "How was this person functioning before the event?" While brief, the answer at least gives therapists a general sense clients' history.

Education about the situation starts with the history of the locale and continues up to the current moment. Some relief efforts may be aimed at situations literally "down the street" from the team members and much of the education in this area may be quite familiar to the members. Nonetheless, nothing should be taken for granted.

Some of the best information can be gathered from local mental health professionals. Prior to arrival team members should seek input from their counterparts. Because of their education, training, and experience, as well as the influence of American media, these individuals are likely to be more familiar with the cultures and backgrounds of Western team members than the team members will be with the local culture. This kind of information-gathering, supplemented by outside sources, serves not only to educate the team but also to reassure their counterparts that the team is not coming in with an arrogant attitude.

An example of information coming from clinicians outside of a situation occurred when we went to Sarajevo. I (SR) was surprised by how many people chose to work on automobile accidents and, at first, thought they were avoiding the war experiences. It wasn't until they began processing that I found these accidents *were* war experiences. Because of sniper activity in the streets, many people got from place to place by driving very fast and at night to avoid being seen. Traffic lights were, at best, intermittent. The result was that many people were injured in traffic accidents and had trauma reactions from them.

This area of education is especially critical because it begins the process of developing a culturally appropriate model of EMDR processing. Much of the model and most of the metaphors clinicians encounter in EMDR training are biased toward Western ideas and concepts. Careful preparation requires developing methods of communicating the same ideas in ways they can be clearly understood.

For example, a British mental health professional working with Tibetan refugees was seeking to develop a way of presenting EMDR that would be comprehensible to Tibetan Buddhists. After some email discussion, I (SMS) drew on my work with Native American war veterans and discussions I had with their traditional healers. I suggested using a model emphasizing balance. Navajos and Buddhists share a view of life as trying to travel the "Right Path," a path with danger on either side. If your burden is unbalanced, the journey is made risky. Some experiences unbalance us and make it difficult to travel as we once did. EMDR helps us to balance the load by shifting it back and forth until the balance point is discovered. The British clinician found that this metaphor, modified to fit the circumstances of the Tibetan refugees, facilitated their EMDR processing.

Educating team members about the functioning of a team should be an obvious point but it is remarkable how little attention is paid to this. Here again cultural factors must be taken into account. For example, in the generally egalitarian West, members of a team typically interact in a familiar way that in other cultures is often seen as disrespectful of the individual in the role of trainer or team leader. From this point of view, either the other team members are behaving in an inappropriate fashion, and therefore should not be respected, or the trainer is incompetent, and therefore should not be respected. When team members make a point of being respectful to their team leader, he or she may be taken more seriously.

It should be remembered that some private practitioners have limited team experience. One goal of the training is to familiarize the team members with their particular responsibilities and to inculcate them into the team ethos that the entire team—and each individual member—is responsible for the successful completion of the mission. There is no work beneath a relief team member. In addition, procedures, including who speaks for the team, who makes final decisions, how conflict will be handled, how the group will cooperate with other agencies, and so forth, need to be spelled out as clearly as possible before departing.

During the effort we strongly recommend having an informal team discussion about the work at the end of each day. Team members need to debrief rumors and facts they have heard in the course of their work and to "let it go" in safe surroundings. This is a good time to remind everyone of the need for self-care. This discussion can help to head off developing problems and conflicts among team members before they erupt and damage the mission. With the caution that relief work is quite wearing and can affect not only the recipient of a critique but the presenter as well, team members should be encouraged to engage in appropriate critiques and to provide positive comments.

Such discussions also provide educational opportunities. Besides refreshing what the clinicians have already learned about the local situation, leaders can tell them about new developments and changes in the current situation and alert them to therapeutic issues being encountered among the clients being treated. In some instances these may not be what was expected.

WORKING WITH LOCAL
MENTAL HEALTH PROFESSIONALS

Local mental health professionals not only provide a relief team with information and assistance that would be difficult to obtain by other means, but also assist in preparing materials, coordinating on-scene activities, and dealing with other institutions, particularly those of a governmental nature. They know the culture, society, country, and may already know the principles of trauma treatment. But the local mental health professionals may be experiencing their own stressors, including a variety of reactions evoked by having outsiders present: suspicion of the foreigners; embarrassment, even shame, at what is happening in and to their country; and feelings of inadequacy, professionally and personally, regarding coping with what has happened. They may have been traumatized themselves directly or vicariously through their work and have been affected by what they see happening to their country. Their experiences may come up during EMDR training for them. Trainees may have problems with concentration, irritability, and fatigue, all of which need to be taken into consideration during training.

In a country beset by war or terrorism, it is not uncommon for mental health professionals to use their own traumatic experiences in the practicum portions of EMDR training. In conventional EMDR trainings this is not generally encouraged; instead, in the first supervised practicum one chooses a milder experience. However, in relief settings it offers some advantages and should be permitted where there is sufficient coverage by the training staff. Mental health professionals who use significant trauma experiences get an opportunity to see EMDR work with what they are most likely to confront on a day-to-day basis. This increases their confidence in using EMDR. A typical positive cognition for these people is often something along the lines of "I help myself by helping others." It may be necessary to expand their training to include information on the foundations of trauma therapy, including coping skills and tension reduction techniques (safe place exercise, progressive relaxation training, etc.), which are useful not only for their clients but for them as well. Ample opportunity to practice all techniques should be provided.

While many mental health professionals may be quite comfortable with English, many will not be proficient English speakers or will not be sufficiently able to use English in a training workshop. In our experience, resources permitting, it is useful to provide training to those with strong English language skills separately and first. Then we have a training for those with little or no English, using the previously trained English speakers as translators and facilitators. This both increases their knowledge and gives them an opportunity to be involved in the teaching of EMDR, increasing the likelihood that the skills will be sustained after the team leaves. Ideally, translators should have a briefing beforehand, in which all the terms to be used are thoroughly examined, so that they can be clear and accurate.

Translators are critical in a clinical environment, where the mission is not training but treatment. Again, prior briefing of the translator is valuable. Good translators with mental health experience are often rare but can supply useful ideas for getting across various concepts. Where training and clinical work are being done together, having participants from the training assist as translators is beneficial to both clients and participants.

It should be understood that training is not an opportunity to resolve all of a country's problems. In an area of civil strife, bringing together members of opposing factions may satisfy some liberal impulse toward brotherhood but may present the participants with major problems. On the other hand, if the local mental health professionals themselves suggest this and the safety of all can be assured, then there is no reason not to follow through.

With a methodology as complex as EMDR, the training provided to local mental health professionals cannot be limited to a workshop.

Provisions must be made for ongoing consultation and follow-up training. Ideally this is accomplished through multiple team visits along with day-to-day assistance provided through such media as email. Ongoing consultation also provides the training team with feedback useful for subsequent trainings and workshops.

A good model of this approach is that developed for Bangladesh by EMDR-HAP and UNICEF. Originally conceived as a series of team visits extending over six months, the program was briefly interrupted by severe flooding. The project started with an EMDR training that was conducted over the course of a week rather than the usual two and a half days. The training team then sought input from the participants and recommended modifications to the project coordinator. The next team provided specialty presentations and case consultation. The team after that, benefiting from what the previous teams had learned, provided a basic training for a new group and an advanced training for the first group.

At the same time, training team members sought opportunities to demonstrate EMDR through clinical applications. In several of these, their Bangladeshi counterparts took over the work the team members initiated. The Bangladeshis themselves served as facilitator assistants at subsequent trainings, improving their own skills and greatly assisting the whole process.

PROGRAM EVALUATION

Program evaluation of relief work efforts might be the sole topic of an entire book. Here let us merely outline the considerations for such evaluations, since these have an impact on the team mission.

All relief efforts, whether involving direct clinical intervention or training, should be subjected to an evaluation process of some kind. In some circumstances this process must be fairly informal. Ideally, however it is conducted, the evaluation process should be built into the relief team effort. Coordinating and host agencies should be carefully consulted as to how the evaluation can be conducted. What is to be avoided is the impression that the evaluation is about the local people. Its primary focus is on the work of the team. Did it accomplish what it set out to do?

Several questions are relevant to program evaluation:

- What are the needs?
- What are the goals and specific outcomes of the program?
- How do you measure outcomes?
- Who does the data-gathering?
- How will the evaluation results be used?

Identification of needs runs into the issue of who determines those needs. There may very well be needs that are more pressing than trauma treatment, such as those for food and shelter, but outside of our mission. Also, providing training in EMDR is based on the supposition that the intended audience has basic therapy skills. Someone in an administrative position may not realize this.

Once the needs are identified, the outcomes generated by attempting to meet them are the obvious primary focus of program evaluation. Additional areas may include participant satisfaction with the training provided or patient satisfaction with the treatment provided. Program evaluation should also include input from the team members covering all aspects of the experience.

The issue of data-gathering is very important. Beyond the ethical issue of providing a service that results in positive change, resource management requires appropriate substantiation that the effort was worthwhile. Clearly, there are some areas that the team and its agency will be interested in exploring. Ideally, the long-term evaluation of the work should be conducted by an independent body. Local academics trained in evaluative methods are often quite helpful in this regard. This has the added advantages of involving more of the local professional community and of utilizing a resource capable of long term follow-up.

Relief work seems to attract both the best and the worst in the mental health field. While those with the strong desire to be of help are very much in the majority, the reality is that there is a substantial minority of people who should not be allowed anywhere near a relief project. Only careful selection protects both the providers and the recipients of the effort.

It is foolish to assume that all the answers in this field are known. Wherever possible, local mental health professionals should be engaged in the work. After all, they will be remaining after all the relief teams have gone home. More importantly, they are the people most likely to understand the situation on the ground. It makes sense to involve them in EMDR work wherever possible.

It is appropriate to ask if what is being done is succeeding. Not all efforts will. Discovering the reasons for success or failure is vital and may have a profound impact on current or future efforts. Participants in relief work should be persistent demanding that evaluations be conducted.

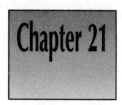

CROSS-CULTURAL ISSUES

"Grandfather, hear my prayer: for all my people . . . "

We have used EMDR literally around the world, as have many other clinicians, with similar therapeutic effects. While the challenge of describing the model varies from place to place, there are some broad principles to keep in mind as well as special circumstances to consider.

PRESENTING TREATMENT

It is important to remember that psychotherapy in general, and EMDR in particular, originated in Western culture. The practice of psychotherapy is not common to all cultures. In some places or with some clients it may be necessary to introduce and gain acceptance of the concept of psychological trauma and treatment before introducing EMDR. One psychologist working in Rwanda likened the psychological aftermath of genocide to a shock wave propagating depression, somatization, relational problems, and self-defeating behavior. "Those who are (conscious) that a psychological trauma is at the base of their discomfort are lucky. Most of the population lives in pain without recognizing the origin and so without the idea that they may get help."

It some situations, it may be important to provide information about trauma reactions and a range of possible interventions to program coordinators and government officials providing services to traumatized individuals. It can be helpful to point out that there are social, public health, and even economic benefits to treating psychological trauma. It is not always easy to find a vocabulary for these presentations, since much of the Western terminology used for discussing psychological trauma evolved from medicine and carries its own set of connotations. Even terms such as "trauma" and "stress" may have to be modified to fit a particular cultural context.

Howard Lipke developed an educational presentation that has been used successfully with populations as varied as American veterans and Kosovar Albanians (Lipke & Glang, 2000). By describing common trauma reactions, instructors can gain credibility with the members of the audience. When they have accurately described the negative consequences of trauma, their description of what might be done about the problem may be more acceptable. Taking the position of a teacher first can also enable one to gain respect in some cultures.

While the role of psychotherapist may be limited to certain cultures, the role of healer is not. In some cultures, psychotherapists may span several different social positions. For example, among Native Americans a person who serves the role of traditional healer may function as a psychotherapist, legal authority, teacher, and medical healer, as well as other positions. This gives a particular authority to such individuals. The educational presentation noted above can include information about the role of the therapist. Wherever possible the description of that role should be in culturally familiar and respectful terms, but should be done in a way that will be perceived as an addition to, rather than as a substitute for, the resources already existing in the community (Silver, 1992, 1994; Silver & Wilson, 1988).

A brief case history illustrates this. I (SMS) was asked to consult with a psychologist who had been approached by a Navajo Vietnam War veteran complaining of symptoms of posttraumatic stress disorder. The psychologist was unfamiliar with Native Americans in general and Navajo in particular. The clinician thought the veteran was a good candidate for EMDR and was wondering what would be the best way to present the treatment to him.

The first suggestion was to ask the client about the degree to which he was traditional in his upbringing, values, and outlook, and then to use his answers as a guide for the discussion of EMDR. The veteran had been raised on the reservation primarily by his grand-mother. English was a second language until he began formal school-ing. He began to drift away from his tribal traditions as he entered high school. By the time he entered the service, he described himself as "not at all traditional."

However, after his war experience, he had returned to the reserva-tion. He shunned the outside world and tried to bury himself in his culture and tribe. He was unsuccessful in forgetting the past and eventually developed a major problem with alcohol. Though he had maintained several months of sobriety by the time he contacted the psychologist, he felt that the pressure of his PTSD symptoms would eventually drive him back to drinking.

The client was asked if he had made use of any traditional healing practices, such as an Enemy Way ceremony, or Sing, and if this was something he might want to do. I recommended that the clinician learn about these practices at least in a general way. As it happened, the veteran wanted to have an Enemy Way Sing done, but felt that he was unworthy.

The psychologist thought this sense of unworthiness would be a good initial target for processing. He presented a model of EMDR using the idea of a Natural Way or Right Path discussed earlier. Fo-cusing processing on the sense of unworthiness quickly got into sur-vivor guilt. With that resolved, the veteran felt able to approach his family and friends to have an Enemy Way Sing performed. On fol-low-up with me, the psychologist surmised the ceremony had the ef-fect of reintegrating the veteran into his social milieu after the processing and resolution of his negative information with EMDR. I added that, from a Navajo point of view, "information" is contained in and a part of the body, heart, mind, and spirit, and that resolution occurs when all these parts come together. "Isn't that what I just said?" the psychologist asked.

PRESENTING A MODEL

Presenting the model in culturally appropriate terms is the initial challenge for an EMDR clinician away from home. In many circum-stances, this means avoiding discussion of neurophysiology and using metaphors drawn from the culture of the client. One should remem-ber, however, that a particular client may be fully cognizant of the concepts you are using, and so not require an elaborate cultural metaphor. To make a presumption based on cultural stereotyping is always a mistake. Metaphor is employed in virtually all settings where EMDR is used and is often the primary vehicle for explaining EMDR processing. Metaphor may be a useful way of reminding clients of information that was presented to them in the preparation phase. It may be that to devise culturally appropriate metaphors, clinicians need to be familiar with the culture of the client. There are many sources for cultural information, e.g., universities, the Internet, and local personnel.

It may be helpful to take a more thorough history than you would with someone from your own culture. This requires sensitivity, since in some cultures the development of a client history may be considered an intrusion unless you are a well-regarded individual. Even then some questions should not be asked. Generally, these kinds of questions, insofar as our discussion of developing a model for presenting EMDR, are not critical. What we are interested in are the answers to questions about familiarity with the concepts of psychotherapy. These answers will guide us in the presentation of a model for EMDR processing.

In any case, the model should be developed prior to meeting with clients, so that the therapist can receive input on it from those already familiar with the culture. Contact with the relief effort organizers, other relief workers and agencies, and indigenous mental health professionals can be of great assistance in this regard. An additional and often excellent source of such input and information may be the person working as a translator.

USING TRANSLATORS

When working with a translator, it is important to take the time beforehand to educate the translator about EMDR terms and procedures, so she or he understands what is going on and has had a chance to figure out equivalent and appropriate terms. An individual who has become skilled in a foreign language has often learned a great deal about the culture of that language. In turn, this can be a very useful resource for clinicians providing treatment. Time for working with the translator should be allowed, both to develop the needed terminology and to educate the clinician.

There are two other issues to be considered when working with translators. The first has to do with indigenous translators who may have been subjected to traumatic stress themselves. Since, when in the role of translator, such people are going to be exposed to the sometimes disturbing stories of other survivors, it makes sense to assist them in resolving their own experiences first. This can be presented as an opportunity to achieve resolution of experiences, to gain familiarity with EMDR, and to assist in the development of a way to present the method to clients. Depending on the individual, the culture, and the nature of the stressors the translator has been through, various past experiences might be used. Ideally, even if we begin on a relatively minor experience, success with resolving that experience will lead to addressing and resolving major traumas. This may be a good time to remind the translator that specifics of the event do not need to be shared.

During briefing a very well-educated Bangladeshi woman who was going to serve as a translator for working with traumatized women, I (SMS) offered to demonstrate EMDR with her. I asked her deliberately to withhold the specifics of what she wished to work on, with the idea that some of the women they were to treat might have major inhibitions about discussing certain experiences with a foreign male. The demonstration was effective, somewhat to the surprise of the translator, and she reported that it did help her understand the concepts of EMDR. (On the other hand, another translator, an equally well-educated Bangladeshi woman, waived the demonstration, noting that she had received a great deal of information about EMDR already from the local UNICEF office and was ready to get to work.)

The other issue to keep in mind when working with translators is the possibility that they might be disturbed by what they hear during the session. Translators should be both briefed and debriefed. The briefing should prepare them for hearing the various experiences of the clients and should also explain why it is important to keep one's own reactions out of the therapy process. The tools offered to clients for dealing with disturbance, such as the safe place, should also be explained for the translator. During the debriefing the therapist should ascertain whether the translators need any assistance and give them a chance to use those tools if needed.

Post-session debriefing is extremely important as a way of evaluating the work with a view toward improving clinician-translator-client communication in the future. It is always polite to begin by asking the translator to describe any errors or problems arising from the manner, style, or words of the therapist. In some cultures therapists may be perceived as occupying the respected position of teachers who are not to be subjected to criticism. Genuine concern for welfare of clients, as well as an expressed respect for the client's culture and a desire not to inadvertently violate the norms, is usually sufficient to elicit useful feedback.

Once the translator has given feedback, the therapist can provide the same for the translator. Again, local cultural norms come into play and phrasing should take these into account. As a general rule of thumb, changing statements into questions prefaced by a desire to understand the appropriate way to do things will more likely provide for an open dialogue.

We recommend not using foreign language phrases and words that clinicians do not understand. In other words, do not try to parrot the translator. However, it is a good idea to learn the equivalents of such terms as *go with that, keep going, good, thank you, hello,* and *goodbye.* These simple phrases are fairly easy to learn and are useful in clinical work.

THE THERAPEUTIC RELATIONSHIP

While rapport between therapist and client is important to any therapy, solid relationships are often more important in non-western therapeutic situations. Therefore it is often beneficial for clients, peer therapists, translators, or other coworkers to spend time getting to know each other. In some settings clients may want to learn about the therapist on a personal level, about his or her family in multigenerational terms, status and functioning as a teacher, or other details. Care should be taken in how this information is presented.

In the therapeutic relationship, boundary issues of physical proximity, as well as what may be discussed or how it is presented, may vary as a result of cultural influences. The cultural impact on sex roles may make it difficult for a client to discuss certain issues or experiences with a member of the opposite sex. Utilizing a translator of the client's sex can be useful in reassuring a client that it is permissible to discuss certain issues.

CULTURE AND THE ASSESSMENT PHASE

Recently, within the EMDR clinician community there has been some discussion around the concept that cognitions fit into three categories of responsibility—defectiveness, safety, or choices. It has been proposed, for example, that underlying the negative cognition of "I am disgusting" is the schema of "I am responsible for this trauma." The positive cognition should then follow this schema. EMDR clinician Gerry Puk, a member of the first EMDR training teams to go to the Balkans, has noted that culture may play a major role in the negative and positive cognitions portions of the assessment phase. Puk further notes that the negative cognition of "I am disgusting" may have powerful cultural meaning not relating to responsibility. For example, "I am disgusting" may be related to the victimization of the client. For example, a Muslim woman who is assaulted and raped may see herself as worthless or disgusting based on the cultural perception of her as stigmatized in a way that has little to do with issues of safety or responsibility.

He also reminds us that even within Western cultures there may be differences in the meanings of such terms as "powerlessness" and "helplessness." In Germany, a client who presents the negative cognition reflecting powerlessness (*machtlos*) is describing a perception of self as unable to affect the world or surrounding environment. On the other hand, a negative cognition about helplessness (*hiflos*) is about a perception of self as vulnerable to others.

The very statement of a negative cognition may be influenced by the client's culture as well. Describing personal attributes, particularly those of a negative type, may not be a usual activity. Indeed, the concept of a negative cognition, much less its description to another person, may be unfamiliar. During assessment, a more open phrasing may be needed, such as, "When you think of that image, what words define your sense of who you are?" Understanding these distinctions and not being bound by theoretical constructs developed in American culture will enable EMDR clinicians to have a clearer perception of the underlying issues and to provide clients with more useful assistance during the assessment phase.

CULTURE AND PROCESSING

The points made about the influence of culture on assessment carry over to desensitization and installation, since culture may influence what and how much a client may be willing or able to report. An EMDR clinician may need to rely on other indicators of change.

One area where this is often the case is in the reporting of emotions. Culturally, clients may have learned that expressing any or certain emotions, or levels of those emotions, is inappropriate. Even when they begin to experience them, their lack of familiarity with them or their culturally based inhibitions on their expression may lead them to not report processing in emotional terms. It may be far easier for such clients to describe physical sensations and their changes than to present emotional changes.

Cultural limits on the expression of emotion might mislead a clinician into believing significant material was not being addressed. Gerry Puk found that clients in Croatia and Bosnia during the war gave what were clearly horrific situations only a five on the SUD scale. In part, the apparent muting of emotional response reflected the effect of even worse experiences, a repression of emotion as a defense in a environment of continuing danger, and, as they explained later, of clients culturally based reticence to be self-revealing.

Such differences can arise within the multicultural context of American society as well. While working with a Puerto Rican veteran on the memory of the deaths of friends, I (SR) observed that processing became blocked at one point. I asked the client what was happening and he reported that he was beginning to feel tearful and was thinking about his father's telling him that it was not appropriate for a man to show such feelings, especially in front of a woman. We agreed to stop processing for the moment, so he could have more privacy with his feelings, and resume work later.

EXPANDING THE THERAPIST'S VIEW

Westerners tend to use a cultural shorthand and view everyone from a particular area as the same. For an American reader of this book, think about the wide range of groups making up America today—one label, one culture, really does not describe all the groups and subgroups. Among refugees from Southeast Asia, for example, there are a wide variety of different ethnic peoples. Their cultures, especially in terms of world views, vary significantly. In the area of religion, to cite just one item, beliefs range from Buddhism to animism. Physical contact boundaries likewise vary; in one group men hold hands while walking as a gesture of friendship, while in another men do not.

Spending time, conditions permitting, with a client to ascertain these things helps develop the therapeutic relationship by demonstrating that the therapist has a desire to be respectful and accommodating. During EMDR trainings in Bangladesh, many of the female facilitators made a point of purchasing and wearing items of traditional dress, and all women, whether they were from America, Israel, Scotland, or South Africa, made a point of dressing modestly. The participants in the workshops were well aware that many of the local cultural values were not shared by these Western women, and the fact they were making an effort to accommodate those values was appreciated.

Western clinicians sometimes make the mistake, in their effort to be perceived as appreciative of the client's culture, of downgrading their own. Typically this is done with comments like, "We have the same (or worse) problem in my country." This is not a good way to establish rapport for several reasons. First, it may cost clinicians the respect of their clients. People who disparage their own culture and home may be viewed as being disrespectful of their heritage by clients who hold respect of one's heritage as a value. Second, clients may feel that the uniqueness of their experience and situation is not being recognized. Third, the comments may be untrue from the client's perspective and may be perceived as patronizing and ignorant, in that there may be additional elements compounding the clients' difficulties that have not as yet been identified.

Likewise, references to how particular problems were or are handled in the West may be heard as implicit criticisms of the client's country and culture. Care must be taken with such references. Even when made to professional groups, descriptions of resources and programs can seem condescending to people who at present could not possibly develop the same kinds of things.

An appreciation of the client's culture has a direct role in EMDR processing as the resolution of the problem takes place. A therapist accustomed to hearing certain kinds of resolutions of similar trauma experiences may not appreciate how much of those typical resolutions are culturally influenced. For example, in America resolutions involving clients' perceiving themselves in a more assertive role may be relatively more common than among clients from South Asia, even for similar trauma experiences and symptom clusters. As always, the client is the best guide.

The client-centered and flexible focus that guides much of EMDR practice is a good one to maintain when entering into other cultures. Clients, when approached respectfully, will often prove to be an excellent and understanding guide for therapists whose genuine desire to be of assistance is shown by their presence and their efforts to understand.

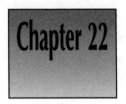

RESEARCH

"How do you know this stuff can do me any good?"

This chapter contains a review of research related to the use of EMDR as a treatment for trauma reactions. We include this review for several reasons, not the least of which is to give EMDR clinicians the basis for justifying the use of EMDR to the various institutions with which they must cooperate in order to work with survivors of war and terrorism. We refer to this chapter as the basis, given the amount of ongoing research on EMDR now taking place. Much of that research will both bolster the case for using EMDR and answer some of the questions still being asked about this fascinating new therapy.

While the investigation of EMDR has been extended to a variety of problems, such as addictions, phobias, and panic disorder, such issues are beyond the scope of this book. This chapter focuses primarily on studies using trauma or PTSD subjects. There are separate sections for the review of outcome studies with civilian and combat subjects, a distinction that is also made in the American Psychological Association Division 12 update on empirically validated therapies (Chambless et al., 1998). While it is likely that the critical distinction will be found between single-stressor PTSD and multiple-stressor PTSD, at this point it is only possible to separate studies on the basis of their use of civilian samples (which are likely to have a greater proportion of subjects who have experienced a single traumatic experience) and war veteran samples (which are likely to have a greater proportion of subjects who have experienced multiple traumatic experiences).

CIVILIAN PTSD STUDIES

EMDR Compared to Waitlist

In this type of study, subjects receiving EMDR are compared to un-treated control subjects. The inclusion of untreated controls makes it possible to examine the effects of EMDR while controlling for the effects of time and retesting.

Wilson, Becker, and Tinker (1995) compared patients treated with three sessions of EMDR with waitlist controls. The EMDR group showed significant improvements on PTSD, depression, and anxiety compared to controls. The improvements were maintained at three-month follow-up. At that point the waitlist patients were treated with EMDR and showed similar improvement. The study used a sample of traumatized individuals, not all of whom had PTSD. Though all subjects met the *DSM-IV* stressor criterion, only 47% of the subjects met full diagnostic criteria for PTSD. Subsequent analysis showed that EMDR was as effective for the PTSD subjects as for the non-PTSD subjects. A 15-month follow-up showed maintenance of treat-ment effects, with 84% of PTSD diagnosed subjects no longer meeting diagnostic criterion (Wilson, Becker, & Tinker, 1997).

In a study of rape victims, Rothbaum (1997) compared those treated with four sessions of EMDR with waitlist controls. The EMDR group showed a significantly greater improvement on measures of PTSD and depression. At posttest 90% of the EMDR and 12% of the wait-list subjects no longer met diagnostic criteria for PTSD. Though this is a strong study, the sample size was small and three of the EMDR subjects and two of the waitlist subjects received some concurrent treatment, which may account for the apparent remission of symp-toms among some of the controls.

EMDR Compared to
Counseling and Relaxation

In these studies, EMDR has been compared to some form of support-ive counseling or relaxation training. This design makes it possible to examine the effects of EMDR while controlling for time, retesting, and nonspecific therapeutic effects. In a study of traumatized women, 77% of whom met full PTSD criteria, (Scheck, Schaeffer, & Gillette, 1998), two sessions of EMDR were compared with two sessions of active listening focused on the traumatic experience. Significant improvements were found for both treatments on PTSD, anxiety, depression, and self-concept. EMDR resulted in significantly greater improvements than active listening on all but self-concept. Effect sizes for EMDR were twice as large as for active listening. A three-month follow-up showed continued improvements in depression and PTSD in both groups, though results may have been influenced by the manner of follow-up (telephone interview).

A study of PTSD treatment in a health maintenance organization setting (Marcus, Marquis, & Sakai, 1997) compared EMDR with standard care consisting of cognitive, psychodynamic, or behavioral therapy and group therapy. Both groups included subjects who were on medication. Unlike most of the studies reviewed in this chapter, the number of sessions was not predetermined. In order to more fully conform to the way treatment is delivered in HMO settings, individual therapy sessions were limited to 50 minutes. The EMDR group showed greater improvement in global distress, PTSD, depression, and anxiety than the standard care group within the first three sessions. Fewer EMDR subjects met PTSD diagnostic criteria after three sessions (only 16 of 32 in the EMDR group, compared to 23 of 29 in the standard care group) and at the completion of treatment (7 of 28 in EMDR vs. 15 of 30 in standard care). The EMDR group also used significantly fewer medication sessions, group sessions and total appointments. The study demonstrated that EMDR is not only clinically effective, but cost-effective as well.

EMDR Compared to
Cognitive-Behavioral Therapy

Prior to the introduction of EMDR, the form of PTSD treatment with the greatest amount of empirical support was cognitive-behavioral therapy (CBT). These treatments include prolonged exposure (also known as flooding or direct therapeutic exposure), stress inoculation training, and cognitive restructuring. Interest in the investigation of the comparative effects of these treatment methods has grown along with empirical support for both EMDR and CBT. Shapiro's (1989a) original study involved the comparison of EMD and a simple exposure control. Her finding of superior effects on process measures such as the SUD and VOC scales has been supported by the findings of our own research (Rogers et al., 1999) showing significantly great-er decreases in within-session SUD with EMDR compared to simple exposure to trauma memories. However, the relationship between within-session SUD levels and treatment outcome is uncertain (Foa & Kozak, 1998.) and both Shapiro (1989a) and Rogers et al. (1999) conducted single-session studies that did not allow for the comparison of a reasonable trial of EMDR with full exposure therapy as it is typically conducted.

Vaughan et al. (1994) compared three to five sessions of EMDR, image habituation training (IHT), applied muscle relaxation (AMR), and waitlist. IHT is a form of exposure therapy in which subjects are asked to audiotape and then listen to six brief descriptions of recur-ring trauma-related images, with a 30-second silence between each description during which they are to visualize the memory. Subjects were trained in the procedure during treatment sessions and were instructed to practice imagery with the tape for one hour a day. All three treatments resulted in significant improvements in PTSD and depression compared to the waitlist. The EMDR group showed sig-nificantly greater reduction in intrusive symptoms. Treatment gains were maintained at three-month follow-up, with 70% of all subjects no longer meeting diagnostic criteria for PTSD. IHT and AMR sub-jects did 40–60 minutes of daily homework, which was not required of the EMDR subjects. The study lacked fidelity checks and em-ployed a mixed sample (78% of the subjects met full criteria for PTSD prior to treatment while the remaining 22% met all but the avoidance criterion).

Lee, Gavriel, Drummond, Richards, and Greenwald (in press) compared seven sessions of EMDR to stress inoculation therapy plus prolonged exposure (SITPE). Though both groups showed substan-tial improvements on measures of PTSD and depression, the EMDR group showed significantly greater reductions in intrusive symptoms. At three-month follow-up, 83% of the EMDR group and 75% of the SITPE group no longer met PTSD diagnostic criteria. While there were no significant differences in outcome, EMDR required a total of three hours of homework while SITPE required 28 hours. The study employed random assignment, fidelity checks for both treatments, and comparison of EMDR with an empirically validated PTSD treat-ment. However, it lacked blind assessment, and the sample size was small.

Devilly and Spence (1999) compared eight sessions of EMDR to a trauma treatment protocol (TTP). Like many of the treatments referred to in this chapter, TTP combined elements of prolonged exposure and stress inoculation training. However, a new element was added, in that subjects' irrational cognitions were challenged *during* exposure. Both treatments were effective, but TTP was found to be more effective on combined PTSD measures and a global functioning scale. The study lacked random assignment and blind assessment.

Ironson, Freund, Strauss, and Williams (in press) compared three to six sessions of EMDR to prolonged exposure (PE). Unlike other studies in this chapter, in-vivo exposure homework was done by both groups in an attempt to equalize treatment time. Both treatments yielded a significant reduction in PTSD and depression which was maintained at a three-month follow-up. EMDR appeared to be faster, as evidenced by a larger number of subjects reaching a 70% reduction in symptoms after three active treatment sessions (seven of ten for EMDR, compared to only two of twelve for PE). The EMDR group had a significantly lower dropout rate. Subjects in the EMDR group experienced a significant reduction in SUD levels during the first session, while the PE group showed a slight increase. Response to EMDR appeared to be more variable than that to PE. Though nine of ten EMDR subjects were ultimately successfully treated, two of them showed an increase in PTSD symptoms after three active treatment sessions. Of the two EMDR "slow responders," both were working on memories in which someone close to them had been hurt or killed and guilt was the primary emotional response. The two slowest responders to PE were also working on memories that elicited feelings of guilt. The individual whose PTSD symptoms increased the most with EMDR showed the greatest difficulty accessing his feelings. Though measurement of PE effect size was compromised by dropouts, EMDR plus exposure homework yielded an average effect size of 1.52. The study's sample was small, and it lacked blind assessment. Therapists had been trained in both therapies and had displayed no previous allegiance to one method or the other.

Powell, McGoldrick, and Brown (2000) compared 10 sessions of EMDR with exposure plus cognitive restructuring (PE+CR) and with a waitlist. Results showed substantial improvements for both treatment groups but no change for the waitlist group on standardized measures of PTSD, depression, anxiety, and social functioning.

Dropout rates for the treatment groups were similar. The EMDR group showed a significantly greater improvement on depression and a faster response to treatment (50% fewer sessions needed) compared to the PE+CR group. Treatment effects were maintained at fifteen-month follow-up, with continued improvement in the EMDR group and some deterioration in the PE+CR group. The study used blind assessment and random assignment and is notable for its large sample (N = 105) and good subject retention at follow-up (72%).

Of the five EMDR vs. CBT comparisons completed to date, four have shown EMDR to be as effective but more efficient than the CBT, while one has shown EMDR to be less effective than the CBT condition. While it is possible that the TTP procedure developed by Devilly and Spence is a superior treatment, there are several aspects of their study that should be considered. First, though the authors stated that the therapists had been fully trained in EMDR and that fidelity was checked by an expert, the procedure as they described it (Devilly, Spence, & Rapee, 1998) contained obvious errors. Second, the average effect size reported for EMDR was very small (.75) compared to that reported in numerous other efficacy studies with similar subjects and shorter treatment trials, which ranged from a low of 1.38 to a high of 2.22. Only 18% of the EMDR subjects in this study no longer met diagnostic criteria after treatment, compared to 83% in Lee et al. (in press) and 90% in Rothbaum (1997). Third, expectancy measures for EMDR in this study were strongly negative, while four other studies showed positive expectancies for EMDR (Bauman & Melnyk, 1994; Feske & Goldstein, 1997; Gosselin & Matthews, 1995; Hekmat, Groth, & Rogers, 1994).

To date there have been no direct comparisons of EMDR and cognitive restructuring, possibly due to the prevailing belief that prolonged exposure is a necessary element in the effective treatment of anxiety disorders. The existence of several studies showing comparable effects of exposure and cognitive restructuring have called this belief into question. Several studies in this section have compared EMDR with combinations of exposure and cognitive restructuring, but none has compared EMDR with cognitive restructuring by itself.

It should be noted that in the majority of these efficacy studies, EMDR, while having its most noticeable effects on intrusive symptoms, has a broad effect across symptom clusters of intrusion, avoidance, and hyperarousal. The fact that several studies have shown decreases in general measures of anxiety and depression, as well as increases in psychological well-being, indicates that EMDR's effects are not limited to the mere desensitization of traumatic imagery.

STUDIES OF COMBAT-RELATED PTSD

In her original study, Shapiro (1989a) cautioned that her impressive single-session results had been obtained with a sample of subjects who, in the majority of cases, were civilians experiencing a single traumatic event. She went on to state that individuals who had experienced multiple traumas might need longer treatment trials to achieve comparable results. Nevertheless, several of the studies of combat-related PTSD that followed were limited by the use of very brief treatment trials.

Jensen (1994) compared two sessions of EMDR to a "no treatment" control condition. Both groups showed increased symptoms with no significant differences between groups. The study lacked fidelity for the EMDR condition (fidelity checks were failed) and blind assessment. Control subjects may have received some sort of treatment during the study.

Devilly et al. (1998) compared two sessions of EMDR to "standard psychiatric support." Both groups showed significant improvement on measures of PTSD, anxiety, depression, and coping, with no significant differences between group means. However, 67% of the EMDR group reliably improved compared to only 10% of the controls. The study lacked random assignment and blind assessment. Fidelity problems were the same as identified previously for Devilly and Spence (1999). This study also included a comparison of EMDR with an analog condition that did not involve eye movements (nonEM), which will be discussed in the following section on treatment mechanisms.

Boudewyns and Hyer (1996) added five to eight sessions of EMDR or an analog condition to an existing PTSD treatment program that combined medication, psychoeducation, and group therapy. Both groups showed significantly greater improvements on PTSD symptoms and physiological reactivity to trauma narratives than those receiving the program only. The study included random assignment and blind assessment, but fidelity checks were mixed.

Carlson, Chemtob, Rusnak, Hedlund, and Muraoka (1998) compared 12 sessions of EMDR to biofeedback-assisted relaxation and a waitlist control. At posttest, EMDR was shown to have a significantly greater effect on PTSD and depression than the waitlist control. At three-month follow-up the EMDR group had significantly greater improvements on PTSD than the relaxation group. All three groups showed significant decreases in reactivity to trauma narratives; the improvements were maintained at follow-up. The finding of decreased reactivity among control subjects is unexpected in light of previous studies with long trials of exposure therapy that showed no change in reactivity. Average effect size for EMDR was large (1.53). The study lacked blind assessment, but therapist allegiance, if present, favored the relaxation condition. A separate blind assessment at nine-month follow-up showed maintenance of the improvements in the EMDR group, 78% of whom no longer met diagnostic criteria for PTSD. It should be noted that, according to the "gold standard" described by Foa and Meadows (1997), this is the most rigorous study of treatment outcome for war-related PTSD conducted to date.

These studies support Shapiro's original statement that brief treatment trials may be insufficient to resolve PTSD based on multiple traumas. The fact that large and lasting treatment effects were obtained on standardized measures of PTSD, anxiety, and depression in a study of combat veterans conflicts with the view that combat-related PTSD is a chronic and treatment-resistant disorder (Johnson et al., 1996). While it has been suggested that EMDR's effects on combat-related PTSD are only transitory (Macklin et al., 2000), this conclusion was based on a five-year follow-up of a dismantling study (Pitman et al., 1996) in which subjects received sessions of EMDR or an analog procedure focused on only one of their trauma memories. As long-term follow-up on the effects of CBT are also lacking, the durability of treatment effects with this population remains to be investigated.

It has been noted that prolonged exposure seems to have a limited effect on the guilt that often accompanies PTSD (Foa & McNally, 1996; Foa & Rothbaum, 1998). Noting the disparity between the effects of prolonged exposure on rape victims and combat veterans, Foa concluded that the difference was due to the fact that veterans have a high degree of guilt about their involvement in violence against others. She observed that rape victims who experienced guilt were also more resistant to exposure therapy. Further, while guilt is a com-

mon response of traumatized combatants, it is not always about killing, but about surviving when so many comrades died.

It is not clear why guilt should be resistant to the effects of exposure therapy, since the theoretical basis of exposure is the extinction
of conditioned emotional responses. Perhaps the difference in treatment response between civilians and veterans is due to the number
of traumatic stressors experienced rather than specific history of those
stressors. In any case, one of the few studies to specifically address
the issue of guilt in a PTSD population, the study of combat veterans
conducted by Cerone (2000), showed significant decreases in trauma-
related guilt after EMDR treatment.

Since research suggests a significant degree of correlation between
trauma exposure and other clinical syndromes such as depression
(Shalev et al., 1998) and phobia (Ost & Hugdahl, 1981), it makes
sense that the exploration of the boundaries of EMDR's clinical util-
ity begin with these disorders. Sanderson and Carpenter (1992) compared brief trials of a simplified version of Shapiro's original EMD and
a nonEM analog of the same procedure. Both procedures resulted in
reductions in SUD ratings. However, subjects whose phobias originated in traumatic experiences showed a significantly greater response
to treatment than phobics who were unable to identify an etiological
trauma. While nontrauma subjects' SUD ratings dropped an average
of 28 points, trauma subjects' SUD ratings dropped an average of 69
points. EMD was more effective than the analog with trauma phobics,
but not significantly so. The lack of significance may have been due to
the small number of trauma subjects, eight, available for comparison.
While several preliminary studies of the use of EMDR with trauma-
based phobia have been published (e.g., Lohr, Tolin, & Kleinknecht,
1996), fully controlled studies are lacking.

INVESTIGATION OF THE MECHANISMS
INVOLVED IN EMDR

Evidence Against a Specific Effect
for Eye Movements

Numerous dismantling studies of the eye movement component of
EMDR have been conducted (Bauman & Melnyk, 1994; Devilly,
Spence, & Rapee, 1998; Dunn, Schwartz, Hatfield, & Wiegele, 1996;

Feske & Goldstein, 1997; Foley & Spates, 1995; Gosselin & Matthews, 1995; Pitman et al., 1996; Renfrey & Spates, 1994; Sanderson & Carpenter, 1992; Wilson, Silver, Covi, & Foster, 1996). In these studies subjects receiving an eye movement procedure are compared to subjects who receive the same procedure without eye movements, who are instructed at stare at a point, or who experience an alternative form of stimulation such as alternating sounds or hand taps. In the majority of these studies, the nonEM conditions were found to be as effective as the EMDR condition.

While some, though not all, of these results might suggest that the eye movement is an inert component, several limitations of this group of studies should be considered. Many of these studies used nonclinical samples (often recruiting undergraduates with significant scores on measures of test anxiety or fear of public speaking), which calls in to question the generalizability of the results to clinical, traumatized populations. Several of the studies used truncated versions of the EMD procedure rather than the full EMD or EMDR procedure, which again limits the generalizability of the findings. Some of the studies used extremely brief treatment trials, such as seven to nine sets of eye movements.

By far the most serious shortcoming of these studies as a group is the use of small sample sizes, ranging from six to eighteen subjects per group, which reduces statistical power and increases the probability of an erroneous "no difference" conclusion. While small samples can also be problematic in comparative outcome studies, they are critical when the study is being used to assess the contribution of a single component such as eye movements. Appropriate sample size is usually determined in advance by estimating probable effect sizes and calculating the number of subjects needed to reliably protect against Type II error. For example, as we discuss below, a treatment component with a moderate effect size would require a sample size of approximately 25 subjects per group.

Investigators have typically either failed to address the issue of power in dismantling studies at all or, like Devilly, Spence, and Rapee (1998), have assumed that sample sizes were sufficient because they based their estimates on the large effect sizes obtained in previous studies for the EMDR procedure as a whole rather than an estimate of the effect of the eye movements themselves. If one uses Gosselin and Matthews' (1995) comparison of EMD and a nonEM analog on the most sensitive measure (SUD), the sample size needed for sufficient statistical power is at least 25 subjects per group (see Cohen, 1988). It is interesting to note that the only study to show a significant advantage for eye movements on standardized outcome measures (Feske & Goldstein, 1997) used a clinical sample (panic disorder), a long treatment time (five sessions), and one of the largest samples (12–18 per group).

There are several potential solutions to the problem of power in dismantling studies. One approach is to design studies with clinical samples, reasonable treatment times, and sufficient sample size. Another is to group the small studies together for meta-analysis. Another is to evaluate the effects of eye movement by removing them from the EMDR procedure and studying them in isolation. While it may be some time before large studies are completed, the latter approaches have been used with positive results.

Evidence Supporting a Specific Effect for Eye Movements

While Shapiro (1998a, 1989b) originally posited a specific effect for eye movements, as early as 1991 she was reporting that clinicians using her method had also achieved positive results with other forms of bilateral stimulation such as hand taps or alternating sounds (Shapiro, 1991). Nevertheless, meta-analysis of EMDR trauma treatment studies shows a significantly greater effect when eye movements are included in the procedure (Marzano & Marzano, 2000).

Single-case designs have also been used in the dismantling of EMDR (Montgomery & Ayllon, 1994a, 1994b). These studies, while falling short of demonstrating that eye movements contribute definitively to treatment outcome, do show a convincing association between the initiation of eye movements and sharp declines in SUD ratings.

One of the more intriguing of the dismantling studies done to date is Lohr, Tolin, and Kleinknecht's (1996) single-case comparison of EMDR and a nonEM analogue in the treatment of claustrophobia. The study monitored two claustrophobic subjects' subjective distress (SUD) and heart rate through baseline, nonEM analog, EMDR and follow-up phases. Both subjects reported traumatic experiences as the origin of their phobic symptoms. Both received EMDR treatment for these scenes as well as other recent situations in which they had the phobic response, such as elevators and airplanes. The first subject showed a pattern of increasing subjective distress during analog treatment of the first three memories, including the original trauma. The onset of eye movements resulted in an abrupt change of slope, with rapidly decreasing SUD levels. The only scene to respond to the analog condition was the one that was treated last, which may be due to generalization of the desensitization of the previous three scenes. The second subject responded positively to the analog condition during treatment of recent examples of the phobic response but failed to show any evidence of desensitization of the original trauma until eye movements were added to the procedure. Another interesting aspect of this study was the finding that, though EMDR resulted in changes in subjective distress and avoidant behavior, heart rates were unchanged during treatment.

In addition to the dismantling approach to the investigation of EMDR mechanisms, researchers are also investigating the effects of eye movements in isolation. Since this approach eliminates the "noise" generated by the other active elements of EMDR, such as exposure, cognitive restructuring, free association, and nonspecific therapeutic effects, it may permit researchers to distinguish the effects of eye movement.

In a study of the effects of a variety of tasks on the vividness and emotional intensity of mental images, Andrade, Kavanagh, and Baddely (1997) compared imagery alone or accompanied by counting aloud, tapping, or eye movements similar to those used in EMDR. Eye movements made images less vivid than the other conditions, whether the images were neutral or negative, and whether they were images of recently presented photographs or actual life experiences. Eye movements also resulted in reductions in the emotional intensity of both negative and positive mental images. Tapping had a similar but weaker effect on vividness and emotional intensity, but it took a complex tapping task to begin to equal the effect of eye movements.

The effects of eye movement on the stream of consciousness were investigated in a study by Nugent and Tinker (2000). Subjects were asked to identify a positive or negative target thought and rate their focus of attention (internal vs. external) and intensity of emotion over a ten-minute period. Three different conditions were compared— eyes closed, eyes open, or eye movements similar to those used in

EMDR. Overall, subjects showed a "wandering" of attention over time, in that their focus on the external environment remained stable while their attention to the target thought decreased over time. Eye condition had no effect on the focus of attention or intensity of emotion when the target thought was happy. However, differences were observed when the target thought was sad. Focus on attention to the sad target thought was highest with the eyes closed and lowest with eye movements. Intensity of negative emotion was greatest with eyes closed and lowest with eyes open. Intensity of negative emotion with eye movements fell midway between eyes closed and eyes open. From these results the authors concluded that eye movements do not produce flooding or complete distraction, but that they allow the individuals to experience their emotions in "tolerable doses." An alternative conclusion is that eye movements facilitate associating to thoughts that are related to the target and may be relevant to its resolution.

Christman and Garvey (2000) compared the effects of saccadic eye movements, smooth-pursuit eye movements, or no eye movements on word tasks involving either semantic memory or episodic memory. Results showed that while eye condition had no effect on semantic memory, it did have an effect on episodic memory. Saccadic eye movements resulted in the best performance on the episodic memory task, followed by smooth pursuit and no eye movements. Results suggest that the eye movements used in EMDR result in bilateral cortical activation, which enhances retrieval of explicit memory for life events. Since previous research had shown that dissociative amnesia is related to decreased interaction between hemispheres (Christman & Ammann, 1995), the authors suggested that the eye movement component of EMDR may be particularly useful in overcoming the dissociative aspects of traumatic memory.

EMDR AND "PLACEBO EFFECT"

It has been suggested (Feske & Goldstein, 1997) that the effects of EMDR can be attributed to a combination of exposure and elevated expectancy due to the unusual nature of eye movements. There may be some confusion about EMDR because several researchers have used the term "placebo" to refer to nonEM analogs in component studies. Since the analog probably has some active components in it, such as exposure and cognitive restructuring as well as its own effects, the use of the term placebo may be misleading. It could be argued that eye movements could actually serve to make the EMDR procedure seem *less* credible to clients (Silver recalls having a psychology doctoral candidate with a severe blood and needle phobia laugh out loud when EMDR was described to her; treatment was nonetheless successful). Several studies have addressed this issue. It has further been argued that the scale most sensitive to EMDR, the SUD, is uniquely vulnerable to expectancy effects.

There have been five EMDR studies examining expectancy effects. In Bauman and Melnyk's (1994) dismantling study of EMD, no correlation was found between subject's expectancies and treatment outcome. Devilly, Spence, and Rapee (1998) compared EMDR and an analog in the treatment of combat veterans with PTSD. Because they were concerned that the eye movements would elicit a positive expectancy, they tried to equalize expectancy by using a machine that generated an unmoving blinking light. As expected, no differences in credibility/expectancy were found between groups. But when subjects were analyzed as a whole, there was also no correlation between credibility/expectancy and treatment outcome. Gosselin and Matthews (1995) attempted to manipulate expectancy by giving half their subjects a rationale that described EMDR as a "powerful new technique that has remarkably positive results" and giving the other have a rationale that described it as a "procedure about which we know very little or even if it works." Not only did the manipulation fail to affect expectancies (subjects in both groups rated their own belief in the procedure as neutral to slightly positive), but it also did not affect their ratings of the researcher's belief in the procedure (rated by both groups as positive). We must conclude, then, that the fact that subjects in the EM group had greater decreases in subjective anxiety was not related to differences in pretreatment expectancy. Hekmat, Groth, and Rogers (1994) tested subjects' hypnotic susceptibility as part of a study of EMDR and pain sensitivity. Once again, they found no correlation between susceptibility and treatment response.

In Feske and Goldstein's (1997) comparison of EMDR and a non-EM analog in the treatment of panic disorder, the effects of expectancy were also assessed. EMDR outperformed the analog on several measures at the posttest, but the differences disappeared at the three-month follow-up due to convergence (the EMDR group deteriorated slightly while the analog group continued to improve). In an effort to interpret that posttest difference, they suggested that the eye movements created a positive expectancy that eventually wore off. However, deterioration occurred on only a few of the scales, while subjects showed continuing improvement on the other measures. Subjects in both groups rated the credibility of the procedure and their expectation of improvement after hearing a description of the treatment, and no differences were found between the eye movement and fixed gaze conditions.

CONCLUSIONS

Definitive research into the contribution of eye movements to treatment outcomes is still pending, though the state of the research thus far suggests a potentially powerful role for them. Having said that, a review of the available research on the effects of EMDR on trauma indicates that it is an effective treatment, that the effects are beyond those nonspecific effects shared by all treatments, and that these effects are independent of clients' expectations. Results also show that the effects of EMDR are at least equal to those found with cognitive-behavioral therapy, often with less treatment time and with fewer dropouts.

REFERENCES

Adelaja, C. (1976). Patterns of psychiatric illness in the Nigerian army. *Military Medicine, 141*, 323–326.

American Psychiatric Association. (1980). *Diagnostic and statistical manual of mental disorders (3rd ed.)*. Washington, DC: Author.

American Psychiatric Association. (1994). *Diagnostic and statistical manual of mental disorders (4th ed.)*. Washington, DC: Author.

Andrade, J., Kavanagh, D., & Baddely, A. (1997). Eye-movements and visual imagery: A working memory approach to the treatment of post traumatic stress disorder. *British Journal of Clinical Psychology, 36*, 209–223.

Archibald, H. C., Long, D. M., Miller, C., & Tuddenham, R. D. (1962). Gross stress reaction in combat—A 15-year follow-up. *American Journal of Psychiatry, 119*, 317–322.

Bauman, W., & Melnyk, W. T. (1994). A controlled comparison of eye movements and finger tapping in the treatment of test anxiety. *Journal of Behavior Therapy and Experimental Psychiatry, 25*, 29–33.

Benight, C. C., Swift, E., Sanger, J., Smith, A., & Zeppeling, D. (1999). Coping self-efficacy as a mediator of distress following a natural disaster. *Journal of Applied Social Psychology, 29*, 2443–2464.

Boudewyns, P. A., & Hyer, L. A. (1996). Eye movement desensitization and reprocessing (EMDR) as treatment for posttraumatic stress disorder (PTSD). *Clinical Psychology and Psychotherapy, 3*, 185–195.

Burkett, B. G., & Whitley, G. (1998). *Stolen valor*. Dallas, TX: Verity.

Carlson, J. G., Chemtob, C. M., Rusnak, K., Hedlund, N. L., & Muraoka, M. Y. (1998). Eye movement desensitization and reprocessing for combat-related posttraumatic stress disorder. *Journal of Traumatic Stress, 11*, 3–24.

Cerone, M. (2000). *Eye movement desensitization and reprocessing in the treatment of combat-related guilt: A study of the effects of eye movements*. Unpublished doctoral dissertation, Temple University, Philadelphia.

Chambless, D. L., Baker, M. J., Baucom, D. H., Beutler, L. E., Calhoun, K. S., Crits-Christoph, P., Daiuto, A., Derubeis, R., Detweiler, J., Haaga, D. A. F., Bennett Johnson, S., McCurry, S., Mueser, K. T., Pope, K.S., Sanderson, W. C., Shoham, V., Stickle, T., Williams, D. A., & Woody, S. R. (1998). Update on empirically validated therapies II. *The Clinical Psychologist, 51,* 3–16.

Christman, S., & Ammann, D. (1995). *Dissociative experiences and handedness.* Paper presented at the Sixty-Seventh Annual Meeting of the Midwestern Psychological Association, Chicago, IL.

Christman, S., & Garvey, K. (2000). *Episodic versus semantic memory: eye movements and cortical activation.* Paper presented at the Forty-First Annual Meeting of the Psychonomic Society, New Orleans, LA.

Cohen, J. (1988). *Statistical power analysis for the behavioral sciences.* Hillsdale, NJ: Erlbaum.

DeFazio, V. J. (1978). Dynamic perspectives on the nature and effects of combat stress. In C. R. Figley (Ed.), *Stress disorders among Vietnam veterans.* New York: Brunner/Mazel.

Devilly, G. J., & Spence, S. H. (1999). The relative efficacy and treatment distress of EMDR and a cognitive-behavioral trauma treatment protocol in the amelioration of posttraumatic stress disorder. *Journal of Anxiety Disorders, 13,* 131–157.

Devilly, G. J., Spence, S. H., & Rapee, R. M. (1998). Statistical and reliable change with eye movement desensitization and reprocessing: Treating trauma within a veteran population. *Behavior Therapy, 29,* 435–455.

Dunn, T. M., Schwartz, M., Hatfield, R. W., & Wiegele, M. (1996). Measuring effectiveness of eye movement desensitization and reprocessing (EMDR) in nonclinical anxiety: A multi-subject, yoked control design. *Journal of Behavior Therapy & Experimental Psychiatry, 27,* 231–239.

Feske, U., & Goldstein, A. (1997). Eye movement desensitization and reprocessing for panic disorder: A controlled outcome and partial dismantling study. *Journal of Consulting and Clinical Psychology, 65,* 1026–1035.

Figley, C. R. (Ed.). (1995). *Compassion fatigue.* Bristol, PA: Brunner/Mazel.

Foa, E. B., & Kozak, M. J. (1998). Clinical applications of bioinformational theory: Understanding anxiety and its treatment. *Behavior Therapy, 29,* 675–690.

Foa, E. B., & Meadows, E. A. (1997). Psychosocial treatments for post-traumatic stress disorder: A critical review. *Annual Review of Psychology, 48,* 449–480.

Foa, E. B., & McNally, R. J. (1996). Mechanisms of change in exposure therapy. In R. M. Rapee (Ed.), *Current controversies in the anxiety disorders* (pp. 329–343). New York: Guilford.

Foa, E. B., & Rothbaum, B. O. (1998). *Treating the trauma of rape: Cognitive behavioral therapy for PTSD.* New York: Guilford.

Foa, E. B., Rothbaum, B. O., Riggs, D. S., & Murdock, T. B. (1991). Treatment of posttraumatic stress disorder in rape victims: A comparison between cognitive-behavioral procedures and counseling. *Journal of Consulting and Clinical Psychology, 59,* 715–723.

Foa, E. B., Zinbarg, R., & Rothbaum, B. O. (1992). Uncontrollability and unpredictability in post-traumatic stress disorder: An animal model. *Psychological Bulletin, 112,* 218–238.

Foley, T., & Spates, C. R. (1995). Eye movement desensitization of public speaking anxiety: A partial dismantling. *Journal of Behavior Therapy and Experimental Psychiatry, 26,* 321–329.

Gosselin, P., & Matthews, W. (1995). Eye movement desensitization and reprocessing in the treatment of test anxiety: a study of the effects of expectancy and eye movement. *Journal of Behavior Therapy and Experimental Psychiatry, 26*, 331–337.

Grand, D. (1998). Emerging from the coffin: Treatment of a masochistic personality disorder. In P. Manfield (Ed.), *Extending EMDR: A casebook of innovative applications* (pp. 65–90). New York: W. W. Norton.

Greenwald, R. (1999). *Eye Movement Desensitization and Reprocessing (EMDR) in childhood and adolescent psychotherapy*. Northvale, NJ: Jason Aronson.

Grinker, R. R. & Spiegel, J. P. (1979). *War neuroses*. New York: Arno.

Haley, S. A. (1974). When the patient reports atrocities: Specific treatment considerations of the Vietnam veteran. *Archives of General Psychiatry, 30*, 191–196.

Haley, S. A. (1978). Treatment implications of post-combat stress response syndromes for mental health professionals. In C. R. Figley (Ed.), *Stress disorders among Vietnam veterans*. New York: Brunner/Mazel.

Haley, S. A. (1979). *Countertransference toward the Vietnam veteran: A case presentation*. Paper presented at the American Psychiatric Association Annual meeting, Chicago.

Hekmat, H., Groth, S., & Rogers, D. (1994). Pain ameliorating effect of eye movement desensitization. *Journal of Behavior Therapy and Experimental Psychiatry, 25*, 121–130.

Ironson, G. L., Freund, B., Strauss, J. L., & Williams (in press). A comparison of two treatments for traumatic stress: A pilot study of EMDR and prolonged exposure. *Journal of Clinical Psychology*.

Janoff-Bulman, R. (1985). The aftermath of victimization: rebuilding shattered assumptions. In C. R. Figley (Ed.), *Trauma and its wake* (pp. 15–35). New York: Brunner/Mazel.

Jensen, J. A. (1994). An investigation of eye movement desensitization and reprocessing (EMD/R) as a treatment for posttraumatic stress disorder (PTSD) symptoms of Vietnam combat veterans. *Behavior Therapy, 25*, 311–326.

Johnson, D. R., Rosenheck, R., Fontana, A., Lubin, H., Charney, D., & Southwick, S. (1996). Outcome of intensive inpatient treatment for combat-related posttraumatic stress disorder. *American Journal of Psychiatry, 153*, 771–777.

Keane, T. M., Zimering, R. T., & Caddell, J. M. (1985). A behavioral formulation of posttraumatic stress disorder in Vietnam veterans. *Behavior Therapist, 8*, 9–12.

Kishur, R. (1984). *Chiasmal effects of traumatic stressors: The emotional costs of support*. Unpublished master's thesis, Purdue University, West Lafayette, IN.

Klonoff, H., McDougal, G., Clark, C., Kramer, P., & Horgan, J. (1976). The neuropsychological, psychiatric, and physical effects of prolonged and severe stress: Thirty years later. *Journal of Nervous and Mental Disease, 163*, 246–252.

Kubany, E. S. (1994). A cognitive model of guilt typology in combat-related PTSD. *Journal of Traumatic Stress, 7*, 3–19.

Lee, C., Gavriel, H., Drummond, P., Richards, J., & Greenwald, R. (in press). Treatment of post-traumatic stress disorder: A comparison of stress inoculation training with prolonged exposure and eye movement desensitization and reprocessing. *Journal of Clinical Psychology*.

Leeds, A. (1998). Lifting the burden of shame: Using EMDR resource installation to resolve a therapeutic impasse. In P. Manfield (Ed.), *Extending EMDR: A casebook of innovative applications* (pp. 256–281). New York: W.W. Norton.

Lipke, H., & Glang, C. (2000). Psychological approach to Albanian Kosovar refugees with considerations for brief post-crisis services in general. *Traumatology, 6*(4), www.fsu.edu/~trauma.

Lohr, J., Tolin, D., & Kleinknecht, R. (1996). An intensive investigation of eye movement desensitization and reprocessing of claustrophobia. *Journal of Anxiety Disorders, 10*, 73–88.

Macklin, M. L., Metzger, L. J., Lasko, N. B., Berry, N. J., Orr, S. P., & Pitman, R. K. (2000). Five-year follow-up study of eye movement desensitization and reprocessing therapy for combat-related posttraumatic stress disorder. *Comprehensive Psychiatry, 41*, 24–27.

Marcus, S., Marquis, P., & Sakai, C. (1997). Controlled study of treatment of PTSD using EMDR in an HMO setting. *Psychotherapy, 34*, 307–315.

Marzano, R. J., & Marzano, J. S. (2000). *A meta-analysis of EMDR research*. Unpublished manuscript.

McCann, I. L., & Pearlman, L. A. (1990). Vicarious traumatization: A framework for understanding the psychological effects of working with victims. *Journal of Traumatic Stress, 3*, 131–150.

McNally, R. J., Kaspi, S. P., Riemann, B. C., & Zeitlin, S. B. (1990). Selective processing of threat cues in posttraumatic stress disorder. *Journal of Abnormal Psychology, 94*, 398–402.

Meguro, K. (1972). War neurosis: A 20-year follow-up study. *Foreign Psychiatry, 1*, 165–203.

Merbaum, M. (1977). Some personality characteristics of soldiers exposed to extreme war stress: A follow-up study of posthospital adjustment. *Journal of Clinical Psychology, 33*, 558–562.

Montgomery, R. W., & Ayllon, T. (1994a). Eye movement desensitization and reprocessing across subjects: Subjective and physiological measures of treatment efficacy. *Journal of Behavior Therapy and Experimental Psychiatry, 25*, 217–230.

Montgomery, R. W., & Ayllon, T. (1994b). Eye movement desensitization across images: A single case design. *Journal of Behavior Therapy and Experimental Psychiatry, 25*, 23–28.

Noyes, R., & Klettie, R. (1977). Depersonalization in response to life-threatening danger. *Comprehensive Psychiatry, 18*, 375–384.

Nugent, N., & Tinker, R. (2000). *What about eye movements in EMDR?* Paper presented at the Annual Meeting of the EMDR International Association, Toronto.

Ost, L. G., & Hugdahl, K. (1981). Acquisition of phobias and anxiety response patterns in clinical patients. *Behaviour Research & Therapy, 16*, 439–447.

Pennebaker, J. W. (1985). Inhibition and cognition: Toward an understanding of trauma and disease. *Canadian Psychology, 26*, 82–95.

Pitman, R. K., Orr, S. P., Altman, B., Longpre, R. E., Poire, R. E., & Macklin, M. L. (1996). Emotional processing during eye movement desensitization and reprocessing therapy of Vietnam veterans with chronic posttraumatic stress disorder. *Comprehensive Psychiatry, 37*, 419–429.

Powell, K. G., McGoldrick, T., & Brown, K. W. (2000). *A controlled comparison of eye movement desensitization and reprocessing versus exposure plus cognitive restructuring versus waiting list in the treatment of post traumatic stress disorder*. Paper presented at the Annual Meeting of the EMDR International Association, Toronto.

Puk, G., & Silver, S. (1997). The EMDR Humanitarian Assistance Program: Training in psychosocial trauma relief. In D. Ajdukovic (Ed.), *Trauma recovery training: Lessons learned*. Zagreb, Croatia: Society for Psychological Assistance.

Renfrey, G., & Spates, C. R. (1994). Eye movement desensitization and reprocessing: A partial dismantling procedure. *Journal of Behavior Therapy and Experimental Psychiatry, 25*, 231–239.

Rogers, S., Silver, S. M., Goss, J., Obenchain, J., Willis, A., & Whitney, R. (1999). A single session, controlled group study of flooding and eye movement desensitization and reprocessing in treating posttraumatic stress disorder among Vietnam War veterans: Preliminary data. *Journal of Anxiety Disorders, 13,* 119–130.

Rothbaum, B. O. (1997). A controlled study of eye movement desensitization and reprocessing for posttraumatic stress disordered sexual assault victims. *Bulletin of the Menninger Clinic, 61,* 317–334.

Rothschild, B. (1999). Making trauma therapy safe. *Self and Society, 27,* 17–23.

Sanderson, A., & Carpenter, R. (1992). Eye movement desensitization versus image confrontation: A single-session crossover study of 58 phobic subjects. *Journal of Behavior Therapy & Experimental Psychiatry, 23,* 269–275.

Sargant, W. (1997). *Battle for the mind.* Cambridge, MA: Malor.

Scheck, M. M., Schaeffer, J. A., & Gillete, C. S. (1998). Brief psychological intervention with traumatized young women: The efficacy of eye movement desensitization and reprocessing. *Journal of Traumatic Stress, 11,* 25–44.

Shalev, A., Sahar, T., Freedman, S., Peri, T., Glick, N., Brandes, D., Orr, S., & Pitman, R. K. (1998). Prospective study of posttraumatic stress disorder and depression following trauma. *American Journal of Psychiatry, 155,* 630–637.

Shapiro, F. (1989a). Efficacy of the eye movement desensitization procedure in the treatment of traumatic memories. *Journal of Traumatic Stress, 2,* 199–223.

Shapiro, F. (1989b). Eye movement desensitization: A new treatment for posttraumatic stress disorder. *Journal of Behavior Therapy & Experimental Psychiatry, 20,* 211–217.

Shapiro, F. (1991). Eye movement desensitization and reprocessing procedure: From EMD to EMDR: A new treatment model for anxiety and related traumata. *Behavior Therapist, 14,* 133–135.

Shapiro, F. (1995). *Eye movement desensitization and reprocessing: Basic principles, protocols and procedures.* New York: Guilford.

Silver, S. M. (1992). Cultural perspectives: Philosophy of war. In F. Montour (Ed.), *Report of the working group on American Indian Vietnam Era veterans.* Washington, DC: Department of Veterans Affairs.

Silver, S. M. (1994). Lessons from Child of Water. *American Indian and Alaska Native Mental Health Research, 6,* 4–17.

Silver, S. M. (Spring 2000). Countertransference in the treatment of trauma reactions: Some issues for therapists and their supervisors. *Voices: The Art and Science of Psychotherapy, 36,* 55–63.

Silver, S. M., Brooks, A., & Obenchain, J. V. (1995). Treatment of Vietnam War veterans with PTSD: A comparison of eye movement desensitization and reprocessing, biofeedback, and relaxation training. *Journal of Traumatic Stress, 8,* 337–342.

Silver, S. M., & Rogers, S. (1996a, January). Report from Sarajevo. *Traumatology* [On-line journal], 2(1), majordomo@mailer.fsu.edu.

Silver, S. M., & Rogers, S. (1996b, Summer). Teaching trauma treatment in Sarajevo. *OEMP Information Update, 4,* 4.

Silver, S. M., & Wilson, J. (1988). Native American healing and purification rituals for war stress. In J. Wilson, Z. Harel, & B. Kahana (Eds.), *Human adaptation to extreme stress: From the Holocaust to Vietnam.* New York: Plenum.

Southard, E. E. (1973). *Shell-shock and other neuropsychiatric problems.* New York: Arno.

Sohlberg, S. C. (1976). Stress experience and combat fatigue during the Yom Kippur War (1973). *Psychological Reports, 38,* 523–529.

Stamm, B. H. (Ed.). (1995). *Secondary traumatic stress*. Lutherville, MD: Sidran.

Trandel, D. V., & McNally, R. J. (1987). Perception of threat cues in posttraumatic stress disorder: Semantic processing without awareness? *Behavioural Research and Therapy, 25*, 469–476.

Vaughan, K., Armstrong, M. S., Gold, R., O'Connor, N., Jenneke, W., & Tarrier, N. (1994). A trial of eye movement desensitization compared to image habituation training and applied muscle relaxation in posttraumatic stress disorder. *Journal of Behavior Therapy and Experimental Psychiatry, 25*, 283–291.

Volkan, V. D. (1979). Symptom formations and character changes due to upheavals in war: Examples from Cyprus. *American Journal of Psychotherapy, 33*, 239–262.

Wildwind, L. (1992). *Working with depression*. Paper presented at the Advanced Clinical Applications of EMDR Conference, Sunnyvale, CA.

Wildwind, L. (1998). *It's never to late to have a happy childhood: Using EMDR to create and install essential experiences*. Paper presented at the 1998 EMDR International Association Conference, Baltimore.

Wilson, D. L., Silver, S. M., Covi, W., & Foster, S. (1996). Eye movement desensitization and reprocessing: Effectiveness and autonomic correlates. *Journal of Behavior Therapy and Experimental Psychiatry, 27*, 219–229.

Wilson, S. A., Becker, L. A., & Tinker, R. H. (1995). Eye movement desensitization and reprocessing (EMDR) treatment for psychologically traumatized individuals. *Journal of Consulting and Clinical Psychology, 63*, 928–937.

Wilson, S. A., Becker, L. A., & Tinker, R. H. (1997). Fifteen-month follow-up of eye movement desensitization and reprocessing (EMDR) treatment for PTSD and psychological trauma. *Journal of Consulting and Clinical Psychology, 65*, 1047–1056.

Wilson, S. A., Tinker, R. H., Hoffman, A., Becker, L., & Kleiner, K. (2000). *A field study of EMDR with Kosovar-Albanian refugee children using a group treatment protocol*. Paper presented at the EMDR International Association Conference, Toronto.

Wolpe, J. (1991). *The practice of behavior therapy (4th ed.)* New York: Pergamon.

APPENDIX A

PARTICIPATING CLINICIANS

As we noted in the acknowledgments, we solicited comments from other EMDR clinicians working with war and terrorism survivors. Throughout the text of this book you have seen their ideas, experiences, and innovations noted and described. Frequently these points were made by more than one of these clinicians or were duplications of our own experiences. We have not attempted to work out who came up with what first—one of the positives of working in this field is the willingness of other clinicians to share their ideas with each other without worrying about "proprietary rights." For readers familiar with the field of psychotherapy, this may appear remarkable.

Below we describe the work of these colleagues and provide readers with the means to locate them so they may continue the education and dialogue we hope this book encourages. We take full responsibility for the use of their input and any error in interpretation and context of their thoughts is ours.

Ernest Baringer, B.S., E.M.T., airforce@delanet.com Ernie worked in the U.S. Vet Center program and other settings for 20 years providing counseling to war survivors. He also has been active in critical incident stress work and is a paramedic. In that capacity he was a volunteer with a canine search and rescue team.

Alan Cohen, M.Sc., accspc@isdn.net.il Alan was one of the first trained by Francine Shapiro in EMDR during her 1989 visit to Israel.

He is been active in the famous Community Stress Prevention Center at Kryat Shmona, which provides training in trauma reaction treatment. He has been particularly interested in training teams to respond to disasters and has been involved in EMDR-HAP work, including the UNICEF-sponsored training program for Bangladesh.

Ricky Greenwald, Psy.D., rg@childtrauma.com Ricky was one of the first pioneers in the area of children and EMDR and his book, *Eye Movement Desensitization and Reprocessing (EMDR) in Child and Adolescent Psychotherapy*, is an excellent practical guide for EMDR clinicians, whether or not they work with children.

Howard Lipke, Ph.D., hlipke@aol.com Howard was the director of one of the first inpatient PTSD programs and convinced the senior author that EMDR was worth a serious look. While continuing his work with war veterans as an outpatient therapist, he has begun to explore the integration of EMDR with other therapeutic perspectives, most notably in his book, *EMDR and Psychotherapy Integration.*

Robert O'Brien, Ph.D., obrien@austin.rr.com Bob works as a psychologist with outpatient war survivors for the Department of Veterans Affairs in Texas. He has also been a participant in EMDR-HAP trainings, including in Bangladesh. He often assists at EMDR Institute trainings in the American Southwest.

Michael Paterson, Ph.D., D.Clin.Psych., paterson@mindclinic.co.uk Michael's background is well covered in the interview in chapter 4. He is a pioneer in using EMDR with survivors of terrorism and both writes and presents on the subject.

Gerry Puk, Ph.D., 102027.3303@compuserve.com Besides having excellent taste in motorcycles, Gerry was a pioneer in developing the application of EMDR to dissociative disorders. He has been heavily involved in work with EMDR-HAP and was a member of the first team to go to Croatia and Bosnia in 1995.

Gene Schwartz, M.S.W., janwalker@home.com Until recently the director of a PTSD treatment program for war veterans for the Department of Veterans Affairs, Gene now has a private practice in Baltimore specializing in treatment of anxiety disorders. He remains active with the EMDR Institute, assisting at trainings.

Roger Solomon, Ph.D., rogersol@ix.netcom.com Roger is a senior trainer for the EMDR Institute and has been greatly involved in working with police and emergency service providers throughout the United States. He has pioneered, with Jeff Mitchell, the integration of EMDR with critical incident stress management. Besides assisting after the Oklahoma City bombing, as a trainer for the EMDR Humanitarian Assistance Programs he provided training for counselors working in Rwanda in the aftermath of their civil war.

Jeanne Varrasse, R.N., C.S.Psych., quilter236@aol.com Jeanne is a primary therapist in the PTSD program of the DVA Medical Center in Coatesville, Pennsylvania. In addition to her work with traumatized war survivors, she has developed interests in program evaluation research.

Frances R. Yoeli, S.W., M.F.T., C.A.C., yoeli@maoz.org.il Frances began using EMDR on the basis of a prepublication article and has used it in a wide range of settings as a family therapist and trauma and drug counselor in Israel. She has also been very active with EMDR-HAP, assisting in the providing of training in EMDR in Israel, Bangladesh, Turkey, and in Bethlehem for Palestinians.

APPENDIX B

EMDR HUMANITARIAN ASSISTANCE

PROGRAMS (EMDR-HAP)

EMDR-HAP is a registered 501-(c)(3) nonprofit organization. Readers interested in obtaining more information about EMDR-HAP can use the Web site at www.emdrhap.org
   EMDR-HAP can be contacted through the following:

E-mail: *HAPnewhope@aol.com*

Telephone: 215-862-4310

Fax: 215-862-4312

136 South Main Street, Suite 1
New Hope, PA 18938

or

PO Box 52164
Pacific Grove, CA 93950

INDEX